Learning BASIC
Programming Essentials

Carl Grame

Dan O'Donnell

De Anza College
Cupertino, California

 ® SCIENCE RESEARCH ASSOCIATES, INC.
Chicago, Henley-on-Tnames, Sydney, Toronto

A Subsidiary of IBM

Acquisition Editor	Alan W. Lowe
Project Editors	Ruth Cottrell
	Gretchen Hargis
Editor	Judith Starnes
Compositor	Jonathan Peck Typographers, Ltd.
Illustrator	Jonathan Peck Typographers, Ltd.
Cover and Text Designer	Naomi Takigawa
Cover Photo by	Marni Burlingame

Library of Congress Cataloging in Publication Data

Grame, Carl, 1927-
  Learning BASIC programming essentials.

  Bibliography: p.
  Includes index.
  1. Basic (Computer program language)   2. Microcomputers
—Programming.   I. O'Donnell, Dan, 1931-   .   II. Title.
QA76.73.B3G68   1984   001.64′24   84-5322
ISBN 0-574-21370-8

10 9 8 7 6 5 4 3 2

Contents

Preface xi

UNIT 1 Introduction to BASIC Programming 1

Objectives 1
Introduction 1
  What Is a Computer? 1
  What Is BASIC? 2
  What Is a BASIC Program? 2
  What Is a Statement? 2
  What Is a Command? 2
  Using BASIC Language Programs with a Computer 2
  Using Statements and Commands 2
Flowcharts 3
  What Is a Flowchart? 3
  Using Flowcharts 3
Computer Overview 4
General Procedure for Programming in BASIC 5
  REMARK Statement 7
  Displaying Literal Characters 7
  Displaying Calculated Results 7
  Displaying a Blank Line 8
  END Statement 8
Mechanics of BASIC Programming 9
  Typing the Sample Program 9
  Displaying the Sample Program 10
  Executing the Sample Program 11
  Making Changes in the Sample Program 11
  Listing and Running the Revised Sample Program 12
  INPUT Statement 12
  GO TO Statement 13
In Closing 13

UNIT 2 Writing Assignment Statements and Altering Program Control 14

Objectives 14
Introduction 14
  What Is an Assignment Statement? 14
  What Is a Numeric Constant? 14
  What Is a Numeric Variable? 14
  What Is an Operator? 14

What Is an Expression? 15
What Is a String Variable? 15
What Is a GO TO Statement? 15
Using Assignment Statements 15
Using GO TO Statements 15
Constants 15
Variables 16
Arithmetic Operations 16
Priority of Operations 16
Algebra Review 17
Flowcharting 17
Assignment Statements 17
Writing Assignment Statements 18
Computer Simulation 19

GO TO Statement 20
Printing a Variable 21
Summing Numbers 21
Scientific Notation 23
Interpreting Scientific Notation 23
Programming Techniques 24
Debugging Aids 25
Reference 26
Constant/Variable Summary 26
Statement Summary 26
Priority of Operations Summary 27
Algebra Rules 27
Rules for Converting Numbers Represented in E Notation to Real Numbers 28
Application Exercises 28
Answers to Application Exercises 30
Programming Problems 31
Mileage-Conversion Program 31
Grade Program 32

UNIT 3 Input and Output 33

Objectives 33
Introduction 33
What Is Input/Output? 33
What Is a PRINT Statement? 33
What Is an INPUT Statement? 34
What Is a READ Statement? 34
What Is a DATA Statement? 34
Using INPUT and OUTPUT Statements 34
Using a PRINT Statement 34
Using an INPUT Statement 34
Using READ and DATA Statements 34
PRINT Statements 35
Displaying Variables Close Together on the Same Line 36
Displaying Variables Far Apart on the Same Line 36
Displaying a String Constant and a String Variable on the Same Line 37
Program Using PRINT Statements 37
Using PRINT Statements Emphasizing Semicolons and Commas 38
Using PRINT Statements Emphasizing a Space for a Sign 38

INPUT Statements   39
  Miscellaneous Uses of INPUT Statements   39
  Finding an Average of INPUT Values   41
READ and DATA Statements   42
  Miscellaneous Uses of READ and DATA Statements   43
  Summing Numbers Read from a DATA Statement   45
  Compounding Savings-Account Interest   46
Programming Techniques   50
Debugging Aids   51
Reference   52
  Statement Summary   52
  Output Spacing   53
Application Exercises   53
  Answers to Application Exercises   54
Programming Problems   54
  Program for Finding Standard and Actual Values   54
  Program for Periodic Savings Deposits   55

UNIT 4   Conditional Branching   59

Objectives   59
Introduction   59
  What Is a Conditional Branch Statement?   59
  What Is a RESTORE Statement?   59
  What Is the STOP Statement?   59
  Using a Conditional Branch   60
  Using a RESTORE Statement   60
Relational Operators   60
The IF-THEN Statement   60
  Additional IF-THEN Statements   61
The STOP Statement   62
The RESTORE Statement   62
Calculating an Average   63
Using the IF-THEN Statement   65
Comparing Values   66
  Savings-Deposit Growth Program   68
Programming Techniques   71
Debugging Aids   72
Reference   72
  Statement Summary   72
Application Exercises   73
  Answers to Application Exercises   75
Programming Problems   75
  Jogging Program   75
  Mortgage Program   77

UNIT 5   Strings   78

Objectives   78
Introduction   78
  What Is a String Variable?   78
Using Strings   78
  Assigning a String Constant to a String Variable   79
  Assigning One String Variable to Another String Variable   79

Reading a String Constant 80
Inputting a String Constant 80
Comparing a String Variable to a String Constant 80
Comparing One String Variable to Another 81
Displaying a String Constant 82
Displaying String Variables and Constants on the Same Line 82
Using Strings in a Complete Program 82
Strings and LET Statements 85
Incorrect Uses of Strings with LET Statements 85
Additional Examples of Strings with LET Statements 86
Strings and READ/DATA Statements 87
Additional Examples of Strings with READ and DATA Statements 87
Strings and INPUT Statements 88
Additional Examples of Strings with INPUT Statements 88
Strings and IF Statements 89
Collating Hierarchy 89
Additional Examples of Strings with IF Statements 89
Strings and PRINT Statements 92
Additional Examples of Strings with PRINT Statements 92
Finding a Date 93
Programming Techniques 97
Debugging Aids 98
Reference 98
Statement Summary 98
Collating Hierarchy of Selected ASCII Characters 100
Application Exercises 100
Answers to Application Exercises 102
Programming Problems 104
Program for Personalized Dating Letter 104
Program for Personalized Sales Letter 107

UNIT 6 BASIC Built-in Functions 111

Objectives 111
Introduction 111
What Is a BASIC Built-in Function? 111
Using BASIC Built-in Functions 111
Sample BASIC Built-in Function 111
General BASIC Built-in Functions 112
Absolute-Value Function (ABS) 113
Truncation Function (INT) 113
Square-Root Function (SQR) 113
Tabulation Function (TAB) 113
Random-Number Function (RND) 113
Trigonometric Functions 114
Using TAB, ABS, INT, and SQR 114
Using SIN, COS, and TAN 117
Rounding Positive Numbers 118
Rounding to a Fixed Number of Decimal Places 118
Rounding to a Varying Number of Decimal Places 123
Random-Number Function 123
Generating Random Numbers Between But Not Including 0 and 1 123
Generating Random Whole Numbers Between and Including Various Limits 125
Guessing Game 126

Programming Techniques 133
Debugging Aids 133
Reference 133
  Some General BASIC Built-in Functions 133
  Some Trigonometric BASIC Built-in Functions 134
Application Exercises 135
  Answers to Application Exercises 135
Programming Problems 136
  Program for Average, Variance, and Standard Deviation 136
  Program for Coin-Flipping Simulation 138

UNIT 7 Looping 141

Objectives 141
Introduction 141
  What Are FOR and NEXT Statements? 141
  Using FOR and NEXT Statements 141
FOR and NEXT Statements 141
Summing Numbers 144
Averaging Values 147
Decrementing with a FOR Statement 147
Using a STEP Variable in a FOR Statement 150
Using a FOR-NEXT Loop to Calculate an Average 151
FOR-NEXT Loop Rules 151
Other Forms of the FOR-NEXT Loop 154
Programming Techniques 154
Debugging Aids 156
Reference 157
Application Exercises 157
  Answers to Application Exercises 158
Programming Problems 159
  Team-Scheduling Program 159
  Currency-Exchange Program 161

UNIT 8 One-Dimensional Arrays 163

Objectives 163
Introduction 163
  What Is an Array? 163
Types of Arrays 164
Subscripts 164
  Subscript Forms 165
Defining Arrays 165
Using Arrays 167
  A Program with Two Numeric Arrays 168
  A Program with a Numeric Array and a String Array 172
  Counting with Arrays 175
Programming Techniques 176
Debugging Aids 177
Reference 178
  DIM Statement Summary 178
  Subscript Summary 178
Application Exercises 178
  Answers to Application Exercises 179

Programming Problems 180
   Calories Program 180
   Golf-Handicap Program 183

UNIT 9 Two-Dimensional Arrays 185

Objectives 185
Introduction 185
   What Are Two-Dimensional Arrays? 185
Nested FOR-NEXT Loops 185
Two-Dimensional Arrays 187
Subscripts 188
The DIM Statement 188
Programs with Two-Dimensional Arrays 189
The Budget Array 191
Partially Completed Budget Program 196
Counting with a Two-Dimensional Array 196
Programming Techniques 202
Debugging Aids 204
Reference 204
   Processing Two-Dimensional Arrays 204
   FOR-NEXT Loop Rules 204
Application Exercises 205
   Answers to Application Exercises 206
Programming Problems 209
   Inflationary-Budget Program 209
   Checkbook-Reconciliation Program 210

UNIT 10 User-Defined Functions and Subroutines 213

Objectives 213
Introduction 213
   What Is a User-Defined Function? 213
   What Is a Subroutine? 213
   Using User-Defined Functions and Subroutines 213
The User-Defined Function 214
The Rounding Function 215
The Subroutine 215
Using User-Defined Functions 216
   The Punch Program 216
   The Baseball-Averages Program 223
Programming Techniques 231
Debugging Aids 232
Reference 232
   Summary of the User-Defined Function 232
   Summary of the Subroutine 233
Application Exercises 233
   Answers to Application Exercises 235
Programming Problems 239
   Prediction Program 239
   Questionnaire Program 242

UNIT 11   Data Files   245

Objectives   245
Introduction   245
   What Is a Data File?   245
   What Is a Record?   245
   What Is a Field?   245
Using a Data File   246
Sequential-File Operations   246
Overview of Processing a Household-Budget File   246
File Loading   248
File Retrieval and Display   251
File Inquiry   254
File Maintenance   257
   Master Budget Code Is Less Than Transaction Code   263
   Master Budget Code Is Greater Than Transaction Code   263
   Master Budget Code Is Equal to Transaction Code   263
Application Exercise   270
   Answers to Application Exercise   272
Programming Problems   273
   Program for Loading a Sequential File   273
   Program for Maintaining a Sequential File   274
   Program for Retrieving and Printing a Sequential File   277
   Program for Inquiring with a Sequential File   278

Index   281

Preface

Using the traditional lecture approach to teach computer programming in our classes, we noticed that students progressed at different rates and learned in different ways. We decided, therefore, to introduce a learning approach that meets the needs of most students, whether enrolled in a self-paced program or a traditional class. We designed a course that enables beginners to start programming almost immediately. To achieve this goal, we simplified the approach by presenting only the most commonly used BASIC statements in the early units and adding other statements gradually as the course progresses. We chose nontechnical programming problems, used examples throughout, and explained the examples with flowcharts. These gradual steps enable students to learn within the classroom environment or independently at their own pace. We have provided audio tapes of the material for those who learn best by listening and printed material for those who prefer reading. The application exercises and programming problems encourage learning by doing.

All program illustrations in this *Programming Essentials* text have been run using standard BASIC. A student should have access to a computer to complete the programming assignments in this text. We have made the material machine-independent wherever possible, so that the course can be used with various computers.

Using this approach, we have taught computer programming to a variety of students, including high-school and college students and returning students in training for second careers. The responses of students have been positive because of the various training methods and the self-paced option.

We have concluded that any motivated student who has passed a course in elementary algebra can successfully achieve the objectives of this text.

The author and publisher would like to thank the following reviewers for their valuable feedback:

Eddy E. Pollock, *Cabrillo College*
William D. Wesnor, *John C. Calhoun Community College*
Patricia L. Leonard, *Rider College*
Arthur D. Polen, *Cuyahoga Community College*
Robert L. Arndt, *Belleville Area College*

Carl Grame
Dan O'Donnell

Introduction

This text is divided into eleven computer-independent units. Systems Specifics booklets supplementing Units 1 and 11 for various computers are under separate cover. In using this text and the appropriate System Specifics booklet, you should proceed in the following way.

Learning Activities

The following procedures should be used to learn BASIC with this text. To acquaint yourself with the various parts of this text, you should refer now to the page numbers cited in Unit 2. Unit 2 is used as an example because it is a typical unit.

1. Read the Objectives and the Introduction (pages 14 and 15).
2. Listen to the audio tape and refer to the illustrations in this text as directed (beginning on page 16).
3. Read the text material (beginning on page 15).
4. Attend lectures if and when scheduled. Bring your text.
5. Read the Programming Techniques (pages 24 and 25).
6. Read the Debugging Aids (page 25).
7. Read the Reference section, which summarizes the material in the unit and may be used as a quick reference (pages 26–27).
8. Complete the Application Exercises (pages 28–30).
9. Compare your answers with the Answers to the Application Exercises (page 30).
10. Review the Objectives (page 14).
11. Write a solution to a programming problem (problem 1 is on page 31. Use the flowchart on page 31 as an aid. *Note:* There are two programming problems in each unit, but only one of them has a flowchart provided.)
12. Run your program on a computer. Your results should match those in the text (page 32). However, due to differences in various versions of BASIC, slight variations may occur.
13. Take the test for the unit and submit your computer program list and results to the instructor as directed.
14. Review the corrected test as scheduled.
15. Consult with the instructor and/or supplementary resources as necessary at any point in this procedure.
16. Go back to step 1 and follow the same procedure for the next unit. *Note:* Units 1 and 11 are supplemented by a System Specifics booklet. Thus the detailed steps will vary somewhat from those outlined here. Therefore, for these units 1 and 11, you will be given appropriate directions in the unit.

Advantages of Various Learning Activities

One important advantage of having various learning methods is that you can concentrate on the method that works best for you. Some students prefer to learn by reading, others by listening, and others by doing practical exercises. We have provided opportunities in this *Programming Essentials* text for all three types of learners. The explanatory material for the illustrations in this text is available on audio tapes as well as in printed form for each unit. Practical application exercises let you work with the material, and programming problems acquaint you with the computer. Regardless of your particular preference, we recommend that you use all three methods to learn BASIC.

Perhaps the most important advantage of audio-tape study is that you set your own pace. When listening to a lecture, you must proceed at the instructor's pace. But you can replay a tape, or any part of it, as often as you wish, or you can stop it at any point to review, to consult with your instructor, or to use additional resources. Furthermore, while listening to the tape, you are actively involved in studying illustrations or writing entries in the text. You can concentrate on the illustrations without diverting your attention to look back and forth between the illustrations and the printed text.

The advantage of printed material is that it allows more extensive examination and review of the material presented in the illustrations.

The practical exercises offer the advantage of immediate feedback. You complete Application Exercises in this text and/or the System Specifics booklet and check the answers that follow. The output that you should produce is always shown for programming problems with feedback directly from the computer. When you are listening to the audio tape or reading the text, feedback is provided whenever you are asked to make an entry in this text. Even when you make a mistake, you learn by correcting it.

Reinforcement is available in the form of Programming Techniques, Debugging Aids, and Reference sections in each unit. The Objectives at the beginning of each unit provide a statement of the performance expected of you for that unit. Although you might not completely understand the Objectives when you first read them, they should be clearer when you review them after listening to the tape and reading the text.

Responsibility of the Student

The approach to learning in this text provides you with much to do and many choices to make. This places a great deal of responsibility upon you. You must pace yourself and set some of your own deadlines. You must check your own progress and decide whether to repeat material, go on to new material, or consult with your instructor to meet the objectives.

Depending on how your course is set up, the instructor might not always know what point you have reached in the text or the System Specifics booklet or what problems you are having. Therefore, you should ask for help when you need it. Your instructor will tell you when and how help is available through conferences, additional reading, and lab practice.

1 Introduction to BASIC Programming

OBJECTIVES

When you complete this unit, you will be able to:

1. Name at least two examples each of input and output devices
2. Name the major steps in running a successful program
3. Correct various types of errors that you discover when programming
4. Type a simple BASIC program into memory
5. Display a program in memory on a screen or printer
6. Execute or run a program in memory
7. Delete a program from memory
8. Transfer a program from memory onto magnetic tape or disk
9. Transfer a program from magnetic tape or disk into memory
10. Delete a program from magnetic tape or disk
11. Stop execution of a program while the computer is:
    a. Continuously repeating the same steps (that is, repeating an endless loop)
    b. Waiting for an entry from the keyboard
12. Predict the appropriate logical path to follow in a flowchart, after being given a set of conditions

INTRODUCTION

The purpose of this unit is to introduce you to the use of the BASIC language in writing computer programs.

What Is a Computer?

A computer is a data processor that can perform computation, including numerical or logical operations, under control of a stored program. For purposes of our discussion, a computer consists of the following components: central processing unit (CPU), arithmetic logical unit (ALU), input/output devices, memory, and magnetic tape or disk.

The CPU includes circuits that control the interpretation and execution (carrying out) of BASIC program statements (instructions) and system commands in memory (storage) and the operation of input/output devices and the arithmetic logical unit (ALU).

1

The arithmetic logical unit (ALU) includes circuits that perform arithmetic and logical operations.

Memory is the unit in which all program statements, data, and system commands must be stored before they can be acted upon by the CPU.

Input devices such as keyboards are used to enter program statements, data, and system commands into memory.

Output devices such as screens or printers are used to receive data from memory.

Permanent online storage devices, such as magnetic disks and tapes, are special input/output media on which programs and data are stored for long-term use.

A keyboard and screen or printer are the most common input/output devices used by individuals for sending and receiving information to and from memory.

What Is BASIC?

BASIC is a programming language used for problem solving on a computer by people who are not necessarily professional computer programmers. The letters stand for Beginners All-purpose Symbolic Instruction Code.

What Is a BASIC Program?

A BASIC program consists of a sequence of statements written in the BASIC language by a computer programmer for execution on a computer.

What Is a Statement?

A statement is an instruction contained within a BASIC program that is used to perform operations on data, define data, or include narrative comments in the program. Example:

```
40 PRINT "SAMPLE PROGRAM"
```

This statement displays the words within quotation marks on the screen when the program is executed.

What Is a Command?

A command is an instruction usually not contained within a BASIC program. It is used to perform system control or utility tasks such as running or listing a BASIC program. Examples:

LIST *(Displays program on screen or printer)*
RUN   *(Executes program and displays results on screen or printer)*

Using BASIC Language Programs with a Computer

Computers are used to solve problems. To get a computer to solve a problem, a computer programmer must give the computer a detailed set of instructions called *a computer program*. Various programming languages are available to programmers. BASIC is one of the more popular languages used to write programs. In this unit you will be introduced to the general process of preparing BASIC programs for execution on a computer.

The main computer components that you will use personally include a typewriterlike keyboard for typing instructions or data entries into the computer's memory and a screen or printer to display the contents of memory. The display usually consists of either a printer for printed information or a televisionlike screen for viewing the information.

Using Statements and Commands

Both statements and commands are necessary for programming in the BASIC language; they differ, however, in form and purpose. If a statement is included as part of the program, it has a line number. If it is not included as part of the program and does not have a line number, it is a command.

The following is a brief comparison of statements and commands:

Statement	*Command*
1. Must be preceded by a line number.	1. Need not be preceded by a line number unless program mode.
2. Generally the same regardless of the make of computer.	2. Frequently vary on different makes of computers.
3. When entered they become part of the program and perform their action later when the program is executed.	3. When entered they do not become part of the program and they perform their action immediately.

Examples:

```
10 REM THIS IS A SIMPLE PROGRAM
20 PRINT "2+2=4"
30 END
```

Examples:

```
LIST
RUN
```

The BASIC statements introduced in this unit should be essentially the same on any computer system you might be using. Commands other than LIST and RUN usually vary with different makes of computers. For that reason we only introduce here the various functions to be performed by these commands. Then, in the exercises in the System Specifics booklet for this unit, we will introduce the precise commands and techniques for your computer system. The terms *line number* and *statement number* will be used interchangeably from this point on; the terms *print* and *display* will also be used interchangeably.

Flowcharts

What Is a Flowchart?

A flowchart is a diagram that illustrates a sequence of steps for carrying out an activity. Example:

START

TYPE PROGRAM

DISPLAY PROGRAM

EXECUTE PROGRAM

STOP

Using Flowcharts

Programmers often use a flowchart to describe the logical solution to a problem in graphic form, before writing the program.

Flowcharts appear extensively throughout this manual to help you understand the explanations of the computer programs being discussed. Some assignments ask you to write partial or complete programs from given flowcharts. Other assignments require that you write a complete program from a written description of a problem. You will find it helpful to draw a flowchart of the solution before writing the program.

In this unit we will introduce the general concept of following a flowchart path, but not the exact form of program flowcharts that you will use to write programs. Beginning with Unit 2 and in each subsequent unit, we will introduce program flowchart symbols as they apply to the subject matter of the unit rather than offering a separate unit on flowcharting.

In this unit our main concern is to introduce the use of the BASIC language in writing computer programs. Many people think of computers as giant electronic brains. Let's forget this concept. We are going to consider the computer as a fast problem solver. A computer can't do anything unless it's told exactly what to do by a computer programmer, and you are going to be the computer programmer. You will write programs using the BASIC language, which—as we mentioned in the Introduction—is a programming language used for problem solving on a computer by people who are not necessarily professional programmers.

Computer Overview

Before we start programming, though, let's take a brief look at the computer itself.

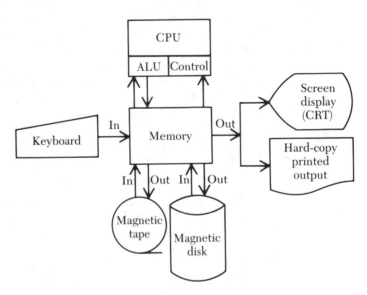

Figure 1-1   Computer overview

In Figure 1-1 you see a diagram of some computer components. You will notice on the left a keyboard symbol. Through this typewriterlike keyboard, programs and data are entered into the computer. On the right side of the figure you see the various ways by which the computer can output, or display, information. One way is by printing it on paper. This is often referred to as *hard copy*. Another way to display it is on a televisionlike screen frequently called a *CRT*, which stands for cathode-ray tube. The computer system you will be using for BASIC will probably have both types of output. The keyboard input and the screen output are often housed in the same unit and on larger computer systems are referred to as *terminals*.

Keyboards, screens, and printers will be the principal input/output devices that you will use to communicate with the computer. Note, however, two symbols for magnetic tape and magnetic disk, labeled "in" and "out," at the bottom of the figure. The computer you will be using could have one or both of these additional devices. It is important to realize that they do exist, and they could sometimes be preferable methods of input or output, when you want to store or retrieve programs and data.

Let's look at a typical flow of program instructions and data that could result from your programming effort. First, you would input your program by typing one statement at a time on a keyboard until the entire program is stored in memory, sometimes referred to as *main storage* or *working storage*. Then you could run, or execute, the program in memory. This means that one instruction at a time is transferred from memory into the CPU (remember, this means central processing unit). The instruction is then analyzed and executed (that is, carried out). It might be an instruction requesting that data be input into memory—by having it typed on a keyboard. The next instruction in memory might be an arithmetic instruction that causes data from memory to be transferred into the ALU (arithmetic logical unit), where the requested operation is performed and the resulting answer is transferred to memory. The next instruction to be executed by the CPU might cause the resulting answer in memory to be displayed on a printer or screen.

When all instructions have been executed, you might want to have your program transferred from memory and listed on a printer or output from memory and stored on some form of storage (such as magnetic tape or magnetic disk) that can later be input into memory without being retyped. Tape or disk storage is sometimes referred to as *auxiliary* or *secondary storage*. Although this is a very general description, it will be helpful for you to keep these relationships in mind as you begin writing programs that cause their interaction.

General Procedure for Programming in BASIC

In Figure 1-2 we present the general procedure for programming in BASIC.

Symbol 1 is a terminal symbol used here to start the flowchart. Symbol 2 requires that you decide what is to be accomplished by your program. For example, find the sum of two numbers and display it. You might determine that the two numbers would be input from the keyboard and the answer should be output on the printer.

Symbol 3 calls for you to develop a flowchart showing the logical steps to be followed in reaching your solution. Symbol 4 covers the process of translating your flowchart into a program of BASIC language statements, recording them on paper, and proofreading for mistakes before typing them into the computer memory. Proofreading is often referred to as *desk checking*. In symbol 5 you enter the program statements into memory by typing them on a keyboard, correcting known errors as you go.

Next, symbol 6 indicates that, when you have finished typing your program, you should display it and check for errors. Symbol 7 is a decision symbol indicating that one of two actions will be taken, depending on the error conditions. A variety of errors can occur when you are programming. These will be discussed in later units. For the present you should be aware of the importance of checking for them. If there are errors, you take the branch or flow to the right to symbol 8. Symbol 8 says to determine the corrections and go back to symbol 5, repeating steps 5 through 7. On the other hand, if there are no errors in symbol 7, then you take the branch downward and continue to symbol 9.

Symbol 9 calls for you to run or execute the program to produce the desired results and check it for errors. Symbol 10 asks if there are any errors in the results produced when the program is run. If there are errors, you take the branch to the right to symbol 11. In symbol 11 you determine the necessary corrections to your

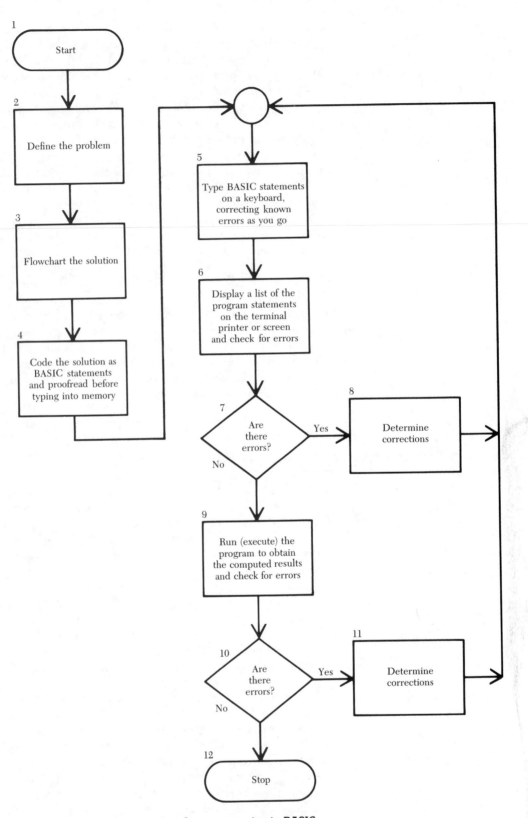

Figure 1-2   General procedure for programming in BASIC

program and then go back to symbol 5, repeating steps 5 through 10 until there are no errors. At this point, you take the downward branch to symbol 12. Symbol 12 is another terminal symbol, used here to stop the flowchart. In the remainder of this unit, we will introduce the activities covered in symbols 5 through 12. The procedures in symbols 1 through 4 will be covered in subsequent units.

REMARK Statement

You will use the REMARK statement illustrated in Figure 1-3 to record explanatory comments within your program. These comments make your program understandable to you or to someone else reading it.

Line number	Statement name	*This explanatory comment will be displayed (printed on paper or shown on a screen) when the program is listed*
10	REM	THIS IS A SIMPLE PROGRAM

("Display the words THIS IS A SIMPLE PROGRAM when the program is listed")

Figure 1-3   REMARK statement

It's very easy to forget details about your program. The REMARK statement helps you to overcome this difficulty. It consists of (1) a line number, in this case 10, followed by a space; (2) the statement name, REM, followed by a space; and finally (3) the comments you want to be displayed when the program is listed. In this example, you want to display the words "THIS IS A SIMPLE PROGRAM". The effect of this particular statement is described in the parentheses as "Display the words 'THIS IS A SIMPLE PROGRAM' when the program is listed."

Displaying Literal Characters

There are many variations of the PRINT statement. In this unit we will see three of them. The first is shown in Figure 1-4.

Line number	Statement name	*The string constant (i.e., literal characters) appearing between quotation marks will be displayed when the program is executed (run)*
40	PRINT	"SAMPLE PROGRAM RESULTS"

("Display the words SAMPLE PROGRAM RESULTS when the program is executed")

Figure 1-4   PRINT statement displaying a string constant (literal characters)

The PRINT statement in this figure consists of the line number 40, the statement name PRINT, and a string constant of literal characters contained within quotation marks. The effect of this statement is described in the parentheses as: "Display the words 'SAMPLE PROGRAM RESULTS' when the program is executed." Messages such as this can be used for headings, for instructions to people using the program, or for making the output of the program more understandable.

Displaying Calculated Results

Figure 1-5 at the top of the next page is an example of a PRINT statement that performs arithmetic and displays the answer.

Line number	Statement name	The indicated operation is performed on the numeric constants and the result is displayed as a single value
60	PRINT	2+3

("Add 2 and 3 and display the answer 5 when the program is executed")

Figure 1-5   PRINT statement performing arithmetic and displaying the answer

As usual, there is a line number, 60, and a statement name, PRINT. Next, the numeric constant 2 is followed by a plus (+) sign, which indicates the operation to be performed. This is followed by another numeric constant, 3. Note that 2+3 is not enclosed within quotation marks, so the expression will not be printed. Instead, the effect is described within the parentheses as "Add 2 and 3 and display the answer 5 when the program is executed."

Displaying a Blank Line

Figure 1-6, an example of a PRINT statement, consists simply of the line number 45 and the statement name PRINT with nothing following it—that is, without an operand.

Line number	Statement name
45	PRINT

("Display a blank line")

Figure 1-6   PRINT statement displaying a blank line, causing a vertical line space before the next line is printed

The effect of executing this instruction is to display a blank line. For now, this will be your way of causing the computer to provide extra space between printed lines. Every such PRINT statement will cause an additional line feed (vertical line space) in the output display.

END Statement

In Figure 1-7 the END statement consists simply of the statement number and the word "END."

Line number	Statement name
999	END

("Define the end of the BASIC program and stop execution of the program")

Figure 1-7   END statement

There must be one, and only one, END statement for each program, and it should have the highest line number in the program. For this reason it is usually advisable to make it a very large number. The purpose of the END statement is to define the end of the BASIC program and stop execution of the program.

We will use these few statements to acquaint you with your computer.

Mechanics of BASIC Programming

We will devote the remainder of this unit to teaching you the mechanics of using BASIC programs on your computer. Computer manufacturers have different methods for accomplishing many of the functions covered in this unit. For that reason we have left many of the details that apply to your computer to be covered in the appropriate System Specifics booklet for Unit 1. One word of encouragement: if you find your early contacts with the computer a little confusing, you have lots of company. With a little experience, however, these routines will become second nature, and you will be on your way to becoming a computer programmer. Rule 1 for the novice, therefore, is: if in doubt, ask. People are usually eager to help if they know you need it, but you must let them know. Consult your instructor, other students, members of your computer center staff, or your manufacturer's reference manual. One answer can save you frustrating loss of time.

Now let's examine some general points about a sample program we will use to introduce you to the computer. The sample program will cover only techniques that apply to all computers. Later, in the System Specifics booklet we will cover particulars about your individual computer.

We will assume that this sample program will be entered by typing it at a keyboard and that it will be displayed on a screen. We will also assume that the proper start-up procedure has been accomplished and that memory has been cleared. When you are finished typing a line, you must signal the computer to record it in memory. Since this technique varies among computers, we will assume it is done properly in the sample. All the preceding assumptions will be covered in the System Specifics booklet.

Typing the Sample Program

Now let's look at some specific aspects of the sample program. (Refer to Figure 1-8.)

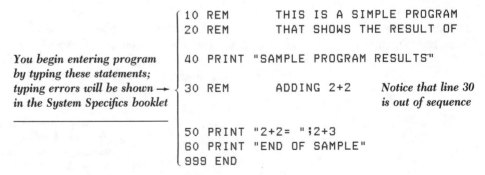

You begin entering program by typing these statements; typing errors will be shown → in the System Specifics booklet

```
10 REM        THIS IS A SIMPLE PROGRAM
20 REM        THAT SHOWS THE RESULT OF

40 PRINT "SAMPLE PROGRAM RESULTS"

30 REM          ADDING 2+2
```
Notice that line 30 is out of sequence
```
50 PRINT "2+2= ";2+3
60 PRINT "END OF SAMPLE"
999 END
```

Figure 1-8   Typing the sample program

Begin by typing the BASIC statements shown in Figure 1-8. The first is line number 10, the REMARK statement. Type 10 REM THIS IS A SIMPLE PROGRAM, and then signal the computer that you are finished typing that line. In many computers this is accomplished by pressing the **RETURN** key; in others the **ENTER** key is used. The System Specifics booklet for this unit will discuss the appropriate method for your computer.

There are a few things you should know about this first statement. First, on the keyboard you must type the numeric key for one, not the lowercase letter "l" as you would on some conventional typewriters. The *one* key is located with the other numeric keys zero through nine. Also, be sure you press the zero key for zero and not the letter "O." The space before and after the statement name REM is caused by pressing the space bar. Although this is not required in all computers, it improves readability of the statements. BASIC statements appear all in capital letters in this *Programming Essentials* text.

Type line number 20, another REMARK statement. Next type line 40, a PRINT statement that will display the message "SAMPLE PROGRAM RESULTS" when the program is executed. Now we have done something on purpose that you might do accidentally. We forgot to type line number 30. This is not a problem, because BASIC doesn't care in what order it receives the lines. It will store them in the proper sequence in memory. You can now type statement 30, and BASIC will insert it in the proper sequence in memory—that is, between lines 20 and 40. Later, when the program is displayed, the lines will appear in their proper sequence. Also note that we do not use consecutive line numbers, such as 10, 11, and 12. Instead, we leave gaps by numbering in increments of ten, so that, later, if we want to insert a new statement between existing statements, line numbers will be available and we will avoid retyping the program.

Look at line 50 next. The result of line 50, when executed, is that whatever is contained within the quotation marks will be displayed exactly as shown—that is, "2+2 = ". Next, following the semicolon, you will type 2+3 without quotation marks. When line 50 is executed, the computer will perform the addition of 2 and 3, and print out only the answer 5. This is mathematically correct, but it is not what we want to show as an example of adding 2 + 2. We will correct this later. In line 60 the PRINT statement will display the ending message enclosed in quotation marks. Finally, the last statement you will type is the END statement. Since the END statement should have the highest number in your program, we suggest that you get in the habit of giving it a very high number, such as 999. Most computer systems allow statement numbers as large as 9999; some don't, though, so you should check out your system.

Displaying the Sample Program

Occasionally you will want to display the program that is stored in memory. In our example we asked you to make a couple of errors in lines 30 and 50, so you could see how the program actually appears in memory (errors and all). Almost all computers accomplish this the same way, so in Figure 1-9 we show the actual command, which is LIST.

You type   LIST ◄— *Causes computer to display program from memory onto screen in line-number sequence regardless of the sequence entered; notice lines 30 and 40 in particular*

Computer displays
```
10 REM       THIS IS A SIMPLE PROGRAM
20 REM       THAT SHOWS THE RESULT OF
30 REM       ADDING 2+2
40 PRINT "SAMPLE PROGRAM RESULTS"
50 PRINT "2+2= ";2+3
60 PRINT "END OF SAMPLE"
999 END
```

Figure 1-9   Displaying or listing the sample program

Remember, from the Introduction, that one difference between a command and a statement is the line numbers. Statements have them; commands normally do not. Since LIST is a command, you merely type LIST without a line number and signal the computer that you are finished. The computer then displays the program in memory on your screen or printer.

Executing the Sample Program

At this point all you have done is enter instructions for a program and display them. The computer must now be commanded to carry out the instructions. As with the LIST command for displaying programs, most computers use the same method for executing them. This is the RUN command, as shown in Figure 1-10.

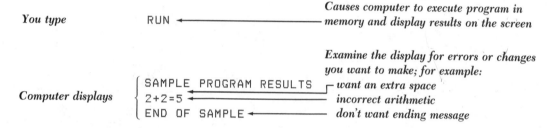

You type   RUN ←   *Causes computer to execute program in memory and display results on the screen*

Computer displays
```
SAMPLE PROGRAM RESULTS
2+2=5
END OF SAMPLE
```
Examine the display for errors or changes you want to make; for example:
— *want an extra space*
— *incorrect arithmetic*
— *don't want ending message*

Figure 1-10 Executing or running the sample program

You type RUN without a line number and signal the computer that you are finished. The computer begins executing the statement with the lowest line number, goes on in sequence to the next highest, and so forth, until it comes to the END statement, or until it is instructed to go to (or branch to) a statement out of sequence. In our program the computer continues in sequence until it executes the END statement. The output results are shown below the word RUN. Review the results of executing your program to see whether it does what you want it to do. In other words, are there errors? If there are, correct the errors by retyping the statement.

Making Changes in the Sample Program

Are there any changes that you want to make? Figure 1-11 shows how to make changes.

Adds line 45 to program to get extra blank line when displaying the results during a run
↓

You type
```
45 PRINT
50 PRINT "2+2= ";2+2
60
```
← *Replaces original line 50 with revised line 50 to correct arithmetic*

↑
Deletes line 60 from program to eliminate ending message

Figure 1-11 Making changes in the sample program

In this case we will assume that you want an extra space in the output between the line that says "SAMPLE PROGRAM RESULTS" and the line that says "2+2= 5." To get the extra space, you type line 45, a PRINT statement with nothing after the word PRINT. This would cause a blank line to be printed, giving you an extra space. Also, let's say that, rather than have 5 be printed as a result of the arithmetic in line 50, you want the answer 4 to be printed. The correction consists of simply typing line 50 in the desired form; it will replace the previous line 50 in memory. Let's assume that you also want to eliminate the message that says "END OF SAMPLE". You simply type the statement number 60, and it is deleted from memory.

Listing and Running the Revised Sample Program

In Figure 1-12 we will display the program as it now appears in memory.

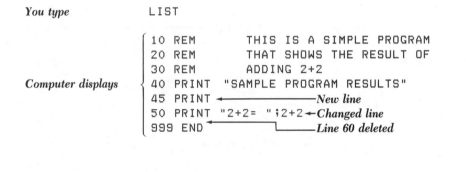

You type   LIST

Computer displays
```
10 REM       THIS IS A SIMPLE PROGRAM
20 REM       THAT SHOWS THE RESULT OF
30 REM       ADDING 2+2
40 PRINT  "SAMPLE PROGRAM RESULTS"
45 PRINT  ────────────New line
50 PRINT "2+2= " ;2+2─Changed line
999 END                └──Line 60 deleted
```

You type   RUN

Computer displays
```
SAMPLE PROGRAM RESULTS ── Compare results with those
                          in the run in Figure 1-10
2+2=4
```

Figure 1-12   Listing and running the revised sample program

The display of the corrected program appears below the word LIST. There are no errors in the display, so we again execute the corrected program in memory. The results appear below the word RUN.

Before proceeding to the System Specifics booklet, we will examine two more statements that will be used to illustrate programs in that booklet: INPUT and GO TO.

INPUT Statement

Figure 1-13 introduces the INPUT statement; you will learn more about it later. We need to use it now, however, to illustrate how to stop the program while it is waiting for an entry from the keyboard.

The INPUT statement consists of a line number and a statement name, IN-PUT, followed by the name of a numeric variable (in this case N). When this particular instruction is executed, the computer types a question mark (?) on the display and then waits for the user to type a numeric value and signal the computer to accept it. For example, if the user types the number 6 and signals the computer, the value of 6 would be stored in memory under the name N.

Line number	Statement name	The variable name under which data will be stored when entered from the keyboard
90	INPUT	N

*("Display a ? signaling the user to enter a value on the keyboard,
which will be stored in memory under the name N")*

Figure 1-13   INPUT statement (explained more completely in a later unit)

GO TO Statement

Earlier we said that the computer begins executing a program with the lowest line number and goes on in sequence to the next higher number, and so on, until it comes to the END statement or until it is instructed to go to (or branch to) a statement out of sequence. The GO TO statement is one example of an instruction that will cause the computer to branch to a statement out of sequence.

Line number	Statement name	Branch to this line number
70	GO TO	60

("Go directly to line 60 and begin executing statements in sequence again")

Figure 1-14   GO TO statement (explained more completely in a later unit)

In Figure 1-14 you can see that the GO TO statement consists of a line number and the statement name GO TO, followed by the line number that the computer should begin executing next (in this case 60). This example says, in effect, go directly to line 60 and begin executing statements in sequence again. You will learn more about this in a later unit. We will use the GO TO statement in the System Specifics booklet for this unit to illustrate more about the mechanics of using your computer— namely, how to stop execution of a program that continuously repeats the same steps over and over. This repetition is called *looping*.

In Closing

The following sections are normally located in this book, the *Programming Essentials* text, at the end of each unit:

Programming Techniques
Debugging Aids
Reference
Application Exercises
Answers to Application Exercises
Programming Problems

However, since the procedures covered in this unit vary significantly among various computers, the closing sections for this unit are located in Unit 1 of the System Specifics booklet.

Now refer to the System Specifics booklet for Unit 1 to become familiar with your particular computer.

2 Writing Assignment Statements and Altering Program Control

OBJECTIVES

When you complete this unit, you will be able to:

1. Demonstrate sufficient knowledge of algebra and BASIC to parallel the computer execution of simple assignment statements typically found in BASIC programs
2. Identify the variable and constant elements of a BASIC assignment statement
3. Convert a given formula to a BASIC assignment statement
4. Predict the arithmetic results of a LET statement
5. Use a GO TO statement in a program
6. Display the contents of a variable
7. Code and execute a BASIC solution, given a program that requires LET and PRINT statements

INTRODUCTION

What Is an Assignment Statement?

An assignment statement is a BASIC statement that directs the computer to perform arithmetic or assigns a value to a variable. Examples:

```
10 LET C=C+1
20 LET T=5
```

What Is a Numeric Constant?

A numeric constant is a number whose value does not change. Examples: 121.65, 37, 1.12345E−2.

What Is a Numeric Variable?

A numeric variable is a symbol representing a value that can be changed. Examples: A, X, B9.

What Is an Operator?

An operator is a symbol that indicates which arithmetic or logical operation is to be performed. Examples: $+$, $-$, $*$, $/$, $\uparrow$, $=$, $<$, $>$.

14

What Is an Expression?

An expression is a combination of one or more variables and/or constants along with arithmetic operators. Examples:

```
X+Y/5
T+1
```

What Is a String Variable?

A string variable is a symbol that represents one or more alphabetic characters that can be changed. Examples:

```
A$
M$
Z$
```

What Is a GO TO Statement?

A GO TO statement is a statement that alters the control of a program. A GO TO statement can transfer control of a program to a statement that follows or precedes it. Examples:

```
30 GO TO 100

70 GO TO 40
```

Using Assignment Statements

A BASIC program consists of a series of instructions called *statements*. Most BASIC programs require mathematical calculations, which are written in the form of statements. These statements contain expressions that can consist of constants, variables, and operators. Assignment statements represent calculations to be performed, and they are used extensively in BASIC programs.

Using GO TO Statements

Computers execute one statement after another, following the order in which the statements appear. But this sequence can be changed. Many BASIC programs require certain statements within the program to be executed more than once. GO TO statements are used to branch to these statements. GO TO statements are also useful when it is necessary to branch past or skip certain statements. In a later unit, you will learn about other statements that alter the control of a program.

Constants

In this unit we will discuss the arithmetic operations of BASIC. Before we get involved in BASIC, though, let's look at some of the similarities between BASIC and elementary algebra, which you probably learned some time ago. BASIC and algebra have some things in common—for example, constants and variables.

Constants can be numbers without decimal points (called *integers*), if they have no fractional part, or they can be decimal numbers with a fractional part to the right of the decimal point (called *real numbers*). Integer numbers are whole numbers; they have no fractional part. Constants can also be expressed in *scientific notation*—a real number with an exponent. However, not all BASIC systems have the capability of handling both integer numbers and real numbers.

Scientific notation is used to describe very large or very small real numbers; integer numbers are used to conserve computer storage. Most programs use real numbers without scientific notation. You might be accustomed to including commas with numbers, or dollar signs with values of money, but these forms will be unacceptable (thus incorrect) in BASIC. Also, there are size limits for constants. These vary among computers, so you should consult the manufacturer's BASIC manual to determine your computer's limits.

Variables

BASIC variables are like the familiar x, y, and z in algebra, which represent changing values. Variables can represent numbers or alphabetic characters. A programmer can choose an alphabetic character or an alphabetic character and a digit (such as A or A1) as a variable to represent a real number; an alphabetic character and a dollar sign (such as A$) can be used as a variable to represent one or more alphabetic characters, called *strings;* and on some systems an alphabetic character followed by a percent sign (such as A%) can represent an integer. Some BASIC systems permit two or more alphabetic characters to represent variables.

Arithmetic Operations

BASIC arithmetic operations—addition, subtraction, and so on—use constants and/ or variables. In BASIC, addition is indicated by a plus sign, subtraction by a minus sign, multiplication by a single asterisk, division by a slash, and exponentiation (or raising to a power) by an upward arrow, caret, or double asterisk. In Figure 2-1 you can see all these symbols used in the BASIC expression at the top of the figure.

BASIC Expression
A – B / C + (D + E) * F ^ 3

PRIORITY	OPERATION SYMBOL	OPERATION
1	( )	Parentheses; innermost first
2	↑, ^, or **	Exponentiation (raising to a power)
3	{*⁄	Multiplication (Operations of equal priority Division are performed from left to right)
4	{+⁻	Addition (Operations of equal priority Subtraction are performed from left to right)

5th	3rd	6th	1st	4th	2nd	Priority
↓	↓	↓	↓	↓	↓	
A – B	/	C+	(D+E)	*	F↑3	

Figure 2-1   Priority of operations

Priority of Operations

To illustrate the order of operations, the same BASIC expression is used in the example at the bottom of Figure 2-1. We have indicated the order in which the various operations are performed based on the rules governing the priority of operations in BASIC, which are similar to those of algebra. Inner parentheses have the highest priority, so operations within them are performed first. Exponentiation is the second level of priority. Multiplication and division are the third level of priority, and addition and subtraction are the fourth level. With operations of the same level, computation proceeds from left to right. A summary of these rules appears in the Reference section at the end of this unit.

Algebra Review

Algebra rules of arithmetic apply to BASIC:

1. When two constants and/or variables with like signs are added, the result is the total of the two elements. The sign of the result is the same as the sign of the elements.
2. When two constants and/or variables with unlike signs are added, the result represents the difference between the two elements. The result will take on the sign of the larger absolute value of the two elements. (The absolute value of any number is that number with a positive sign.)
3. In subtraction, the sign of the number to be subtracted is changed and the rules of addition are followed.
4. In multiplication and division, unlike signs give a negative result; like signs give a positive result.
5. In exponentiation (raising a number to a power), the value is multiplied by itself the number of times indicated by its exponent. The exponent is also referred to as a *superscript*.

These rules, with examples, are summarized at the end of this unit.

Flowcharting

Many programmers find flowcharts to be excellent aids for writing computer programs. A flowchart expresses in a symbolic or pictorial form the solution of a problem to be solved by a computer program. We will be using flowcharts throughout this text to make it easier for you to understand the BASIC programs presented. Most BASIC statements can be represented by a flowchart symbol. As we introduce each BASIC statement, we will also present the flowchart symbol associated with it.

Assignment Statements

One of the statements used most frequently in BASIC programs is the assignment statement (see Figure 2-2). Like all BASIC statements, the assignment statement begins with a line number. The statement name, LET, indicates that an assignment is to be made. A numeric variable, string variable, constant, or any valid BASIC

Line number	Statement name	The value is assigned to this variable	Means "replaced by"	Constant	Operator	Variable	
10	LET	X	=	1.5	*	Z	$X \leftarrow 1.5 * Z$

Process symbol

("Let the value in X be replaced by 1.5 multiplied by the value in Z")

Figure 2-2   Assignment statements

expression can follow the equals sign. There can never be more than one variable to the left of the equals sign. In an assignment statement, the equals sign means "replaced by" rather than "equal to." The statement in Figure 2-2 means "Let the value in the numeric variable X be replaced by the constant 1.5 multiplied by the value in the numeric variable Z." Most BASIC systems permit the programmer to write the assignment statement without the word LET. Figure 2-2 could be written as 10 X=1.5*Z.

To the right of the LET statement in Figure 2-2 is the flowchart symbol that indicates an assignment statement. It is a rectangle called a *process symbol*. The arrow within the symbol points to the variable that will be replaced by the value of the variable, constant, or expression located to the right. Notice the close relationship between the LET statement in the program and the contents of the process symbol.

Writing Assignment Statements

Figure 2-3, line 1, illustrates an assignment statement. It begins with statement number 10 followed by LET G=3.5. This is an illustration of an assignment statement with one constant to the right of the equals sign.

We arbitrarily gave the variable the name G. We then assigned a constant, 3.5, to this variable. This value will remain in G until changed by you, the programmer. This is called an *assignment statement* because it assigns a value to a variable on the left side of the equals sign.

"Variable" usually refers to a numeric variable that contains a numeric value; "string variable" refers to a variable that contains one or more alphanumeric characters

1. 10 LET G = 3.5   *One constant*

2. 10 LET D = R*T   *Two variables*

3. 10 LET T = G*.25   *Variable and a constant*

4. 10 LET M = I/N   *Two variables*

5. 10 LET K = K +1   *Variable and a constant*

6. 10 LET C$ = "Y"   *String variable*

7. 10 LET C = AB   *Invalid multiplication (implied) of A and B*

8. 10 LET C = A*B   *Valid multiplication of A and B*

9. 10 LET C=A(B/D)E   *Invalid multiplication using parentheses*

10. 10 LET C=A*(B/D)*E   *Valid multiplication using parentheses*

Figure 2-3   Writing assignment statements using numeric constants and variables

With a pencil, on line 2 write 10 LET D=R*T. This represents the familiar formula "Distance equals rate multiplied by time." The statement you have written on line 2 shows an expression with two variables on the right side of the equals sign.

Lines 3, 4, and 5 illustrate some other combinations. Look at the statement on line 5. You might think it strange to write K equals K plus 1. We would never do this in algebra. But remember that the equals sign takes on a different meaning in BASIC—it means "replaced by." So this statement really means "K is replaced by K+1."

On line 6 write 10 LET C$="Y". This statement will assign the alphabetic character Y to the string variable C$. String variables will be covered in greater detail in a later unit.

One common mistake of the beginning programmer is to assume that implied multiplication works in BASIC. Look at line 7. In algebra, if you show A and B next to one another as illustrated, it means A times B; the multiplication is implied. This is not true in BASIC. You must place a multiplication sign between the A and the B, if you intend to multiply them. Correct this statement, and write it on line 8.

You should have written 10 LET C=A*B.

On line 9 you can see another example of invalid implied multiplication, using parentheses. Correct this statement, and write it on line 10.

You should have written, 10 LET C=A*(B/D)*E.

Computer Simulation

Figure 2-4 is an example of a sequence of assignment statements that, when used with the scratch area to the right, simulates the computer execution of these statements. Each assignment statement changes the value of a variable in computer memory. Let's go through the statements and see how they affect the variables. Make entries with your pencil in the scratch area. The purpose of this sequence of statements is to accumulate the recorded hours for several days. In addition, you will keep a count of the days for which hours are recorded.

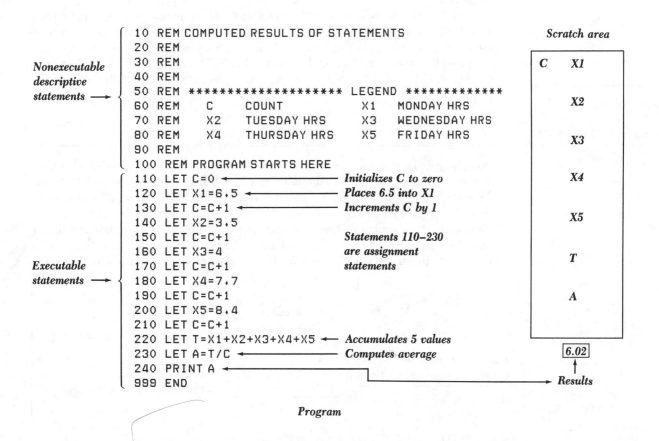

Figure 2-4   Computing results of assignment statements

Statements 10 through 100, beginning with the letters REM, are REMARK statements describing the variables used in the program and what they represent. You will find it helpful to include a legend similar to the one illustrated in the programs that you write. A list of each variable in the program and its use, as shown in statements 60 through 90, will help you remember what each variable represents and can thus reduce programming errors.

The first statement that will cause the computer to take an action is statement 110. This statement and others like it, called *executable statements*, direct the computer to do something, whereas statements such as the REMARK statement are descriptive, not executable. Statement 110 LET C=0 will be used to initialize a counting area to zero. Some BASIC systems automatically assign a zero to all variables, but most do not. In this illustration the variable C will be used to count the number of days. Any variable that will be used as a counter or accumulator should first be cleared to zero, just as you would clear an adding machine before making calculations. In the scratch area, enter a zero under the variable C.

Statement 120 assigns a value to the variable X1. This is the variable name we have chosen to represent the hours for Monday. Write this value in its proper location in the scratch area under the variable name. You should have written 6.5 under the variable X1. Statement 130 says to replace the value in C with the value of C+1. Cross out the original contents of C, and write the new value. You should have crossed out the zero and replaced it with a 1. (Zero plus 1 is 1.) During execution of the program within the computer, the zero would be replaced by the 1. However, so that we can trace our steps if necessary, we will just cross out the replaced value and place the new value below it. At this point, there should be a 1 under C and 6.5 under X1.

Make a check mark to the left of statement 140. From this point, you're on your own. Before you complete the steps in statements 140 through 240, note the final values of C, T, and A, because these are the values you should arrive at when you complete this program. The final value in C is 5, T is 30.1, and A is 6.02. At the conclusion of this unit you will be asked to complete this as part of the Application Exercises.

GO TO Statement

Computer programs operate sequentially unless this sequence is rerouted, or redirected, by the program. A computer executes BASIC statements one at a time, following the order in which the statements appear in the program. If you want to alter this sequential execution in any way, you must insert what is called a *control statement* in your program. A control statement transfers control to a statement other than the next one in sequence. The simplest of all control statements is the GO TO statement, illustrated in Figure 2-5. This statement does exactly what its name

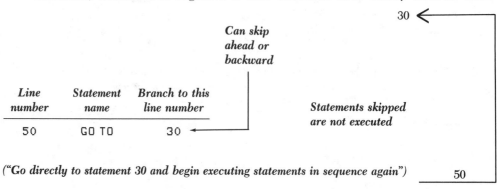

("Go directly to statement 30 and begin executing statements in sequence again")

Figure 2-5   The GO TO statement

implies—it goes to another statement. In this case control passes to statement 30 every time the GO TO statement is encountered. The statement that it goes to can precede or follow the GO TO statement. When the computer transfers control to the statement number specified in the GO TO statement, it then begins executing sequentially again.

There is no flowchart symbol to represent the GO TO statement. The transfer of control from the GO TO statement to another statement is shown by a flowline (as illustrated), which points to the next statement to be executed after the GO TO statement. The GO TO statement is also called an unconditional branch.

Printing a Variable

In Unit 1 you learned how the PRINT statement is used to print or to display the results of an arithmetic computation and literal data. Figure 2-6 shows a more common use of the PRINT statement—that is, to print the contents of a numeric and/or string variable. The parallelogram is the flowchart symbol that describes printing, and it is called the *input/output symbol* because it can be used to represent input as well as output.

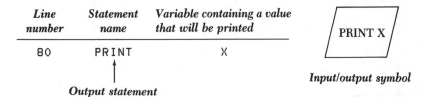

("Print the value contained in the variable X")

Figure 2-6 The PRINT statement

Summing Numbers

Figure 2-7 illustrates a flowchart to sum numbers; the BASIC program written from the flowchart; and the results of summing the numbers 1 through 5. The START symbol at the top of the flowchart represents statement numbers 10 through 100, which describe the program and the variables to be used. We will begin all our flowcharts this way. Symbol 110 indicates that S should be initialized to zero. Statement 110 in the program shows how this is written in BASIC. The program will use S to accumulate the sum of the values.

Process symbol 120 and BASIC statement 120 illustrate that we initialize a count in BASIC by placing a 1 in the variable C. The next symbol below symbol 120 is an input/output symbol that represents three PRINT statements (130–150). Statement 130 prints the first line of the heading, statement 140 prints the second line, and statement 150 produces a blank line after the heading. Look at the "results" section, which shows how the heading printed.

Symbol 160 and statement 160 show how the contents of the count, C, are accumulated in the sum, S. The first time this statement is executed, S will be replaced by the value in S, which is a 0 (zero), plus the value in C, which is 1. Both variables, C and S, now contain 1. This is verified by statement 170, which prints the contents of C and S. Look at the "results" section again. The printed values of C and S are both 1.

22

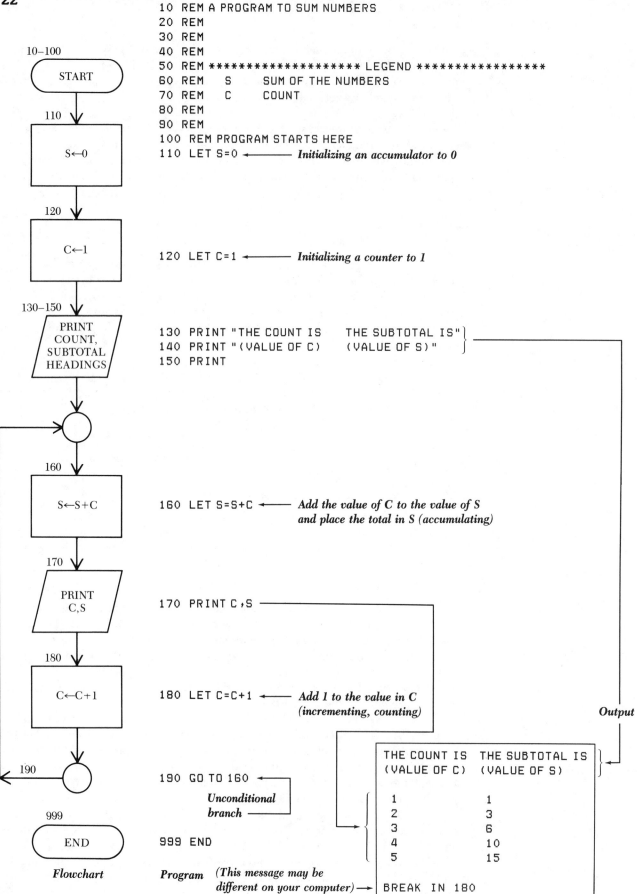

```
 10 REM A PROGRAM TO SUM NUMBERS
 20 REM
 30 REM
 40 REM
 50 REM ******************** LEGEND ****************
 60 REM    S      SUM OF THE NUMBERS
 70 REM    C      COUNT
 80 REM
 90 REM
100 REM PROGRAM STARTS HERE
110 LET S=0  ◄———— Initializing an accumulator to 0
120 LET C=1  ◄———— Initializing a counter to 1
130 PRINT "THE COUNT IS    THE SUBTOTAL IS"
140 PRINT "(VALUE OF C)    (VALUE OF S)"
150 PRINT
160 LET S=S+C  ◄—— Add the value of C to the value of S
                   and place the total in S (accumulating)
170 PRINT C,S
180 LET C=C+1  ◄—— Add 1 to the value in C
                   (incrementing, counting)
190 GO TO 160

     Unconditional
     branch

999 END
```

10–100 START

110 S←0

120 C←1

130–150 PRINT COUNT, SUBTOTAL HEADINGS

160 S←S+C

170 PRINT C,S

180 C←C+1

190

999 END

Flowchart   *Program*   *(This message may be different on your computer)* ➤

Output

```
THE COUNT IS    THE SUBTOTAL IS
(VALUE OF C)    (VALUE OF S)

     1                1
     2                3
     3                6
     4                10
     5                15

BREAK  IN  180
```

Results

Figure 2-7 Flowchart and program to sum numbers

Statement 180 increments the value of C by 1, so that the next number can be added to the sum. Notice where the number 190 is in the flowchart. It is above the flowline that alters control of the program and points to symbol 160. Statement 190 accomplishes this in the program.

When statement 160 is executed the second time, S will be replaced by the value in S (which is 1) plus the value in C (2)—a total of 3. Look at the second line of results after the heading and see what was printed.

This procedure of incrementing by 1 and adding the new count to the previous total will continue until the programmer stops the program at the computer. We stopped this program after it accumulated the numbers 1 through 5. (As you recall, in Unit 1 of the System Specifics booklet you learned to stop a program during execution.) Actually, statement 999, the END statement, will never be executed. In a later unit you will learn how to stop the program under control of the BASIC program rather than stopping it at the computer. Notice that the flowchart symbol used to represent the END statement is the same as that used to show the start of the program. This symbol is called the *terminal symbol*. In a later unit you will learn another use for the terminal symbol.

Scientific Notation

In BASIC, very large and very small numbers are not printed in their familiar forms as real numbers. Instead, they are printed in scientific notation, also called *E notation* (for exponential notation), as illustrated in Figure 2-8. The sign of the number and the decimal point are interpreted as they are in any real number. The E indicates that this number is represented in E notation form. The sign after the E indicates whether the exponent is positive or negative; this is the sign of the exponent, not the sign of the number.

The number after the E and the plus sign, 18 in this illustration, indicates how many places the decimal point is to be moved. If the sign of the exponent is positive, the decimal point is moved to the right the number of places indicated. If the sign of the exponent is negative, the decimal point is moved to the left.

A number expressed in E notation: $-1.234567E+18$

Sign of the number	Decimal point		E-notation indicator	Sign of exponent	Exponent
-	1	.	234567	E	+	18

Figure 2-8   Scientific notation (E notation)

Interpreting Scientific Notation

In example 1 of Figure 2-9, in the first column, the number in E notation represents the real number shown in the second column. The sign of the E-notation number is negative; therefore the sign of the real number is negative. E+18 means move the decimal point (between the 1 and the 2) 18 places to the right and fill in the blank spaces with zeros. Example 2 is similar to example 1. The only difference is that the resulting real number is positive, because the E-notation number is positive.

Example 3 illustrates a negative number with a negative exponent. The resulting real number is negative; in this case (with a negative exponent), the decimal is moved four places to the left. Example 4 is similar to example 3. The only difference is that the resulting real number is positive. Try examples 5 and 6 now.

You should have written −.0000000000001234567 and 12345.67. Rules for converting E-notation numbers to real numbers are listed in the Reference section at the end of this unit.

	Scientific notation (E notation)		Real number
1.	$-1.234567E+18$	Positive exponent—	$-1234567000000000000.$
2.	$1.234567E+18$	move decimal to the right	$1234567000000000000.$
3.	$-1.234567E-04$	Negative exponent—	$-.0001234567$
4.	$1.234567E-04$	move decimal to the left	$.0001234567$
5.	$-1.234567E-13$		_____
6.	$1.234567E+4$		_____

Figure 2-9   Examples of E notation

PROGRAMMING TECHNIQUES

1. Use parentheses to indicate in which order arithmetic operations are to be performed:

```
10  LET C=(((A+B)*D+E)*A+B)/10
```

2. Make variable names mnemonic (look like the values they represent):

```
C    for count
T    for total
W1   for week number 1
S    for sum
P    for pay
```

3. Use remarks to identify and describe your program:

```
10 REM PROGRAM WRITTEN BY JANE ROTH
20 REM A PROGRAM TO TOTAL WEEKLY AMOUNTS
30 REM T=TOTAL, W1=WEEK 1, W2=WEEK 2
40 REM W3=WEEK 3, W4=WEEK 4
50 REM          * * *
60 REM * ASSIGN VALUES TO WEEKS *
70 LET W1=70
80 LET W2=90
90 LET W3=45
100 LET W4=75
110 REM * TOTAL WEEKLY AMOUNTS *
120 LET T=W1+W2+W3+W4
130 REM * PRINT TOTAL *
140 PRINT T
999 END
```

4. If a constant is used repeatedly, assign it to a variable and use the variable in all computations:

Using Constant of 3.14	*Assigning Constant to Variable*
10 LET A=3.14*D	10 LET P=3.14
20 LET B=3.14*R^2*H	20 LET A=P*D
30 LET C=3.14*R^2	30 LET B=P*R^2*H
40 PRINT A,B,C	40 LET C=P*R^2
	50 PRINT A,B,C

Note: Throughout this *Programming Essentials* text you will notice incomplete programs. These incomplete programs will be used to illustrate a particular point, and they will not have an END statement.

DEBUGGING AIDS

ERROR	CAUSE	CORRECTION
Convert to BASIC $z = \dfrac{a + b}{c + d}$: 10 LET Z=A+B/C+D	B/C will be the first operation performed; A and D will then be added to give Z	10 LET Z=(A+B)/(C+D)
Convert to BASIC y times 2 divided by 10: 10 LET X=Y2/10	Implied multiplication of Y by 2	10 LET X=Y*2/10
10 LET A$=Y	String must be within quotes	10 LET A$="Y"
10 LET B="N"	String must be assigned to string variable	10 LET B$="N"
10 LET 1A=50	Variable must start with alphabetic character	10 LET A1=50
10 INPUT A 20 LET M=A*A 30 PRINT M 40 GO TO 15	GO TO statement number invalid	10 INPUT A 20 LET M=A*A 30 PRINT M 40 GO TO 10

REFERENCE

CONSTANT/VARIABLE SUMMARY

TYPE	CONSTANT	VARIABLE[a]
Real	Number with or without a decimal point: 15, 123456., .654321, etc.	An alphabetic character: X, Y, A, Z, etc.; an alphabetic character followed by a digit: A1, C3, X9, etc.
Scientific notation	Number with an exponent: $1.234567E+10$, $-7.654321E+12$, $3.45671E-7$, $-6.543217E-15$, etc.	Same as real variable
Integer[b]	Number without a decimal point: 5, 86321, 97, etc.	An alphabetic character followed by a percent sign: A%, X%, W%, etc.; an alphabetic character followed by a digit and a percent sign: A1%, X5%, W9%, etc.
Character	Any BASIC character not used in an arithmetic computation: "A", "732", "X+Y", "NAME", "12/25/85", etc.	An alphabetic character followed by a dollar sign: X$, M$, A$, etc.; an alphabetic character followed by a digit and a dollar sign: X1$, M6$, A3$, etc.

[a]Some BASIC systems permit variable names of up to 30 characters.
[b]Not available on all BASIC systems.

STATEMENT SUMMARY

ASSIGNMENT STATEMENT	GENERAL FORM
Directs the computer to perform arithmetic	LET variable = constant, variable, or expression *Example:* `50 LET A=Z/2.5 + C1` *Flowchart symbol:* A←Z/2.5+C1

CONTROL STATEMENT	GENERAL FORM

Alters control of the program	GO TO statement number
	Example:
	`20 _____`
	`__ _____`
	`__ _____`
	`__ _____`
	`50 GO TO 20`
	
	Flowchart flowline:
	
	→ 20
	
	50

PRIORITY OF OPERATIONS SUMMARY		
PRIORITY	**SYMBOL**	**OPERATION**
(highest) 1	( )	Parentheses; innermost first
2		Evaluation of functions (covered in a later unit)
3	↑, ^, **	Exponentiation—i.e., raising to a power (symbol varies with different BASIC systems)
4	* /	Multiplication Division } Equal priority
5 (lowest)	+ −	Addition Subtraction } Equal priority

Note: Operations of equal priority are performed from left to right.

Example:

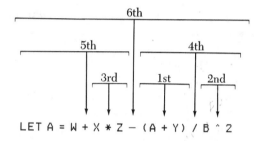

Algebra Rules

1. When two constants and/or variables with like signs are added, the result is the total of the two elements. The sign of the result is the same as the sign of the elements. Examples:

$$
\begin{array}{cc}
 & +5 \\
(+) & +5 \\
\hline
 & +10
\end{array}
\qquad
\begin{array}{cc}
 & -3 \\
(+) & -6 \\
\hline
 & -9
\end{array}
$$

2. When two constants and/or variables with unlike signs are added, the result is the difference between the two elements. The result will take the sign of the larger absolute value of the two elements. Examples:

$$
\begin{array}{cc}
 & +3 \\
(+) & -7 \\
\hline
 & -4
\end{array}
\qquad
\begin{array}{cc}
 & -2 \\
(+) & +5 \\
\hline
 & +3
\end{array}
$$

3. In subtraction, the sign of the number to be subtracted is changed, and the rules of addition are followed. Examples:

$$
\begin{array}{cc}
 & +8 \\
(-) & -3 \\
\hline
 & +11
\end{array}
\qquad
\begin{array}{cc}
 & -6 \\
(-) & +2 \\
\hline
 & -8
\end{array}
$$

4. In multiplication and division, unlike signs give a negative result; like signs give a positive result. Examples:

$$+3 \times -2 = -6 \qquad +3 \times +3 = +9 \qquad -4 \times -3 = +12$$

$$-3\overline{)-6}^{\,+2} \qquad\qquad +2\overline{)-8}^{\,-4} \qquad\qquad -4\overline{)+8}^{\,-2}$$

5. In exponentiation (raising a number to a power), the value is multiplied by itself the number of times indicated by its exponent. Example:

$X = Z^C$ (assume $Z = 5$ and $C = 3$)
$X = 5 \times 5 \times 5$
$X = 125$

Any value raised to the power of 0 equals 1. Example:

$X = 0$
$Z = 8^X$
$Z = 1$

Rules for Converting Numbers Represented in E Notation to Real Numbers

If the exponent is positive:

1. Move the decimal point to the right the number of places indicated by the exponent
2. Fill in zeros to the right between the units position of the number (least-significant digit) and the relocated decimal point
3. The sign of the real number is the same as the sign of the number represented in E notation. Example:

$9.8765 \text{ E} + 6 = 9876500$

If the exponent is negative:

1. Move the decimal point to the left the number of places indicated by the exponent
2. Fill in zeros to the left between the high-order position of the number (most-significant digit) and the relocated decimal point
3. The sign of the real number is the same as the sign of the number represented in E notation. Example:

$9.8765 \text{ E} - 3 = .0098765$

APPLICATION EXERCISES

1. Complete the computed results in Figure 2-4.

2. Circle the answer that identifies the two variables and/or constants involved in the first operation performed within each of the expressions in items (1) through (10). The rules for the priority of performing BASIC operations (hierarchy of operations) are identical to those of algebra.

	a.	b.	c.	d.
Example: LET X=V*W/(X+Y)	V,W	W,X	(X,Y)	
(1) LET X=V/W/(Y*X^3)	V,W	Y,X	(X,3)	W,Y
(2) LET X=U*(S+R)	U,S	(S,R)		
(3) LET X=(U*S+V+W)^R	(U,S)	S,V	V,W	W,R
(4) LET X=V+W+(Y+P)	V,W	W,Y	(Y,P)	
(5) LET X=V+W*Y	V,W	(W,Y)		
(6) LET X=(((V+W)*U+Y)*U+X)*8	X,8	U,X	U,Y	(V,W)
(7) LET X=V/W/Y	V,Y	(V,W)	V,Y	
(8) LET X=X^(J^(K+1))	X,J	J,K	(K,1)	
(9) LET X=U^(V+W)	U,V	(V,W)		
(10) LET X=V*U^3+W*U^2	V,U	(U,3)	W,U	U,2

3. Circle the letter that identifies the numeric value that the variable A would contain after the computer has completed each of the arithmetic statements in items (11) through (19). Assume the following variable values are in effect before each statement is executed:

Variable	Value	Variable	Value
M	1	R	−2
N	−3	S	2
P	5	T	1
Q	2		

	a.	b.	c.
Example: LET A=M+N+P+Q	11	9	(5)
(11) LET A=M+Q-1	0	2	4
(12) LET A=M+N/P	1.6	(.4)	-2.6
(13) LET A=T*S-R	0	4	-4
(14) LET A=3*N^2-N*P-M-Q	9	29	39
(15) LET A=Q+(M+M)^S	12	16	6
(16) LET A=P+Q-M*(N+Q)	6	-6	8
(17) LET A=S*(R+T)	6	3	-2
(18) LET A=N*N/N	-3	3	-27
(19) LET A=(P*N)/Q	-7.5	7.5	8

4. Select one of the choices (a through c) that correctly identifies the "ordinary" notation corresponding to the E notation shown in items (20) and (21).

	a.	b.	c.
(20) $-3.269E-03$	-3.26900	$.003269$	$-.003269$
(21) $-2.36958E+8$	$.00236958$	-236958000	-8.236958

5. Given the following program:

```
10 LET Y=0
20 LET Z=0
30 GO TO 50
40 LET Y=Y+10
50 LET Z=Z+50
60 LET Y=Y+25
70 GO TO 100
80 PRINT Z*Y/2
90 GO TO 110
100 PRINT Z/Y
110 (Program continues)
```

Circle the letter in (22) that indicates what will be printed when statement 80 or 100 is executed.

(22) a. 1.4285   b. 1   c. 2   d. 2.857

6. Given the following program:

```
10 LET M=8
20 LET N=32
30 LET P=-4
40 LET N=N/P
50 LET P=P*P
60 LET M=M/N+P+1
70 PRINT M/2
99 END
```

Circle the letter in (23) that indicates what will be printed after the program has been executed.

(23) a. 16   b. -4   c. -32   d. 8

7. For items (24) and (25), write each formula as a BASIC assignment statement.
   Example: Theory of Relativity
   $$E = mc^2$$
   ```
   LET E=M*C^2
   ```

   (24) Volume of a cylinder: $V = 3.14\ r^2h$
   (25) Calculation of Ohm's law: $I = v \div r$

Answers to Application Exercises

(1) c	(10) b	(18) a
(2) b	(11) b	(19) a
(3) a	(12) b	(20) c
(4) c	(13) b	(21) b
(5) b	(14) c	(22) c
(6) d	(15) c	(23) d
(7) b	(16) c	(24) LET V=3.14*R^2*H
(8) c	(17) c	(25) LET I=V/R
(9) b		

PROGRAMMING PROBLEMS

2-1. Mileage-Conversion Program

Given the distances in miles between four cities, write a program to print the distance in kilometers between each pair of cities. In addition, compute and print the total time required, in hours, to travel between all four cities, if the average speed is 60 kilometers per hour.

Given:

Between	Miles
San Francisco and Chicago	2197
Chicago and New York	814
New York and Dallas	1602
Dallas and San Francisco	1769

1 mile = 1.609 kilometers
Total travel time = total kilometers/average speed

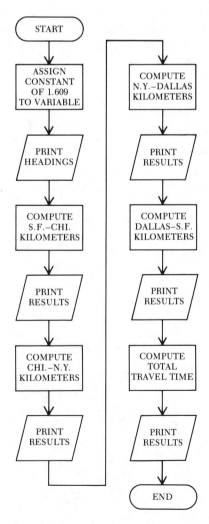

Figure 2-10   Flowchart of the mileage-conversion program

Programming tips:

1. Convert each distance in a LET statement before printing the distance in kilometers.
2. The computation of the total travel time can be done in the PRINT statement.
3. When writing the formula for the total time, be sure to include parentheses around the four amounts to be divided.
4. Use the general flowchart in Figure 2-10 as a guide.

Results:

```
THE DISTANCE IN KILOMETERS
BETWEEN SELECTED CITIES IS

S.F. TO CHI.- 3534.97
CHI. TO N.Y.C.- 1309.73
N.Y.C. TO DALLAS- 2577.62
DALLAS TO S.F.- 2846.32

TOTAL TRAVEL TIME
 171.144     HOURS
```

2-2. Grade Program

Given a student's course, course grade, and the unit value of the course, write a program to print the course, the number of units, the course grade, the grade points per course, the total units taken, and the student's grade-point average.

Given:

Course	Units	Grade
Algebra	4	B
Biology	5	C
Computer Programming	3	A
English Composition	3	B
History of Art	2	C

Programming tips:

1. Draw a flowchart of the solution.
2. Grade points are assigned as follows:

   A—4
   B—3
   C—2
   D—1

3. Print the heading before doing any computation. (Use commas in the PRINT statement to space output.)

Results:

```
COURSE        UNITS      GRADE     GRADE POINTS

ALGEBRA         4          B           12
BIOLOGY         5          C           10
COMP PROG       3          A           12
ENG COMP        3          B            9
ART HIST        2          C            4

TOTAL UNITS= 17   GPA= 2.76471
```

3 Input and Output

OBJECTIVES

When you complete this unit you will be able to:

1. For given problems, write PRINT statements that accomplish the following:
   a. Display a string constant (literal characters)
   b. Perform arithmetic and display the answer
   c. Display a blank line and cause single spacing
   d. Display the contents of a numeric variable
   e. Print more than one value on the same line either close together or far apart
2. Write INPUT statements for a given problem
3. Write READ and DATA statements for a given problem
4. Write and execute a BASIC solution, given a problem that requires PRINT, INPUT, READ, and DATA statements

INTRODUCTION

What Is Input/Output?

Input/output refers to the process of communicating with the computer. It includes sending data into the computer for your program to work on and receiving the results in a usable form. Input/output is frequently abbreviated as I/O.

Input is information (data) that the program receives. It can be received either in the form of data stored as part of the program in DATA statements, when the program is written, or as information entered by the user from the keyboard when the program is executed or run. Input statements, such as INPUT, READ, and DATA, control the receipt of information.

Output is the visible result of a program's execution. It frequently appears in the form of information displayed on a computer printer or screen. An output statement, such as PRINT, controls the display of information from memory.

What Is a PRINT Statement?

A PRINT statement produces various types of displays on a computer printer or screen.

What Is an INPUT Statement?

An INPUT statement displays a question mark on a computer printer's page or screen, and then accepts values entered from the keyboard and stores them in memory under the variable(s) named in the INPUT statement.

What Is a READ Statement?

A READ statement accepts data located in a DATA statement within the same program. Once read, the data is stored in memory under the variable(s) named in the READ statement.

What Is a DATA Statement?

A DATA statement is a source of data for a READ statement located within the same program.

Using INPUT and OUTPUT Statements

Most programs that you write will require the computer to obtain data, process the data, and present results. In BASIC the READ, INPUT, and DATA statements control the entry of data into memory for processing. The PRINT statements control the output or recording of processed results from memory. There are many forms of input/output, such as keyboards, screen and printed (hard copy) displays, paper tape, punch cards, magnetic tapes, and disks.

In this unit we will concentrate on keyboard input and displayed output (either hard copy or screen). Only the most fundamental input/output features are covered in this unit. Additional features will be discussed later.

Using a PRINT Statement

The results of executing a program must be presented to the user in an understandable form. The PRINT statement is used to display values and descriptive information on a computer printer or screen.

Using an INPUT Statement

If the exact values of data to be used by a program are not known when the program is being written, an INPUT statement can be used to accept data from a keyboard. The data is entered on the keyboard by the user when the program is executed. When the program executes an INPUT statement, it prints a question mark (?) and waits for the user to type a value on the keyboard. The value is stored in memory under the name of the variable in the INPUT statement.

Using READ and DATA Statements

If the exact values of data to be used by a program are known when the program is being written, these values can be included as constants in DATA statements in the program. When the program is executed, these values are assigned to the variable(s) named in a READ statement. At the beginning of program execution, BASIC automatically sets a pointer at the first constant in the first or lowest-numbered DATA statement. The pointer indicates which constant in the DATA statement is to be read next. When a constant has been read during the execution of a READ statement, the pointer automatically moves to the next constant. When the last constant in a DATA statement is read, the pointer automatically moves to the DATA statement with the next higher line number. If the pointer has moved past the last constant in the last DATA statement and a READ statement is executed, the program will stop execution because it is out of data. As a programmer, you can reset the pointer yourself. This will be discussed in a later unit.

In this unit we will emphasize some fundamental input and output features, leaving additional features for a later unit. First we will concentrate on the PRINT statement, then the INPUT statement, and finally the READ and DATA statements. All these input/output operations are represented in a flowchart by the parallelogram symbol, as shown in the figures throughout this unit.

PRINT Statements

In Unit 1 we discussed the form of the PRINT statements shown in Figures 3-1, 3-2, and 3-3. By now you should be familiar with PRINT statements that display string constants, perform arithmetic and display the answer, and display a blank line. These examples are presented here as a review. Remember that we are using the terms *display* and *print* interchangeably to mean display on a screen or printer.

Line number	Statement name	*The string constant appearing between quotation marks will be displayed when the program is executed (run)*	
40	PRINT	"SAMPLE PROGRAM"	PRINT MESSAGE

("Display the words 'SAMPLE PROGRAM' when the program is executed")

Input/Output Symbol

Figure 3-1   PRINT statement displaying a string constant

Line number	Statement name	*The indicated operation is performed on the numeric constants and the result is displayed as a single value*	
60	PRINT	2+3	PRINT RESULTS

("Add 2 and 3 and display the answer 5 when the program is executed")

Symbol

Figure 3-2   PRINT statement performing arithmetic and displaying the answer

Line number	Statement name	
45	PRINT	PRINT

("Display a blank line")

Symbol

Figure 3-3   PRINT statement displaying a blank line, causing a single space before the next line is printed

Figure 3-4 presents another form of the PRINT statement that we discussed in a previous unit. The contents of the numeric variable T are displayed on the computer printer or screen. If the value 15 had been stored under the variable named T, then 15 would be displayed.

Line number	Statement name	Variable name containing a numeric value that will be displayed
70	PRINT	T

PRINT
T

Symbol

("Display the numeric value contained in the variable T")

Figure 3-4 PRINT statement displaying a numeric variable

Displaying Variables Close Together on the Same Line

In Figure 3-5 the PRINT statement will display the contents of more than one variable close together on the same line. The amount of space used depends on the particular computer you are using.

Line number	Statement name	Variables containing numeric values that will be displayed close together on the same line
90	PRINT	X;Y;T

PRINT
X;Y;T

Symbol

("Display the values contained in X, Y, and T close together on the same line")

Figure 3-5 PRINT statement displaying variables separated by semicolons on the same line

Displaying Variables Far Apart on the Same Line

In Figure 3-6 the PRINT statement displays the contents of more than one variable far apart on the same line.

Line number	Statement name	Variables names containing numeric values that will be displayed far apart on the same line
100	PRINT	X,Y,T

PRINT
X,Y,T

Symbol

("Display the values contained in X, Y, and T spread out on the same line")

Figure 3-6 PRINT statement displaying variables separated by commas on the same line

The only difference between these two examples is that, in the statement in Figure 3-5 the variables X, Y, and T are separated by semicolons; in Figure 3-6 the variables are separated by commas. Semicolons cause the values to be displayed close together across the same line, whereas commas cause them to be spaced farther apart.

There are five standard print zones in most versions of BASIC. If you separate the variables in a PRINT statement by commas, values will be displayed evenly across the page, starting at the beginning of each zone, with several extra spaces between them. If you want the values closer together, use semicolons to separate the variables in a PRINT statement. The amount of space between values varies among different computers, but it is less when semicolons rather than commas are used. With either commas or semicolons, if the computer runs out of space to display all the variables in a PRINT statement on the same line, it will automatically cause a carriage return and line feed and begin printing on the next line. In a later unit you will learn the TAB method of controlling spacing across the line. Since the spacing varies with different computers, in this section you should determine the following about the computer you are using:

1. Maximum number of print positions in a print line
2. The number of print zones
3. The number of print positions in a print zone
4. The number of print positions required to print the following types of numeric values:
   a. Integer numbers (i.e., without decimal places)
   b. Fixed-point numbers (with fixed number of decimals)
   c. Floating-point numbers (those with a varying number of decimals)

Displaying a String Constant and a String Variable on the Same Line

You can see in Figure 3-7 that it is possible to display both a string constant and a variable in the same PRINT statement.

Line number	*Statement name*	*String constant and variable name containing a numeric value that will be displayed*
110	PRINT	"TOTAL IS"; T

PRINT MESSAGE AND T

("Display the words 'TOTAL IS' and the numeric value contained in the variable T on the same line")

Symbol

Figure 3-7 PRINT statement displaying a string constant and a variable on the same line

In this example the string constant appears first, followed by a semicolon and the variable named T. The items to be printed can appear in any order, as long as they are separated by semicolons or commas. The printing will occur from left to right.

Program Using PRINT Statements

In Figure 3-8 you will get a better idea of what PRINT statements do by looking at the program list and the results it produced.

```
10 PRINT "2+2" ──────────→ 2+2
20 PRINT 2+2 ──────────→     4
30 PRINT ──────────────
40 PRINT "2+2=";2+2 ───→ 2+2= 4        ─ Blank line
50 PRINT ──────────────
60 PRINT "2+2=",2+2 ───→ 2+2=        4
999 END
```

Program   *Results*

Figure 3-8 Program using PRINT statements

We have drawn lines connecting the program line with the output line that it produced in the results. Compare the first line in the program, line number 10, with the first line of the result, which displays the string constant 2+2. Then look at line

20 and the results of the PRINT statement arithmetic, 4, which is on the second line of the results. Line 30 corresponds to the blank space on the third line of the results. In line 40 the string constant 2+2 is separated by a semicolon from the arithmetic operation of 2+2. In the results the 4 is fairly close to the equals sign. Now look at line 60 in the program; it is identical to line 40 except that the separator is a comma instead of a semicolon. Then look at the results of line 60, the last line of the results. Notice how much farther apart the equals sign and the 4 are, because of the comma separating them in the PRINT statement.

Using PRINT Statements Emphasizing Semicolons and Commas

Figure 3-9 gives an additional example of the use of semicolons and commas.

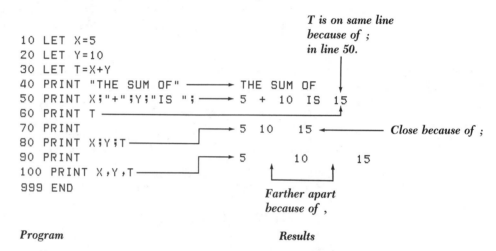

Program   *Results*

Figure 3-9   Using PRINT statements emphasizing semicolons

Lines 10 through 30 of Figure 3-9 assign values to the variables X, Y, and T. Line 40 prints the message "THE SUM OF". Line 50 prints the value of X, which is 5; following the semicolon is a plus (+) sign (this string constant is printed on the same line). Next is the variable Y, which prints as 10, and after the next semicolon, the word IS, which is also printed on the same line. Now look at the last character in line 50. It's another semicolon, but nothing follows it. When a PRINT statement ends with a semicolon, the computer does not perform a carriage return or line feed and go to the next printing line. The effect of this is that the next character the computer prints will be on the same line. Now look at line 60, which says to print the value of T. Because of the trailing semicolon in line 50, the value of T (a 15) is printed on the same line following the word IS. In line 80 the variables X, Y, and T are separated by semicolons in a PRINT statement, whereas in line 100 these three variables are separated by commas. Note the difference in the spacing of the results on the right.

Using PRINT Statements Emphasizing a Space for a Sign

Figure 3-10 demonstrates the difference between printing positive and negative values.

At line 30 in the program in Figure 3-10, a −1 is assigned to C. In line 40 the values for A, B, and C are printed. Note that the positive values have no plus sign in the results, whereas the negative value does have a minus sign. The computer allows one space in front of the value for the sign but doesn't print it if it's positive.

This can be seen more clearly in the results of lines 60 and 80. Line 60 causes the values of C and A, −1 and 15, to be printed on the same line. Line 80 prints the value of B (a 3) on a separate line. Note that the digit 1 from line 60 and the digit 3 from line 80 are aligned in the same PRINT position, whereas the minus sign for the

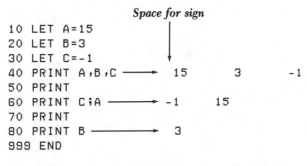

```
                        Space for sign
   10 LET A=15                │
   20 LET B=3                 │
   30 LET C=-1                ↓
   40 PRINT A,B,C ───────→  15        3         -1
   50 PRINT
   60 PRINT C;A ─────────→  -1       15
   70 PRINT
   80 PRINT B ───────────→   3
   999 END
```

Program   *Results*

Figure 3-10   Using PRINT statements emphasizing a space for a sign in output

1 is one PRINT position to the left. Instead of a plus sign in front of the 3, there is a blank space at that print position.

One of the best ways to become familiar with spacing and PRINT statements is to experiment with them on your computer.

INPUT Statements

In Unit 1 we briefly introduced the INPUT statement. Refresh your memory by reviewing Figure 3-11. Then you will be ready to learn more about the INPUT statement in Figure 3-12.

Line number	Statement name	The variable name under which data will be stored when entered from the keyboard
90	INPUT	X

```
  ┌─────────┐
 /  INPUT   /
/     X    /
└─────────┘
```

("Display a ? signaling the user to enter a value on the keyboard, which will be stored in memory under the name X")

Symbol

Figure 3-11   INPUT statement

Miscellaneous Uses of INPUT Statements

Figure 3-12 demonstrates the use of several INPUT statements in one program.

In the flowchart, look at symbol 10–20, which says INPUT X. In the program at the right, statements 10 and 20 show how this is coded in BASIC. Statement 10, the INPUT statement, will cause the computer to type a question mark when the program is run. The person using the program then must type a numeric value for the variable X and press **RETURN** or **ENTER** or whatever the appropriate key is on your computer to signal that you have finished typing. Statement 20 is used to skip a line. The first line in the results displays a question mark, which the computer displays, and the number 5, which the user types as a value for X.

In the flowchart, symbol 30–40 calls for three values—A, B, and C—to be input. In the program, statement 30 will permit the entering of all three values with a single INPUT statement. The variable names A, B, and C are separated by commas, but no comma follows the last variable, C. One question mark will be displayed and the user must type all three values before pressing **RETURN**. When the values are input by the user, they must be separated by commas, but no comma should follow the last value. Statement 40 causes the computer to skip a line. Look at the second line of the results to see the question mark displayed by the computer and the values 15, 3, and −1 typed by the user as the values of A, B, and C. In the flowchart, symbol

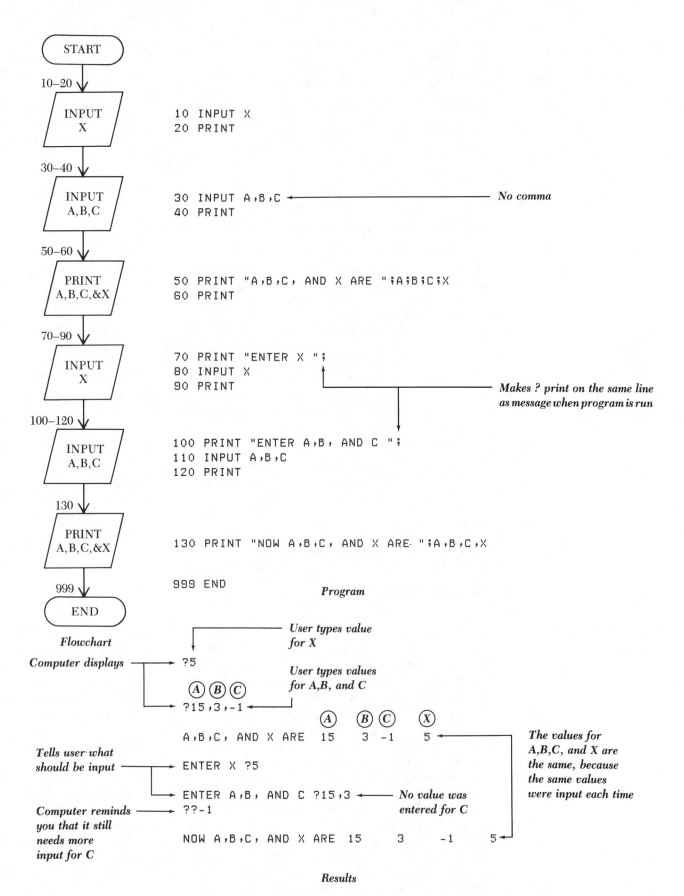

Figure 3-12   Program illustrating miscellaneous uses of INPUT statements

50–60 calls for A, B, C, and X to be printed. In the program, statement 50 displays the third line of results with the values spaced close together because of the semi-colons in the PRINT statement. Statement 60 skips a line.

Now back to the flowchart. Symbol 70–80 says to INPUT X. This looks identical to symbol 10–20, but you can see how the program statements differ. For symbol 10–20 there is simply statement 10, which said INPUT X. For symbol 70–80, statement 70 in the program calls for the printing of the message "ENTER X". The PRINT statement ends with a semicolon. Remember what happens when a PRINT statement ends with a semicolon: The computer does not perform a carriage return and go to the next printing line. We'll see how this works in conjunction with statement 80, which says INPUT X.

Look at the fourth printing line of the results. Notice the words "ENTER X" followed by a question mark on the same line. The message was printed by statement 70 and, since it ended with a semicolon, no carriage return or line feed was performed, so the next time the computer prints a character, it will occur on the same line. Because of the INPUT statement, the computer prints a question mark next, which is therefore on the same line as the message. The user then types the value for X. It is usually a good idea to precede any request for INPUT with a message indicating to the user what is expected after the question mark is typed. Now let's go back to the flowchart at symbol 100–120, which calls for input of A, B, and C.

Statement 100 in the program will print the message "ENTER A, B, AND C". Since line 100 ends with a semicolon, the question mark should print on the same line as the message when the INPUT statement at line 110 is executed. The user should be able to type in the values on the same line, but we have made a deliberate mistake. Look at the fifth line of the results, which says "ENTER A, B, and C". Notice that, following the question mark, the user types 15 for A and 3 for B, but before typing −1 for C, presses the **RETURN** key. This causes two question marks to be displayed on the next line. When an INPUT statement has not received all the values it needs before **RETURN** is pressed, the computer will display two question marks, indicating that it needs more input. The user then types the necessary value(s); in this case, −1. On the other hand, if the computer receives too many values, it will display a warning that it received extra input. The last symbol in the flowchart, number 130, calls for the printing of A, B, C, and X. Statement 130 accomplishes this. The values are printed farther apart, because the variable names are separated by commas rather than semicolons.

Finding an Average of INPUT Values

The program in Figure 3-13 will find the average of five values input by a user on a keyboard.

Symbol 110 in the flowchart sets the variable C to a value of 5, which represents the number of values to be averaged. Line 110 in the program, the LET statement, accomplishes this. Now look back at symbol 120–170 in the flowchart. This calls for the input of five values named X1 through X5.

Look at program lines 120 and 130, which call for the input of X1. Sometimes we will condense the number of symbols in a flowchart for simplicity or brevity and let them represent several statements of the program—in this case, symbol 120–170 represents statements 120 through 170. The second value, X2, is covered by a separate INPUT statement at lines 140 and 150; the next three values, X3, X4, and X5, appear in a single PRINT and INPUT statement at lines 160 and 170.

In the results, examine the first three lines of output produced by this group of program statements. In the flowchart, symbol 180 assigns the total of the values X1 through X5 to T, and symbol 190 divides the total, T, by the count, C, giving the average, A. In the program, these two operations are covered by statements at lines 180 and 190. In symbol 200–220 the values X1 through X5 are printed, and symbol 230 calls for T and A to be printed. Look at the fourth and fifth lines of the results. Both of these lines were printed by statements 200 through 230 in the program.

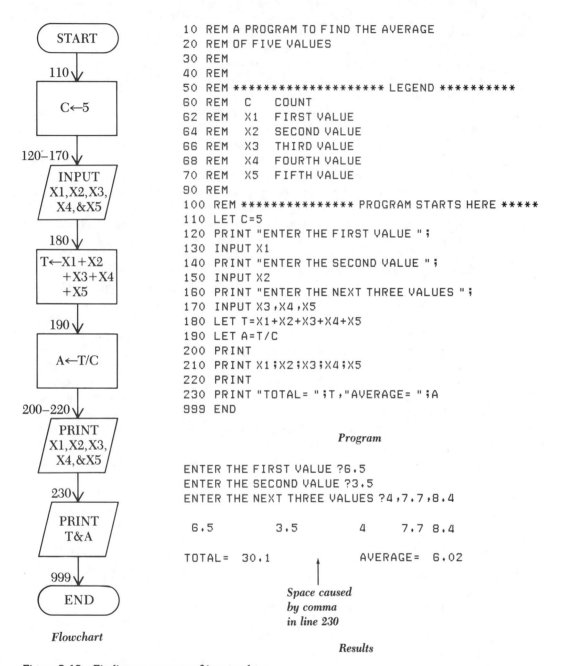

```
10  REM A PROGRAM TO FIND THE AVERAGE
20  REM OF FIVE VALUES
30  REM
40  REM
50  REM ****************** LEGEND **********
60  REM   C     COUNT
62  REM   X1    FIRST VALUE
64  REM   X2    SECOND VALUE
66  REM   X3    THIRD VALUE
68  REM   X4    FOURTH VALUE
70  REM   X5    FIFTH VALUE
90  REM
100 REM ************* PROGRAM STARTS HERE *****
110 LET C=5
120 PRINT "ENTER THE FIRST VALUE ";
130 INPUT X1
140 PRINT "ENTER THE SECOND VALUE ";
150 INPUT X2
160 PRINT "ENTER THE NEXT THREE VALUES ";
170 INPUT X3,X4,X5
180 LET T=X1+X2+X3+X4+X5
190 LET A=T/C
200 PRINT
210 PRINT X1;X2;X3;X4;X5
220 PRINT
230 PRINT "TOTAL= ";T,"AVERAGE= ";A
999 END
```

Program

```
ENTER THE FIRST VALUE ?6.5
ENTER THE SECOND VALUE ?3.5
ENTER THE NEXT THREE VALUES ?4,7.7,8.4

 6.5         3.5         4     7.7 8.4

TOTAL= 30.1              AVERAGE=  6.02
```

Space caused by comma in line 230

Results

Flowchart

Figure 3-13 Finding an average of input values

READ and DATA Statements

In Figure 3-14 we are describing two statements, the READ and DATA statements, because they are so closely related.

Line number 10 is followed by the statement name READ, which is followed by the variable name X, the name by which a value from a DATA statement will be

Line number	Statement name	Variable name under which value from DATA statement will be stored
10	READ	X

Symbol

		Value to be assigned and stored under variable name in READ statement
20	DATA	5

("Read a value for a DATA statement and store it under variable name in READ statement")

Figure 3-14   READ and DATA statements

stored. The DATA statements are the source of information for READ statements. In line 20 the statement name DATA is followed by the value 5, which will be assigned to the variable X named in the READ statements.

If the exact values of data to be used by a program are known when the program is being written, these values can be included as constants in DATA statements in the program. When the program is executed, these values are assigned to the variable or variables named in the READ statements.

At the beginning of program execution, BASIC automatically sets a pointer at the first constant in the first or lowest-numbered DATA statement. The pointer indicates which constant in the DATA statement is to be read next. When a constant has been read during execution of a READ statement, the pointer is automatically moved to the next constant. When the last constant in the DATA statement is read, the pointer moves to the DATA statement with the next higher line number. If the pointer has moved past the last constant in the last DATA statement and a READ statement is then executed, the computer will stop execution because it is out of data. You, as a programmer, can reset the pointer yourself; this technique will be discussed in a later unit.

Several DATA statements can appear in the same program. DATA statements are not executable; they are merely referred to by READ statements. Therefore, DATA statements can be located anywhere in the program before the END statement. They do not have to follow the READ statements that refer to them, and they don't have to be grouped together. In the next figure you will see several examples of READ and DATA statements.

Miscellaneous Uses of READ and DATA Statements

The output results of Figure 3-15 are similar to those of Figure 3-12, in which the values of A, B, C, and X are printed close together on one line and farther apart on another line.

The difference is the manner in which the values are input. Instead of coming from INPUT statements, the values are read from READ and DATA statements. Rather than discuss these flowcharts, we will deal primarily with the program. You might want to look at the flowchart after you have finished studying this illustration. As we go through this program, you should keep track of the DATA statement pointer. Do this in pencil, so that you can erase any mistakes.

Look at the program and circle the constant in the DATA statement where the pointer will be located when the program begins execution.

You should have circled the constant 5 in line 15. Remember that the pointer begins pointing to the first constant in the DATA statement with the lowest line number and it points to the item of data to be read the next time a READ statement is executed.

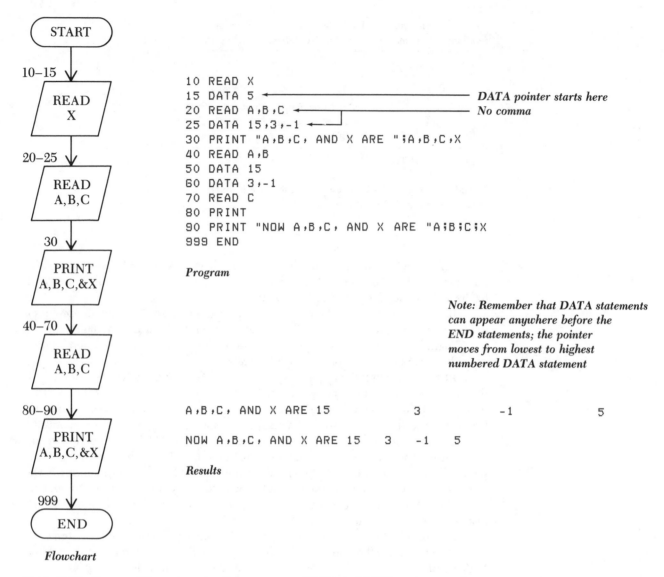

Figure 3-15   Program illustrating miscellaneous uses of READ and DATA statements

Let's go through the execution of the program. Line 10 says READ X. Since the pointer indicates the constant 5 in the DATA statement in line 15, the value 5 will be assigned to the variable X. The pointer will then move to the item to be read the next time a READ statement is executed. Circle the next constant that the pointer will move to.

You should have circled the constant 15 in line 25. The next statement to be executed is line 20, which says READ A, B, and C. Reading more than one variable in a single READ statement is similar to inputing more than one variable in an INPUT statement. You simply separate the variable names with commas in the READ statement. The last variable name is not followed by a comma.

What happens when line 20 is executed? Since the pointer is located at the constant 15 in line 25, this value will be assigned to the variable A. The pointer now moves to the next constant in line 25 (a 3), which will be assigned to the variable B. The pointer then moves to the next constant in line 25 (a −1), which is assigned to the variable C. This concludes the supply of data in line 25. Now circle the constant that the pointer will move to next.

You should have circled the constant 15 in the DATA statement at line 50.

Now let's go back to program execution. Since the READ statement at line 20 is finished, the next statement to be executed is the PRINT statement at line 30. Remember: since line 25 is a DATA statement, it is not executed; it is merely referred to as source of data for the READ statement. Line 30, therefore, causes the values A, B, C, and X to be printed (the first line in the results). The values are spread out on the line because of the commas in the PRINT statement.

Line 40 in the program is the next statement to be executed. It tells the computer to "READ A and B". Since the pointer is at 15 in line 50, this value will be assigned to A. Now circle the constant that the pointer will move to next.

You should have circled the 3 in the DATA statement at line 60, which will be assigned to the variable B. The pointer then moves to −1. Circle this. The execution of the READ statement at line 40 is concluded, because the values have been assigned to A and B.

The next executable statement is line 70, which says READ C. Since the pointer is at −1 in line 60, this value will be assigned to C. The PRINT statement in line 80 skips a line on the display, and line 90 prints the values of A, B, C, and X close together because of the semicolon separating them. Line 999 ends program execution.

Summing Numbers Read from a DATA Statement

The program in Figure 3-16 is similar to the program in Figure 2-7: It sums the numbers and then prints out the numbers and the subtotals of the numbers as they are added to the sum. The program in Unit 2 developed values by using the variable C, which was a count that went from 1 to 5. In this program the values for C, which are still 1 through 5, are read from DATA statements. Also, instead of being stopped at the keyboard as in the Unit 2 program, the program will stop itself by running out of data.

Look at the flowchart for this program in Figure 3-16. Symbol 110 says that S should be initialized to 0. In the program, line 110 shows the LET statement that accomplishes this. S is used as a variable for the sum. Symbol 120–130 in the flowchart calls for the printing of headings, and lines 120 and 130 in the program accomplish this with a PRINT statement.

Symbol 140–145 indicates that a value for C should be READ. Line 140 in the program says READ C. Since the pointer begins with the first constant in the lowest-numbered DATA statement, it will be pointing to the 1 in the DATA statement at line 145. Circle the 1. When line 140 is executed, C takes on a value of 1. Circle the 2 in the DATA statement at line 145 to show the new location of the pointer.

In symbol 150 of the flowchart, the sum, S, is replaced by itself plus the value of C. In line 150 of the program, the LET statement will cause S to be replaced by the value of S, which is 0, plus the value of C, which is 1. Variables C and S both contain the value of 1; therefore, when the PRINT statement at line 160 is executed, two 1s are printed in the first line of the results.

Look at the flowchart below symbol 160 in Figure 3-16. You can see the number 170 above the flowline; this changes the sequence of the program by pointing back to symbol 140–145 to read the value of C. The GO TO statement in line 170 of the program accomplishes this by sending control back to the READ statement at line 140. When the READ statement is executed the second time, C will take on the value of 2, since that is where the pointer is located in the DATA statement at line 145. The pointer then moves to the 3. Circle the 3. The sum S will be replaced by itself (a 1) plus the value of C (a 2). Thus S will now have a value of 3. Both C and S values are again printed in line 160. The program will return to line 140 to read another value of C, and so on, until the last value in the DATA statement, 5, is read and the pointer has nowhere else to go.

The next time that the READ statement in line 140 is executed, the computer

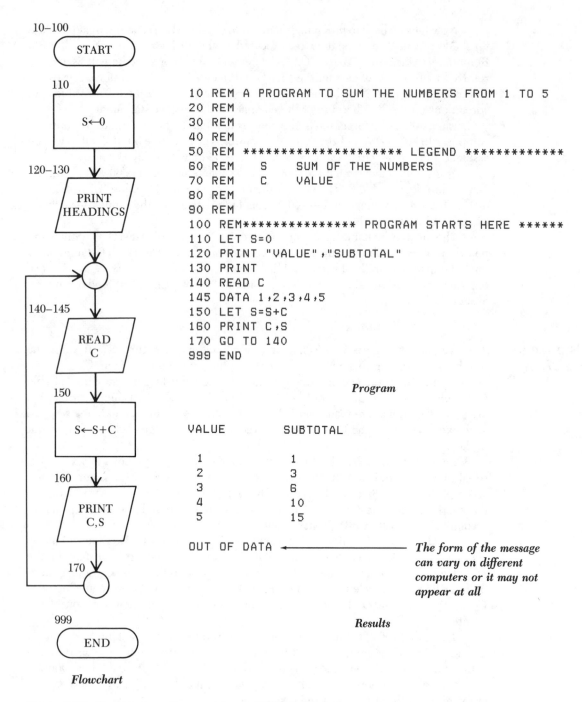

10–100

110

120–130

140–145

150

160

170

999

```
10 REM A PROGRAM TO SUM THE NUMBERS FROM 1 TO 5
20 REM
30 REM
40 REM
50 REM ******************* LEGEND *************
60 REM     S     SUM OF THE NUMBERS
70 REM     C     VALUE
80 REM
90 REM
100 REM************** PROGRAM STARTS HERE ******
110 LET S=0
120 PRINT "VALUE","SUBTOTAL"
130 PRINT
140 READ C
145 DATA 1,2,3,4,5
150 LET S=S+C
160 PRINT C,S
170 GO TO 140
999 END
```

Program

```
VALUE          SUBTOTAL

1              1
2              3
3              6
4              10
5              15

OUT OF DATA  ◄──────────────
```
The form of the message can vary on different computers or it may not appear at all

Results

Flowchart

Figure 3-16 Summing numbers read from a DATA statement

will stop execution and print an "OUT OF DATA" message in the results. Look at the last printed line in the results. This message can vary somewhat with different makes of computers. In a later unit you will learn a technique to permit you to stop the program, under the control of the BASIC program, rather than merely let it run out of data.

Compounding Savings-Account Interest

In Figure 3-17 read the REMARK statements in lines 10 through 100, which explain the program.

To make it easier for you to examine the program and its results, we have numbered and bracketed sections of the program and the corresponding results.

In the flowchart look at the first three symbols after the START symbol: 110–120, 130–140, and 150–160. These call for the input of P, R, and T: the principal, the interest rate, and the number of times per year that the interest is compounded. This is accomplished by section 1 of the program, lines 110 through 160, producing section 1 in the results. Examine both bracketed sections (identified with an encircled 1), to see how P, R, and T are input.

Symbol 170–220 in the flowchart says PRINT HEADINGS. The second section in the program, lines 170 through 220, accomplishes this and produces the headings in section 2 of the results.

Symbol 230–235 in the flowchart calls for the reading of Y, the number of years on deposit. Symbol 240 calculates A, the amount of accumulated principal and interest, using the compound-interest formula shown. Symbol 250 says: PRINT Y, the number of years, and A, the calculated amount. The flow then branches back to symbol 230–235, where a new value for Y is read. The entire process is repeated over and over until there are no more values for Y and the program stops because it is out of data.

Now look at section 3 of both the program and the results, to see how this is accomplished. You might want to experiment with the computer, using different values. If you want to experiment with a different number of years, change the values in the DATA statement at line 235. As we mentioned earlier, you will learn later how to check for an out-of-data condition and how to stop under program control, rather than by merely running out of data.

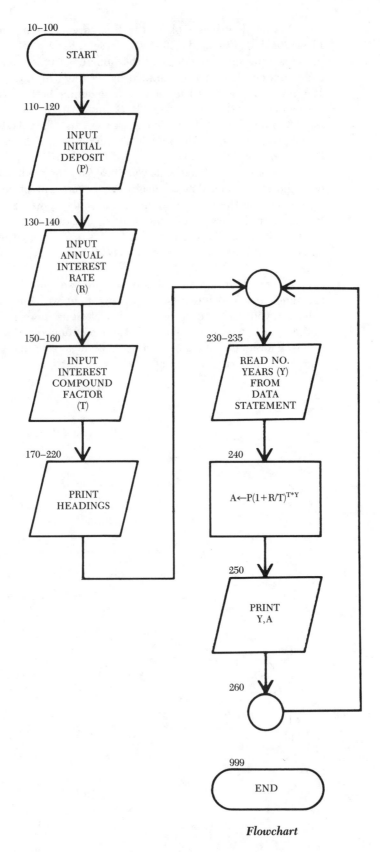

Flowchart

Figure 3-17 Compounding savings-account interest

```
10  REM A PROGRAM THAT WILL DETERMINE HOW MUCH VARIOUS SAVINGS
20  REM   DEPOSITS WILL GROW WITH SELECTED:
30  REM 1) INTEREST RATES
32  REM 2) COMPOUNDING PERIODS
34  REM 3) YEARS LEFT ON DEPOSIT
40  REM   THE FORMULA USED IS A=P*(1+R/T)**(T*Y)
50  REM******************* LEGEND **********
60  REM    P   INITIAL DEPOSIT
70  REM    R   ANNUAL INTEREST RATE
80  REM    T   TIMES PER YEAR COMPOUNDED
90  REM    Y   NUMBER OF YEARS LEFT ON DEPOSIT
100 REM************* PROGRAM STARTS HERE **********
110 PRINT "ENTER INITIAL DEPOSIT ";
120 INPUT P
130 PRINT "ENTER ANNUAL INTEREST RATE IN THE FORM .065 FOR 6 1/2 %";
140 INPUT R
150 PRINT "ENTER NUMBER OF TIMES PER YEAR INTEREST IS COMPOUNDED";
160 INPUT T
170 PRINT
180 PRINT "WILL GROW AS FOLLOWS"
190 PRINT
200 PRINT
210 PRINT " YR      AMOUNT"
220 PRINT
230 READ Y
235 DATA 1,5,10,20
240 LET A=P*(1+R/T)^(T*Y)
250 PRINT Y;A
260 GO TO 230
999 END
```

① (lines 110–160)
② (lines 170–220)
③ (lines 230–999)

Program

```
ENTER INITIAL DEPOSIT ?5000
ENTER ANNUAL INTEREST RATE IN THE FORM .065 FOR 6 1/2 %?.065
ENTER NUMBER OF TIMES PER YEAR INTEREST IS COMPOUNDED?1
```
① (the three ENTER lines)

```
WILL GROW AS FOLLOWS

YR      AMOUNT
```
②

```
1       5325
5       6850.43
10      9385.69
20      17618.2
```
③

```
OUT OF DATA
```

Results

Figure 3-17   Continued

PROGRAMMING TECHNIQUES

1. Follow these *general guidelines* to help you select the appropriate type of statement to use when assigning values to variables:

   a. Consider using a LET statement when the variable value does not change within or between runs:

   ```
   10 LET A=50
   ```

   b. Consider using a READ/DATA statement combination when the variable value does change within a run, but not between runs:

   ```
   10 READ A
   20 DATA 15,3
   ```

   c. Consider using an INPUT statement when the variable value might change within a run or between runs:

   ```
   10 INPUT A
   ```

2. Display values close together on the same line, using semicolons:

   ```
   10 PRINT A;B;C
   ```

3. Display values far apart on the same line, using commas:

   ```
   10 PRINT A,B,C
   ```

4. Plan spacing for output display:

   a. Determine spacing requirements for your particular computer, regarding print positions for numeric values, print zones, and print lines (see Reference section for details).

   b. Lay out your output on a sheet of paper before coding your PRINT statements.

   c. Do not plan the spacing for your headings until you are certain where the numeric values will print. If necessary, execute a trial run of your program. Adjust your headings to align with the location of the numeric values rather than adjusting the numeric values to the location of the headings.

5. Cause the question mark (?) for the INPUT statement to print on the same line as the descriptive message to the user, by using a semicolon at the end of the PRINT statement:

   ```
   70 PRINT "ENTER THE VALUE FOR X";
   80 INPUT X
   ```

6. Cause the question mark (?) for the INPUT statement to print on the next line below the descriptive message to the user, by not including any punctuation at the end of the PRINT statement for the descriptive message:

   ```
   70 PRINT "ENTER THE VALUE FOR X"
   80 INPUT X
   ```

DEBUGGING AIDS

ERROR	CAUSE	CORRECTION
10 PRINT A B C 20 PRINT "AMOUNT 30 PRINT SAMPLE RESULTS	Omitting required delimiters such as semicolons, commas, or quotes in PRINT statements	10 PRINT A,B,C 20 PRINT "AMOUNT" 30 PRINT "SAMPLE RESULTS"
10 LET A=15 20 LET B=3 30 PRINT "THE VALUES ARE"	Omitting a PRINT statement that would display the results	10 LET A=15 20 LET B=3 30 PRINT "THE VALUES ARE" 40 PRINT A,B
10 PRINT A,B,C,D,E,F,G	Values are displayed on different lines rather than the same one, because commas were used instead of semicolons, and as a result they don't fit on one line	10 PRINT A;B;C;D;E;F;G
10 READ A 20 DATA 15,3,70,16 30 PRINT A 40 GO TO 20	Transferring control to DATA statement rather than READ statement	10 READ A 20 DATA 15,3,70,16 30 PRINT A 40 GO TO 10
10 READ A,B,C 20 DATA 15,3	Trying to read C when the pointer has moved past the last item in a DATA statement	10 READ A,B 20 DATA 15,3
10 READ A,B, 20 DATA 15,3	Comma following last variable name in READ statement	10 READ A,B 20 DATA 15,3
10 READ A,B 20 DATA 15,3,	Comma following last value in DATA statement	10 READ A,B 20 DATA 15,3
5 PRINT A,B,C 10 READ A 20 DATA 15 30 INPUT B 40 LET C=70	PRINT statement in line 5 is out of sequence and is attempting to display undefined values for A, B, and C	10 READ A 20 DATA 15 30 INPUT B 40 LET C=70 50 PRINT A,B,C
10 INPUT A,B,	Comma following last variable name in INPUT statement	10 INPUT A,B
10 INPUT A,B,C ? 15,3 ?? (Computer needs more input)	Not enough values entered by the user from the keyboard	10 INPUT A,B,C ? 15,3,70
10 PRINT "ENTER X ";X 20 INPUT X	PRINT statement is attempting to print the value of X before it is input in line 20; usually this happens because the user thinks this is necessary to cause the value for X to appear following the question mark generated by the INPUT statement; actually the value appears after the question mark, because the user types it at the keyboard	10 PRINT "ENTER X "; 20 INPUT X

REFERENCE

STATEMENT SUMMARY

PRINT STATEMENT	GENERAL FORM

1. Any constant or variable to the right of the word PRINT will be displayed
2. If an arithmetic expression occurs to the right of the word PRINT, the arithmetic operation(s) are performed and the result is displayed
3. If nothing appears to the right of word PRINT, a blank line is displayed, thereby causing an extra horizontal space before the next line is printed
	PRINT constant(s) or variables(s) or expression to be displayed
	Examples:
	`110 PRINT "TOTAL IS ";T`
	`120 PRINT 2+2`
	`130 PRINT`
	
	Flowchart symbol:
	
	PRINT

INPUT STATEMENT	GENERAL FORM

1. An INPUT statement causes a display a ? signaling the user to enter a value on the keyboard; this will be stored in memory under the variable name(s) to the right of the word INPUT
2. When two or more variables appear in the same INPUT statement, they should be separated by commas[a]
	INPUT variable name(s)
	Example:
	`10 INPUT X`
	`30 INPUT A,B,C`
	
	Flowchart symbol:
	
	INPUT X

READ/DATA STATEMENTS	GENERAL FORM

1. When a program is run, a data pointer is automatically positioned at the first item of data in the lowest-numbered DATA statement
2. When a READ statement is executed, the first variable to the right of the word READ is the name by which the item of data at the pointer location will be stored in memory; the pointer automatically advances to the next item of data in the same DATA statement or, if there is none, to the next item of data in the next DATA statement in sequence
3. If the computer attempts to read but no item of data remains, execution of the program will be terminated; when two or more variables are read in the same READ statement, both the variable names in the READ statement and the values in the DATA statement must be separated by commas[b]
	READ variable name(s)
	Examples:
	`10 READ A`
	`20 DATA 15`
	`30 READ X,Y,Z`
	`40 DATA 15,25,35`
	
	Flowchart symbol:
	
	READ A

[a] To find the method of stopping program execution while the computer is waiting for input, consult Unit 1 in the System Specifics booklet for your particular computer.

[b] DATA statements can be located anywhere within the program; they do not affect the sequence of execution.

OUTPUT SPACING

Determine the following spacing information about your computer. For each of items 1 through 4 on the left, enter the appropriate information in the space on the right.

DESCRIPTION	NUMBER
1. Maximum number of print positions in a print line	
2. The number of print zones	
3. The number of print positions in a print zone	
4. The number of print positions required to print the following types of numeric values: a. Integer numbers (i.e., without decimals) b. Fixed-point numbers (those with a fixed number of decimal places) c. Floating-point numbers (varying number of decimal places)	

APPLICATION EXERCISES

1. Code a single PRINT statement to print the value of a variable named A preceded by the words "THE AMOUNT IS".

   20 PRINT "THE AMOUNT IS" ; A

2. Code a single PRINT statement to print the average of the variables X, Y, and Z, preceded by the words "THE AVERAGE OF X, Y, AND Z IS".

   30 PRINT "THE AVERAGE OF X Y AND Z IS" ; (X+Y+Z)/3

3. Code PRINT and INPUT statements to produce the following lines, which require the input of the values for variables named B, C, and D from a keyboard. Note that the values 500, 300, and 250 are examples of what the user would type in response to the question mark generated by the INPUT statement.

   ```
   ENTER THE AMOUNT OF YOUR FIRST PAYMENT ? 500
   ENTER THE AMOUNT OF YOUR SECOND AND THIRD PAYMENT
   ?300,250
   ```

   10 PRINT "ENTER THE AMOUNT OF YOUR FIRST PAYMENT" ;

   20 INPUT B

   30 PRINT " ENTER THE AMOUNT OF YOUR SECOND AND THIRD ",

   35 PRINT "PAYMENT"

   40 INPUT C,D

4. Code one READ and two DATA statements to read the values of variables named T, U, V, X, Y, and Z. The first DATA statement should contain 600, 230, and 500 as the values of T, U, and V. The second DATA statement should contain 200, 360, and 220 as the values of X, Y, and Z.

   10. READ T ,U, V, X, Y, Z

   20   DATA 600, 230, 500

   30   DATA 200, 360, 220

5. What would print as a result of the following program segment?

```
10  READ X,Y,Z
20  PRINT X*Y
30  PRINT Z+X^2
40  PRINT X
50  DATA 2
60  DATA 3,8
70  END
```

$\dfrac{X}{2}$ $\dfrac{Y}{3}$ $\dfrac{Z}{8}$

Printed results:

6

12

2

6. Show what the printed output will be after the following program segment is executed.

```
10  PRINT "ABCD";
20  PRINT "EFGH";
30  PRINT
40  PRINT "IJKL"
50  PRINT "MNOP";
60  PRINT "QRST"
70  END
```

ABCDEF GH

IJKL

MNOPQ R ST

Answers to Application Exercises

1. 20 PRINT "THE AMOUNT IS"; A
2. 30 PRINT "THE AVERAGE OF X, Y, AND Z IS"; (X+Y+Z)/3
3. 10 PRINT "ENTER THE AMOUNT OF YOUR FIRST PAYMENT";
   20 INPUT B
   30 PRINT "ENTER THE AMOUNT OF YOUR SECOND AND THIRD ";
   35 PRINT "PAYMENT"
   40 INPUT C,D
4. 10 READ T,U,V,X,Y,Z
   20 DATA 600,230,500
   30 DATA 200,360,220
5. 6
   12
    2
6. ABCDEFGH
   IJKL
   MNOPQRST

PROGRAMMING PROBLEMS

3-1. Program for Finding Standard and Actual Values

Write a program to read a standard value from a DATA statement and allow an actual (new) value to be input from a keyboard. The program should calculate and print the difference between the two in amount and percentage. The printed output should match the output illustrated in Figure 3-18.

Programming tips:

1. You can calculate the percent difference by dividing the amount of difference by the standard amount. Then multiply by 100 to match the results shown (for example, 0.0511308 becomes 5.11308).
2. Since your program will have only three standard amounts, it will run out of data and stop. To process the second set of actual values, run the program a second time. The *OUT OF DATA* error message varies with different computers.
3. Draw a flowchart of the solution.

Results:

```
STD AMT IS  10170    NEW AMT IS ?9650
DIFFERENCE (STD-NEW) IS   520     5.11308 %

STD AMT IS  11020    NEW AMT IS ?11380
DIFFERENCE (STD-NEW) IS  -360    -3.26679 %

STD AMT IS  11900    NEW  AMT IS ?11200
DIFFERENCE (STD-NEW) IS   700     5.88235 %
```

An OUT OF DATA Message

```
STD AMT IS  10170    NEW AMT IS  ?12300
DIFFERENCE (STD-NEW) IS  -2130     -20.944 %

STD AMT IS  11020    NEW AMT IS  ?10900
DIFFERENCE (STD-NEW) IS 120        1.08893 %

STD AMT IS  11900    NEW AMT IS  ?12400
DIFFERENCE (STD-NEW) IS -500      -4.20168 %
```

An OUT OF DATA Message

Figure 3-18 Results for program for finding standard and actual values

3-2. Program for Periodic Savings Deposits

Write a program to produce the output shown in Figure 3-20, as follows:

1. Allow the user to input the following savings information:
   a. Amount of periodic deposit to savings account
   b. Number of deposits per year
   c. Annual (nominal) interest rate
   d. Number of times interest is compounded per year
2. Calculate the effective interest rate and print it along with the information input in item 1.
3. Read from DATA statements the number of years savings are left on deposit.
4. Calculate and print for periods of 1, 5, 10, 15, and 20 years:
   a. Accumulated value of deposits without interest
   b. Accumulated savings value including interest
   c. Accumulated amount of interest

Programming tips:

1. The following definitions apply to the equations in items a and b below:
   R   Nominal annual interest rate
   E   Effective annual interest rate
   T   Number of times interest is compounded   *Note:* T and N must be the
        per year   same for the single equation
   N   Number of deposits per year   used in b below
   A   Accumulated savings balance
   M   Amount of periodic deposits
   Y   Number of years left on deposit

   a. The effective rate of interest can be calculated as follows:

   ```
   E=(1+R/T)^T-1
   ```

   b. The accumulated savings balance can be calculated as follows:

   ```
   A=M*(((1+R/T)^(N*Y)-1)/(R/T))
   ```

2. The accumulated value of deposits can be calculated by multiplying the periodic deposit, the number of deposits per year, and the number of years.
3. Accumulated interest can be calculated by subtracting accumulated deposits from the accumulated savings balance.
4. Your program will run out of data and stop after it has read 20 as the last number of years. To process new input values, run the program a second time. The *OUT OF DATA* error message varies with different computers.
5. Before planning the spacing for your headings, run the program to see where the numeric values print. Then plan the spacing for your headings accordingly. It is much easier to control the spacing of string literals than it is to control the spacing of numeric values.
6. You might want to experiment with values cited in advertisements for various banks and savings-and-loan associations.
7. Use the flowchart in Figure 3-19 as a general guide.

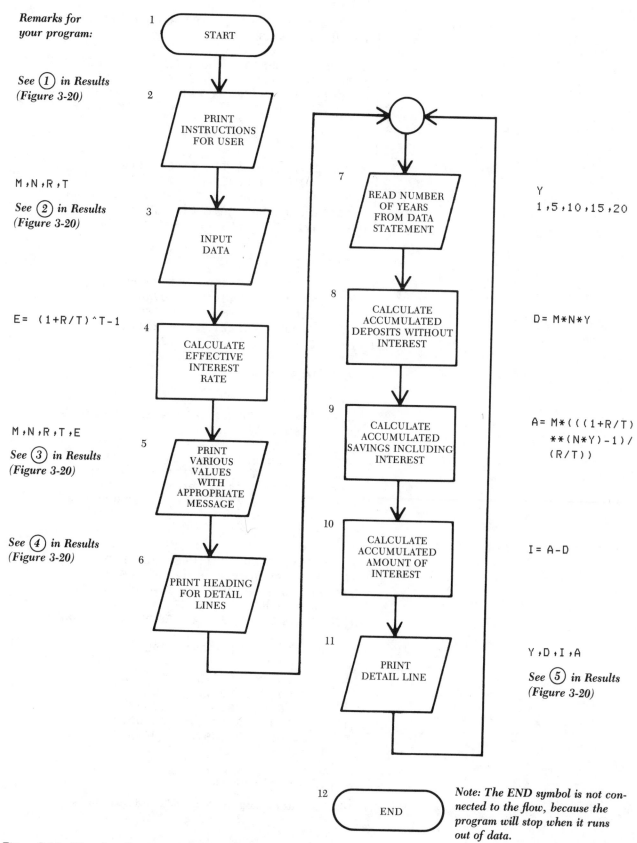

Figure 3-19 Flowchart for program for periodic savings deposits

Results:

① ENTER THE FOLLOWING SEPARATED BY COMMAS
IN THE SEQUENCE SHOWN

AMOUNT OF DEPOSIT	NUMBER OF DEPOSITS PER YEAR	ANNUAL INTEREST RATE	NUMBER OF TIMES COMPOUNDED

② ?400,4,,12,4

③ $ 400 DEPOSITED 4 TIMES PER YEAR
AT A NOMINAL ANNUAL RATE OF .12
COMPOUNDED 4 TIMES PER YEAR,GROWS AT AN
EFFECTIVE ANNUAL RATE OF .125509
OVER VARIOUS NUMBER OF YEARS AS FOLLOWS:

④
YR	DEPOSITS	INTEREST	BALANCE

⑤
YR	DEPOSITS	INTEREST	BALANCE
1	1600	73.4504	1673.45
5	8000	2748.15	10748.2
10	16000	14160.5	30160.5
15	24000	41221.4	65221.4
20	32000	96545.3	128545.

An OUT OF DATA message

ENTER THE FOLLOWING SEPARATED BY COMMAS
IN THE SEQUENCE SHOWN

AMOUNT OF DEPOSIT	NUMBER OF DEPOSITS PER YEAR	ANNUAL INTEREST RATE	NUMBER OF TIMES COMPOUNDED

?100,12,,0925,12

$ 100 DEPOSITED 12 TIMES PER YEAR
AT A NOMINAL ANNUAL RATE OF .0925
COMPOUNDED 12 TIMES PER YEAR,GROWS AT AN
EFFECTIVE ANNUAL RATE OF .096524
OVER VARIOUS NUMBER OF YEARS AS FOLLOWS:

YR	DEPOSITS	INTEREST	BALANCE
1	1200	52.2031	1252.2
5	6000	1592.1	7592.1
10	12000	7627.27	19627.3
15	18000	20705.7	38705.7
20	24000	44949.3	68949.3

An OUT OF DATA message

Figure 3-20 Results for program for periodic savings deposits

4 Conditional Branching

OBJECTIVES

When you complete this unit, you will be able to:

1. Write an IF-THEN statement
   a. For a given problem with a flowchart
   b. For a given problem without a flowchart
2. Write a RESTORE statement
   a. For a given problem with a flowchart
   b. For a given problem without a flowchart
3. Write a STOP statement
   a. For a given problem with a flowchart
   b. For a given problem without a flowchart
4. Code and execute a BASIC solution, given a problem that requires conditional branching

INTRODUCTION

What Is a Conditional Branch Statement?

A conditional branch statement alters the sequence in which program statements are executed, as the result of some condition. The IF-THEN statement discussed in this unit is called a *conditional branch* statement because it permits branching to other statements within the program, depending on a certain condition. Example:

```
10 IF A+B>=15 THEN 50
```

What Is a RESTORE Statement?

The RESTORE statement resets the data pointer to the first item in the first data statement. Example:

```
10 RESTORE
```

What Is the STOP Statement?

The STOP statement ends execution of the program at some point other than at the END statement. Example:

```
100 STOP
```

Using a Conditional Branch

We explained in a previous unit that computers are designed to execute one statement after another, following the order in which the statements appear, unless altered by the GO TO statement. Most BASIC programs require certain statements within the program to be executed more than once, depending on the value of a variable or an expression. The IF-THEN statement is used for this purpose.

Using a RESTORE Statement

Under certain conditions, a programmer might want to reread all entries in a DATA statement. The RESTORE statement allows for this.

Relational Operators

In a previous unit you learned about the GO TO control statement. A more useful control statement is the IF-THEN statement. The IF-THEN statement alters control of the program, depending on one or two conditions. These conditions, called *relational operators,* are summarized in Figure 4-1. The single conditions are less than, $<$, greater than, $>$, and equal to, $=$. The double conditions are not equal to, $<>$, which means either less than or greater than; less than or equal to, $<=$; and finally greater than or equal to, $>=$.

MEANING	ABBREVIATION	BASIC SYMBOL
Less than	LT	$<$
Greater than	GT	$>$
Equal to	EQ	$=$
Not equal to	NE	$<>$
Less than or equal to	LE	$<=$
Greater than or equal to	GE	$>=$

Figure 4-1 Relational operators

The IF-THEN Statement

The IF-THEN statement is illustrated in Figure 4-2. In this example, the expression following the word IF, A+B, is evaluated and compared with 15. If the expression to the left of the relational operators is either greater than or equal to the expression on the right, the condition has been met and control passes to the statement following the word THEN. If the condition is not met, control passes to the next statement following the IF-THEN statement.

The expression between the words IF and THEN is sometimes referred to as a *Boolean expression.* The equals sign in a Boolean expression means "equal to" and not "replaced by," as it does in the LET statement. The values of the variables used in the IF-THEN statement are not changed in any way; they are simply evaluated.

We do not recommend that you compare for an "equal to zero" condition with the IF-THEN statement. Computers convert decimal numbers to binary numbers and then back again to decimal numbers. Not all fractional decimal numbers have exact binary values; therefore, fractional parts of a number are sometimes lost. In the IF-THEN statement, "equal to zero" means *exactly* equal to zero. Any fractional difference caused by the decimal-binary-decimal conversion could cause an equal condition where inequality should exist.

Note: Value of variables not changed

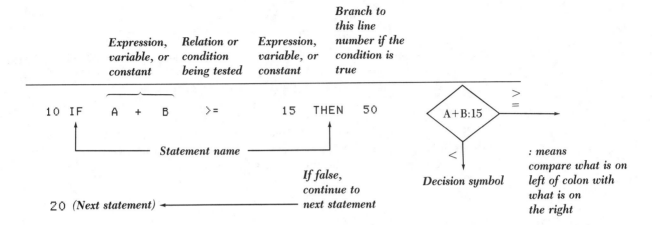

Figure 4-2 The IF-THEN statement

To the right of Figure 4-2 is the flowchart symbol, called the *decision symbol*, used to represent the IF-THEN statement. The expression within the diamond contains a colon and is read as "compared with." The contents of the diamond are read as "A+B compared with 15." There are two exit lines from the diamond. The exit to the right will be taken if the value of A+B is greater than or equal to 15. If A+B is less than 15, the downward exit will be taken.

Following are two examples of the IF-THEN statement:

```
10 IF (A+B-V1)/.25 < > Z1 THEN 110
10 IF X<0 THEN 50
```

The first line shows an IF-THEN statement with a more complex expression. The expressions on either side of the relational operators can be as complex as necessary. The second line shows how a very simple expression, the single variable X, is used in the IF-THEN statement. Its meaning is: "If X is less than 0, go to statement 50; if not, go to the next statement."

All programming examples throughout this unit will use the simplest form of the IF-THEN statement, the form you have just learned. The simple IF-THEN statement is a standard BASIC statement that can be used with any BASIC system.

Additional IF-THEN Statements

Some versions of BASIC have extensions of the standard IF-THEN statement. For example:

```
30 IF A=0 AND B=10 THEN 150
```

This statement can be read as "If A is equal to 0 and B is equal to 10, then go to statement 150; but if *both* these conditions are not met, go to the next statement."

```
50 IF C>15 OR D<=12 THEN 250
```

This statement can be read as "If either of these relational expressions is true—that is, if C is greater than 15 or if D is less than or equal to 12—then statement 250 will be executed." Only if *neither* condition is met will control pass to the next statement. AND and OR are called *Boolean operators.*

Other versions of BASIC permit one or more statements following THEN in the IF-THEN statement.

```
40 IF A>B THEN GO TO 180
50 IF A<C THEN F=50
```

If the relational expression is true, the statement or statements following the word THEN will be executed; if not, the next statement will be executed.

And another extension of the IF-THEN statement:

```
90 IF X>Y THEN 180 ELSE 220
```

If the relational expression is true, statement 180 will be the next statement executed; if it is false, statement 220 will be the next statement executed.

Consult your manufacturer's manual before using any of these extensions of BASIC.

The STOP Statement

All programs written so far have ended with the END statement, which means "stop executing statements at the end of this BASIC program." A programmer might sometimes want to stop at a statement other than the END statement. The STOP statement in Figure 4-3 is used for this purpose. The flowchart symbol for the STOP statement has the same shape as the symbol for the END statement.

Statement name

100 STOP

STOP

Terminal symbol

("Stop execution of the program at this point")
Note: Not available in all versions of BASIC.

Figure 4-3   The STOP statement

The RESTORE Statement

In an earlier unit you learned that the READ statement reads data from the DATA statement by setting the data pointer at the first data item in the lowest-numbered DATA statement. As reading continues, the pointer moves to the next data item until all items in that DATA statement have been read. The pointer then moves to the next highest-numbered DATA statement. This process continues until there is no more data to be read.

Occasionally the programmer might want to begin reading the same data again. The RESTORE statement in Figure 4-4 resets the data pointer at the first data item

Statement name

10 RESTORE

RESTORE

Input/output symbol

("Reset the data pointer to the first item in the
DATA statement with the smallest line number")

Figure 4-4   The RESTORE statement

in the lowest-numbered DATA statement, so that the data can be reread from the beginning the next time a READ statement is executed. Since the RESTORE statement affects input, it is represented by the input/output flowchart symbol. It does not change the execution sequence of the program.

Calculating an Average

We can best illustrate the IF-THEN statement by looking at a flowchart that requires a decision and the associated IF-THEN statement used to represent this decision. Figure 4-5 shows a flowchart and a program to calculate an average.

The flowchart and program show how we can solve the problem of finding the average of a number of values. The start symbol in the flowchart represents statements 10 through 100 in the program. The legends in statements 60 through 90 describe the variables to be used in the program: T will be used to accumulate the total of all values; each input value will be assigned to X; C will contain the count of the number of input values; and A will contain the average of the values.

Symbol 110 in the flowchart and statement 110 in the program assign zero to T, and symbol 120 and statement 120 make the same assignment to C. Since T is to be used as an accumulator and C as a counter, it is necessary to initialize them with zero values. The assignment of zero to T and C could be shown in one flowchart process symbol. Some versions of BASIC allow more than one assignment per statement, but to simplify these illustrations we will show only one statement per line. Other versions automatically assign a zero value to all variables when they are first used in a program. We will *not* assume this automatic assignment in any examples used in this book.

Symbol 130–135 and statements 130 and 135 are used to print a request for an input value. When there are no more values, −1 should be the input value. The −1 is a flag to signal the end of input. It is an arbitrary value; the programmer can choose any number that is not a valid input item. Symbol 140 and statement 140 assign a value to X. Statements 130, 135, and 140 could have been contained within one input/output symbol in the flowchart.

The first use of the decision symbol is shown as a diamond in symbol 150. Within the symbol, X:−1 means "X compared with −1." If X equals −1, the exit to the right (flowing down to symbol 190) is taken. If X does not equal −1, the downward branch is taken to symbol 160. Statement 150 in the program is read as "If X equals −1, go to statement 190; otherwise, go to the next statement—statement 160." Notice how closely the decision symbol corresponds to the IF-THEN statement.

Symbol 160 and statement 160 add 1 to C each time an X value other than −1 is input. It is necessary to keep count of the number of values input, to compute an average. Symbol 170 and statement 170 accumulate the X values. Flowline 180 and statement 180 alter control by branching back to statement 130 to get another X value, and this process is repeated until a −1 is input at statement 140.

When −1 is input, control passes to symbol 190 and statement 190, which compute the average and put the result in A. The input/output symbol represents statements 200 and 210, which skip a line and then print the number of values and their average. Symbol 220 and statement 220 indicate the end of the program. The program corresponds to the flowchart very closely. Writing a program is easier when a flowchart is written first.

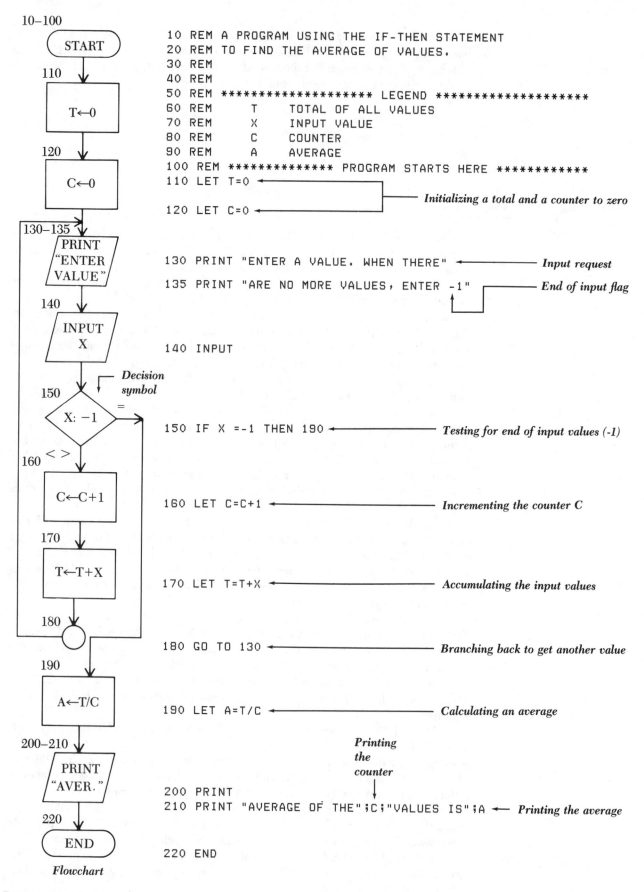

10–100

START

110

T←0

120

C←0

130–135

PRINT
"ENTER
VALUE"

140

INPUT
X

Decision
symbol

150

X: −1 =

160 < >

C←C+1

170

T←T+X

180

190

A←T/C

200–210

PRINT
"AVER."

220

END

Flowchart

```
10 REM A PROGRAM USING THE IF-THEN STATEMENT
20 REM TO FIND THE AVERAGE OF VALUES.
30 REM
40 REM
50 REM ******************* LEGEND *******************
60 REM    T    TOTAL OF ALL VALUES
70 REM    X    INPUT VALUE
80 REM    C    COUNTER
90 REM    A    AVERAGE
100 REM ************* PROGRAM STARTS HERE ***********
110 LET T=0 ◄
                                  Initializing a total and a counter to zero
120 LET C=0 ◄

130 PRINT "ENTER A VALUE, WHEN THERE" ◄          Input request
135 PRINT "ARE NO MORE VALUES, ENTER -1"         End of input flag

140 INPUT


150 IF X =-1 THEN 190 ◄          Testing for end of input values (-1)


160 LET C=C+1 ◄          Incrementing the counter C


170 LET T=T+X ◄          Accumulating the input values


180 GO TO 130 ◄          Branching back to get another value


190 LET A=T/C ◄          Calculating an average

                         Printing
                         the
                         counter

200 PRINT
210 PRINT "AVERAGE OF THE";C;"VALUES IS";A ◄ Printing the average


220 END
```

Figure 4-5 Calculating an average

Using the IF-THEN Statement

Now we will analyze a flowchart, before writing a program to solve the following problem.

Given three variables (J, K, and L) with previously defined values, write a sequence of IF-THEN, STOP, and PRINT statements from the flowchart in Figure 4-6. The program should STOP if each of three variables has the exact value of 100. If one or more variables have a different value, write the values of J, K, and L (symbol 50) and stop.

This flowchart represents only a portion of a program. We must assume that variables J, K, and L were assigned values in a preceding part of the program. The first decision symbol, symbol 10, tests J to see whether it meets the requirement of being equal to 100—that is, the first decision symbol compares J with 100. If the value of J is greater than or less than 100, program control exits to the right and downward to input/output symbol 50. We do not need to check K and L, because the problem states that all three values must equal 100. If J is equal to 100 as a result of the decision in symbol 10, we have more decisions to make. If the first condition is met—that is, if J is equal to 100—then we check the next decision, symbol 20, to determine whether K is equal to 100. If K meets the requirement of being equal to 100, we check L in symbol 30. If L is equal to 100, then we stop the program at this point, because all three values are equal to 100. If one value does not equal 100, at any point, the flowchart branches to symbol 50 and prints the values of J, K, and L. We are presenting only the simplest form of the IF-THEN statement, since it is less confusing to the beginning BASIC programmer. At the conclusion of this unit, return to this example and write the program from the flowchart. Compare your results with the solution given in the Answers to Application Exercises at the end of the unit.

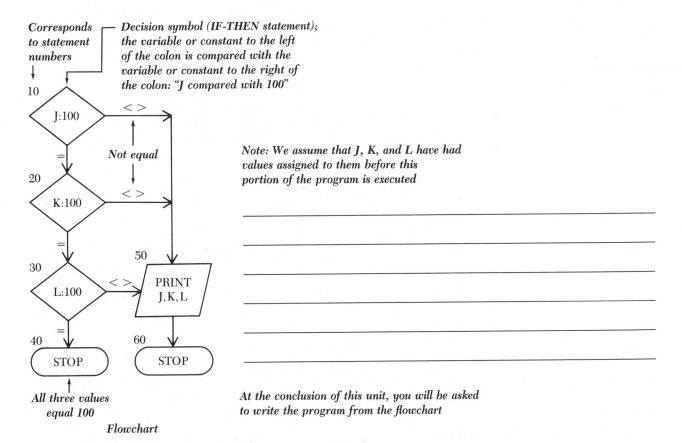

Corresponds to statement numbers → ⎡ *Decision symbol (IF-THEN statement); the variable or constant to the left of the colon is compared with the variable or constant to the right of the colon: "J compared with 100"*

Note: We assume that J, K, and L have had values assigned to them before this portion of the program is executed

All three values equal 100

At the conclusion of this unit, you will be asked to write the program from the flowchart

Flowchart

Figure 4-6   Flowchart for conditional branching

Comparing Values

Using the flowchart in Figure 4-7 as a guide, we will complete the partially written BASIC program to find the largest of three values and then print it.

The first symbol, the start symbol in the flowchart, is used to represent the REMARK statements describing the program and its legend. Read the REMARK statements. The input/output symbol, symbol 110–120, asks for input. Statement 110 asks for three input items. Using the flowchart symbol as a guide, complete statement 120. Begin reading again when you have finished.

You should have written INPUT A,B,C. Look at flowchart symbol 130, which represents our first decision—to compare A with B. It might appear that it would be more efficient to compare all three variables at this point. For this illustration, however, we compare only two variables at a time, to give you more practice in writing IF-THEN statements.

At symbol 130, note which exit is taken if A is greater than B: the exit to the right, which points to symbol 190. Complete statement 130. Begin reading again when you have finished.

You should have written IF A>B. What happens if A is less than B? Look at flowchart symbol 130 again. It indicates that, if A is less than B, the downward exit is taken. Note how this exit is handled in the program at statement 130. If the Boolean expression in the IF-THEN statement is false (that is, in this case, if A is not greater than B) control passes to the next statement—statement 140. If a true condition results from statement 130, control passes to statement 190.

At symbol 190 you can see another decision symbol that compares A with C. If A is less than C, the exit to the left is taken, going to symbol 150. Write statement 190. Begin reading again when you have finished.

You should have written, IF A<C THEN 150. Now look back at flowchart symbol 190. If A is greater than C, the downward exit is taken. If this branch is taken, it means that A is greater than both B and C, and therefore A is to be printed as indicated in input/output symbol 200. Write statement 200 to print A and begin reading again when you have finished.

You should have written PRINT A. Following statement 200 is the usual end-of-program statement. Look again at symbol 190. If A is less than C, control passes to 150 and C is printed, because if A is greater than B and C is greater than A, C is also greater than B. Write statement 150. Begin reading again when you have finished.

The correct statement is PRINT C.

We want to stop the program following statement 150, so we write 160 STOP. This illustrates that it's possible to stop the program at a point other than the END statement. Statement 160 could be GO TO 999. This passes control to the END statement and accomplishes the same thing as a STOP statement.

Look at flowchart symbol 130 at the downward exit—A is less than B. Symbol 140 then compares B with C. Write statement 140. Begin reading again when you have finished.

You should have written IF B>C THEN 170. If this branch is taken, we know that B is the largest of the three values and B is then printed. Write statement 170.

You should have written PRINT B. Now write statement 180.

If you used the flowchart as a guide, you should have written STOP, but GO TO 999 is also correct.

Refer again to symbol 140 in the flowchart. If B is less than C, the downward exit is taken. At this point we know that C is greater than B, and from symbol 130 we know that B is greater than A, so C is the largest value. Note that 150 PRINT C has already been entered in the program. This entry was made as a result of statements 130 and 190, which also resulted in the condition of C being the largest value.

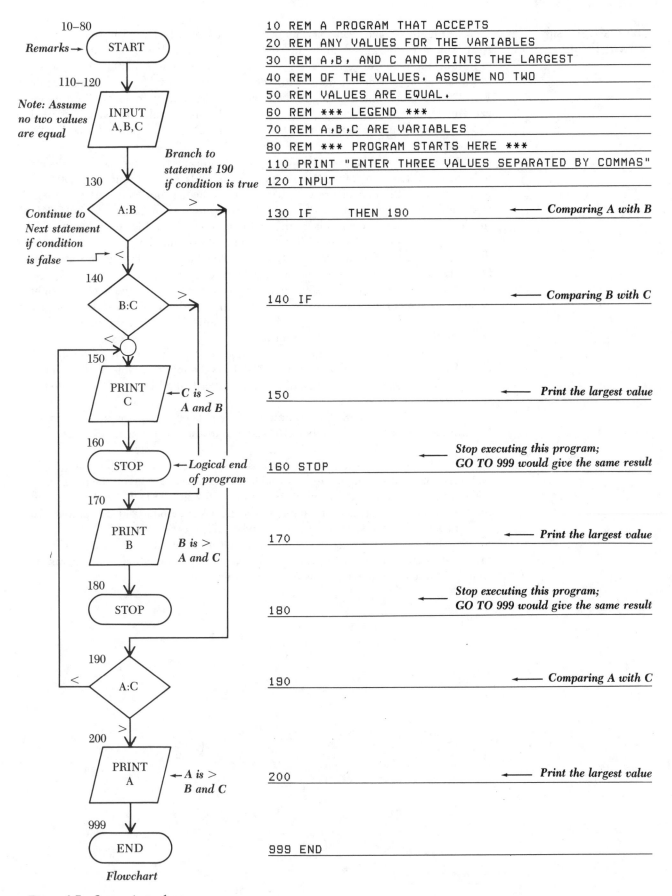

10 REM A PROGRAM THAT ACCEPTS
20 REM ANY VALUES FOR THE VARIABLES
30 REM A,B, AND C AND PRINTS THE LARGEST
40 REM OF THE VALUES. ASSUME NO TWO
50 REM VALUES ARE EQUAL.
60 REM *** LEGEND ***
70 REM A,B,C ARE VARIABLES
80 REM *** PROGRAM STARTS HERE ***
110 PRINT "ENTER THREE VALUES SEPARATED BY COMMAS"
120 INPUT

130 IF   THEN 190   ←—— *Comparing A with B*

140 IF   ←—— *Comparing B with C*

150   ←—— *Print the largest value*

                                 Stop executing this program;
160 STOP   ←—— *GO TO 999 would give the same result*

170   ←—— *Print the largest value*

                                 Stop executing this program;
180   ←—— *GO TO 999 would give the same result*

190   ←—— *Comparing A with C*

200   ←—— *Print the largest value*

999 END

Figure 4-7   Comparing values

Savings-Deposit Growth Program

Look at Figure 4-9 and read statements 10 through 90, which explain the program. Next look at the flowchart in Figure 4-8. The symbol following the start symbol represents input assigning values to P, R, and T. Look at statements 110 through 160 in the program and match them with section 1 of the results. Flowchart symbol 170–220 represents the printing of the headings. Program statements 170 through 220 are used for the heading shown in section 2 of the results. Flowchart symbol 230–240 corresponds to statement 230, used to read the number of years from DATA statement 240.

Flowchart symbol 250 tests for a −1, which indicates that there is no more data to be read. In statement 240 in the program, −1 is the last entry. Statement 250 tests to see whether the end of the data has been reached; if not, the next statement (statement 260) is executed and the amount is computed. Look back at symbol 260 in the flowchart, where the formula for this computation is given. Flowchart symbol 270 and program statement 270 result in a line of output printing the year and amount as illustrated in section 3 of the results. Flowchart flowline 280 and program statement 280 transfer control back to read another data item.

Look at flowchart symbol 250 again. When a −1 is read, the branch to the right is taken to symbol 290–300, which asks for input to determine whether another computation is desired. Look at program statements 290, 295, 300, and 310 and compare them with section 4 of the results.

Flowchart symbol 310 requests that number 1 or 2 be input to represent yes or no and assigned to the variable S. Symbol 320 tests the input variable S. If the input is not 1, the program ends by taking the downward exit. If a 1 is input, the exit to the right is taken.

Symbol 330 represents the restoration of the data pointer to the first data item. Control then passes back to symbol 110–160 to start the process again with different input.

Statement 310 in the program will assign number 1 or 2 to the variable S. Statement 320 tests the input. If the variable S does not equal 1, then the program is ended at statement 999. If 1 is input, statement 330 (the RESTORE statement) will reset the data pointer to the first data item in DATA statement 240. Statement 350 directs control back to statement 110 to repeat the process again.

Section 5 of the results shows output resulting from different input but using the same DATA statement. Section 6 of the results illustrates that the program is ended if a number other than 1 is entered at this point.

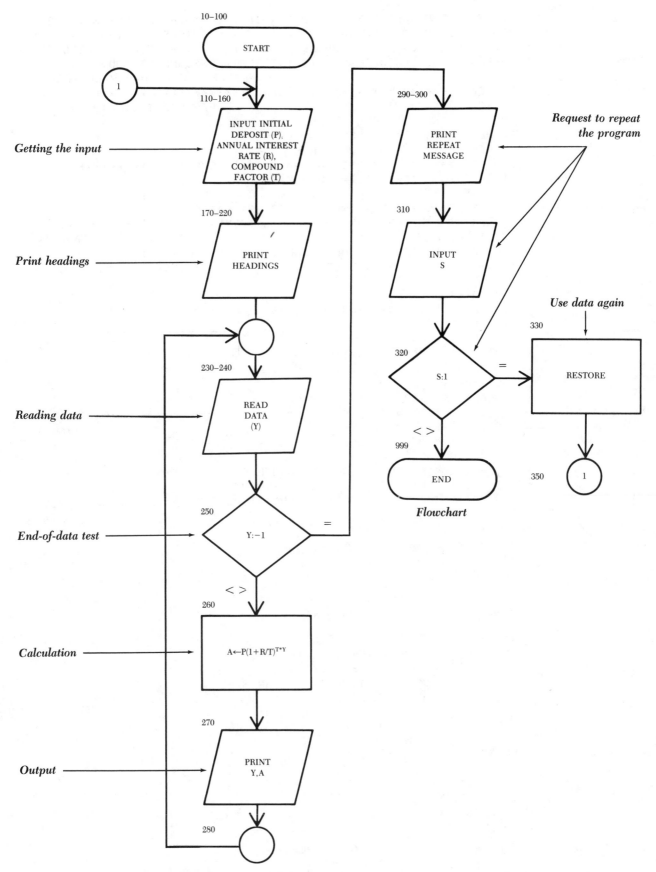

Figure 4-8 Flowchart of the savings-deposit growth program

Explanation of program —→

```
 10 REM A PROGRAM THAT WILL DETERMINE HOW MUCH VARIOUS SAVINGS
 20 REM DEPOSITS WILL GROW WITH SELECTED INTEREST RATES, COMPOUND
 30 REM PERIODS, AND YEARS LEFT ON DEPOSIT. THE FORMULA USED IS
 40 REM AMOUNT=PRINCIPAL * (1+INTEREST/COMPOUND PERIOD)
 45 REM                   ^(COMPOUND PERIODS * NUMBER OF YEARS)
 50 REM ****************** LEGEND ********************
 60 REM      P    INITIAL DEPOSIT        S   RESTORE INDICATOR
 70 REM      R    INTEREST RATE
 80 REM      T    TIMES PER YEAR COMPOUNDED
 90 REM      Y    NUMBER OF YEARS
```

Getting the input —→

```
100 REM ************* PROGRAM STARTS HERE **************
110 PRINT "ENTER INITIAL DEPOSIT";
120 INPUT P
130 PRINT "ENTER THE ANNUAL INTEREST RATE"
135 PRINT "IN THE FORM .065 FOR 6 1/2%";      ←── See ① in results
140 INPUT R
150 PRINT "ENTER THE NUMBER OF TIMES PER YEAR"
155 PRINT "INTEREST IS COMPOUNDED";
160 INPUT T
```

Headings —→

```
170 PRINT
180 PRINT "WILL GROW AS FOLLOWS:"
190 PRINT
200 PRINT                                      ←── See ② in results
210 PRINT "YEARS AMOUNT"
220 PRINT
```

Read data —→
End-of-data test —→
Calculation —→
Output

```
230 READ Y
240 DATA 1,5,10,20,-1
250 IF Y=-1 THEN 290                            ←── See ③ in results
260 LET A=P*(1+R/T)^(T*Y)
270 PRINT Y;A
280 GO TO 230
```

Request to repeat program —→

Reset pointer in DATA statement —→

```
290 PRINT "IF YOU WOULD LIKE ANOTHER"
295 PRINT "COMPUTATION WITH DIFFERENT"
300 PRINT "VALUES, TYPE 1, IF NOT TYPE 2";     ←── See ④ in results
310 INPUT S
320 IF S <> 1 THEN 999
330 RESTORE
340 PRINT
350 GO TO 110
999 END
```

Program

① {
```
ENTER INITIAL DEPOSIT?1000
ENTER THE ANNUAL INTEREST RATE
IN THE FORM .065 FOR 6 1/2%?.12
ENTER THE NUMBER OF TIMES PER YEAR
INTEREST IS COMPOUNDED?365
```
}

② {
```
WILL GROW AS FOLLOWS:

YEARS AMOUNT
```
}

③ {
```
1      1127.46
5      1821.82
10     3319.02
20     11015.9
```
}

Results continue on next page.

Figure 4-9   Results of the savings-deposit growth program

```
   ┌ IF YOU WOULD LIKE ANOTHER
④ ┤ COMPUTATION WITH DIFFERENT
   └ VALUES, TYPE 1, IF NOT TYPE 2?1


   ┌ ENTER INITIAL DEPOSIT?1000
   │ ENTER THE ANNUAL INTEREST RATE
   │ IN THE FORM .065 FOR 6 1/2%?.12
   │ ENTER THE NUMBER OF TIMES PER YEAR
   │ INTEREST IS COMPOUNDED?4
   │
   │ WILL GROW AS FOLLOWS:
⑤ ┤
   │ YEARS AMOUNT
   │
   │ 1    1125.51
   │ 5    1806.11
   │ 10   3262.04
   └ 20   10640.9
   ┌ IF YOU WOULD LIKE ANOTHER
⑥ ┤ COMPUTATION WITH DIFFERENT
   └ VALUES, TYPE 1, IF NOT TYPE 2?2
```

Results

Figure 4–9   Continued

PROGRAMMING TECHNIQUES

1. Testing for end of data:

```
10 DATA 5,10,7,-1   (−1 indicates end of data)
20 READ X
30 IF X=-1 THEN 999
40 (Program continues)
```

2. Testing for end of input:

```
                         ? 5
10 INPUT X               ? 10  ┐
20 IF X=-1 THEN 999      ? 7   ├ Results
30 (Program continues)   ? −1  ┘
```

3. Keeping a count within a loop:

```
        10 LET C=0   (initializing the counter C to 0)
      ┌ 20 INPUT X
      │ 30 IF X=-1  THEN 999
Loop ┤ 40 C=C+1     (incrementing the counter C by 1)
      └ 50 GO TO 20
```

4. Accumulating values within a loop:

```
        10 LET A=0   (initializing the accumulator A to 0)
      ┌ 20 READ Z
      │ 30 DATA _____, _____, _____
Loop ┤ 40 IF Z=-1 THEN 999
      │ 50 LET A=A+Z   (accumulating values of Z in the accumulator A)
      └ 60 GO TO 20
```

DEBUGGING AIDS

ERROR	CAUSE	CORRECTION
10 IF A,B,C=1000 THEN 150	A,B,C is not a valid expression	120 IF A<>1000 THEN 300 130 IF B<>1000 THEN 300 140 IF C<>1000 THEN 300 150 (Program continues) or 120 IF A AND B AND C=1000 THEN 150
10 IF X=Y THEN 20 20 (Program continues)	Statement 20 will always be executed	10 IF X=Y THEN 30 20 LET Z=X*Y 30 (Program continues)
10 INPUT T 20 IF T=1000 THEN 40 30 PRINT T; 40 GO TO 10	Unending loop	10 INPUT T 20 IF T>1000 THEN 40 30 GO TO 10 40 PRINT T;

10 READ D
20 DATA 10,25,20,30,-1
30 PRINT "THE NUMBER OF
   YEARS IS"; D
40 IF D=-1 THEN 60
50 GO TO 10
	-1 end-of-data flag not tested at proper time	10 READ D
		20 DATA 10,25,20,30,-1
		30 IF D=-1 THEN 60
		40 PRINT "THE NUMBER OF
		   YEARS IS"; D
		50 GO TO 10
		60 END

10 READ X 20 DATA 5,20,15,8,7 30 RESTORE 40 GO TO 10	RESTORE within a loop will cause the data pointer to remain at the first data value (5)	10 READ X 20 DATA 5,20,15,8,7,-1 30 IF X=-1 THEN 50 40 GO TO 10 50 RESTORE
10 INPUT T 20 READ Y 30 DATA 100,80,70,0 40 IF Y=0 THEN 70 50 PRINT T/Y; 60 GO TO 20 70 PRINT "TRY AGAIN" 80 INPUT Q 90 IF Q=2 THEN 999 100 RESTORE 999 END	RESTORE does not change the execution sequence of the program	Insert GO TO 10 statement after RESTORE statement

REFERENCE

STATEMENT SUMMARY

STOP STATEMENT	GENERAL FORM
Terminates execution of a program and can be repeated in the program	STOP *Example:* 10 20 30 STOP 40 50 60 STOP 70 80

Terminal Symbol:

STOP

END STATEMENT	GENERAL FORM
Terminates execution of the program	END

Example:
```
10
20
30
99 END
```

Terminal Symbol:

(END)

RESTORE STATEMENT	GENERAL FORM
Resets data pointer to the first data item in the first DATA statement	RESTORE

Example:
```
100 RESTORE
```

Input/Output Symbol:

RESTORE

IF-THEN STATEMENT	GENERAL FORM

		expression,	relation or	expression,		
Passes control to a statement other than the next statement, if the condition is true; if the condition is false, the next statement is executed	IF	variable, or constant	condition tested	variable, or constant	THEN	statement number

Example:
```
30 IF A<B THEN 80
```

Decision Symbol: Expression at left of colon is compared with expression at right of colon

A:B

APPLICATION EXERCISES

1. Write the program from the flowchart in Figure 4-6.
2. Write the program from the flowchart in Figure 4-7.
3. Write IF-THEN statements for the following:
    a. If J is less than or equal to K, branch to statement 90.

   _____

    b. If balance (B) does not equal zero, go to statement 25.

   _____

    c. If mortgage (M) plus taxes (T) plus insurance (I) are greater than balance (B), go to statement 10.

   _____

    d. In the following program segment, select the statement number to which one of the following IF statements will transfer control:

```
10 LET X=80
20 LET Z=X*(-5)
30 IF Z<0 THEN 60
40 IF Z=0 THEN 70
50 GO TO 80
```

(1) 60
(2) 70
(3) 80

4. What value of A will be printed after the following program has been run?

```
5 LET A=10
10 LET L=5
15 LET K=6
20 LET L=K+4
25 IF L=10 THEN 50
30 IF L<10 THEN 60
40 LET A=A+L
45 GO TO 90
50 LET A=A^2
55 GO TO 90
60 LET A=A*A
90 PRINT A
99 END
```

5. Write the appropriate value that is printed for each value of C by the following program (for each new value of C, begin with statement 5 again).

```
5 LET A=2
10 IF C<0 THEN 50
20 IF C=0 THEN 70
30 LET H=A*A
40 IF H-A^2=0 THEN 90
50 LET H=C
60 GO TO 90
70 LET A=A+A
80 LET H=A^2
90 PRINT H
99 END
```

Value of C	Printed value
a. -7.5	_____
b. -3.98	_____
c. 0	_____
d. 6	_____
e. 42	_____

6. Write a program that will input three positive integers represented by the variables X, Y, and Z. If each value is zero, print "all equal zero"; if not, print "all do not equal zero". Continue testing values until $-1, -1, -1$ is input.

_____

_____

_____

_____

_____

_____

_____

_____

Answers to Application Exercises

1. (From Figure 4-6)
```
10  IF J<>100 THEN 50
20  IF K<>100 THEN 50
30  IF L<>100 THEN 50
40  STOP
50  PRINT J,K,L
60  STOP
```

2. (From Figure 4-7)
```
120  INPUT A,B,C
130  IF A>B THEN 190
140  IF B>C THEN 170
150  PRINT C
160  STOP
170  PRINT B
180  STOP
190  IF A<C THEN 150
200  PRINT A
999  END
```

3. a. IF J<=K THEN 90
   b. IF B<>0 THEN 25
   c. IF M+T+I>B THEN 10
   d. 60

4. 100

5. a. −7.5
   b. −3.98
   c. 16
   d. 4
   e. 4

6.
```
10  INPUT X,Y,Z
20  IF X=-1 THEN 99
30  IF X<>0 THEN 80
40  IF Y<>0 THEN 80
50  IF Z<>0 THEN 80
60  PRINT "ALL EQUAL
    ZERO"
70  GO TO 10
80  PRINT "ALL NOT
    EQUAL TO ZERO"
90  GO TO 10
99  END
```

Note: In this case, it is not necessary to test the values for Y and Z if X = −1.

PROGRAMMING PROBLEMS

4-1. Jogging Program

Given the age and sex of one or more joggers, write a program to print a desired elapsed time for certain joggers and the predicted average time of a four-mile jog for all joggers.

Given:

1. Male joggers between 12 and 25 years old should run four miles in 35 minutes (base time).
2. For female joggers, add five minutes to the base time for four miles.
3. For each year of age over 25 years, add one half minute to the base time for four miles.

Programming tips:

1. Use the flowchart and program results in Figure 4-10 as a guide to your solution.

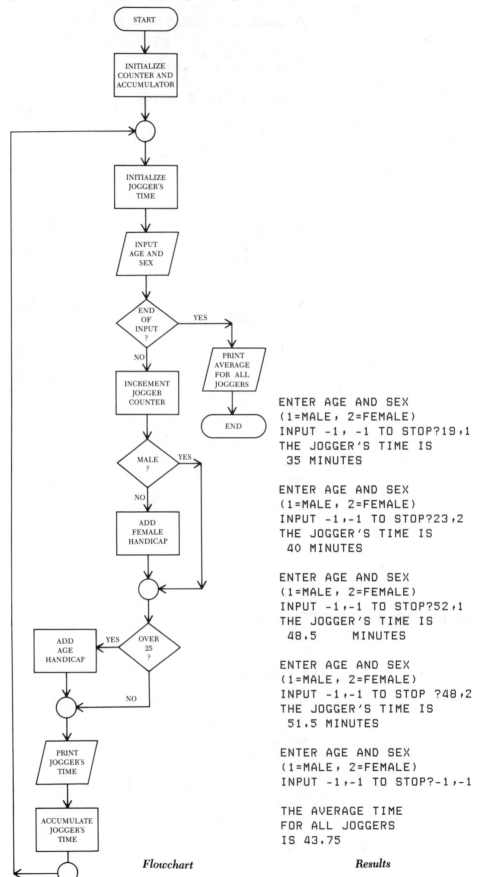

ENTER AGE AND SEX
(1=MALE, 2=FEMALE)
INPUT -1, -1 TO STOP?19,1
THE JOGGER'S TIME IS
 35 MINUTES

ENTER AGE AND SEX
(1=MALE, 2=FEMALE)
INPUT -1,-1 TO STOP?23,2
THE JOGGER'S TIME IS
 40 MINUTES

ENTER AGE AND SEX
(1=MALE, 2=FEMALE)
INPUT -1,-1 TO STOP?52,1
THE JOGGER'S TIME IS
 48,5   MINUTES

ENTER AGE AND SEX
(1=MALE, 2=FEMALE)
INPUT -1,-1 TO STOP ?48,2
THE JOGGER'S TIME IS
 51,5 MINUTES

ENTER AGE AND SEX
(1=MALE, 2=FEMALE)
INPUT -1,-1 TO STOP?-1,-1

THE AVERAGE TIME
FOR ALL JOGGERS
IS 43,75

Figure 4-10
Flowchart and results
of the jogging program

Flowchart   *Results*

2. Each individual jogger's time can be initialized to 35 before each input request.
3. The formula for the age handicap is: (age − 25) ÷ 2.

4-2. Mortgage Program

Given the present value of a mortgage, the length of the debt in years, the number of periodic payments per year, and various interest rates, write a program to print the amount of the periodic payments.

Given:

Periodic rate (P) = annual interest rate / number of payments per year
Total number of payments (T) = number of years × number of payments per year

$$\text{Periodic payment} = \frac{\text{loan amount} \times P}{1 - (1 + P)\,\hat{}\,(-T)}$$

Programming tips:

1. Draw a flowchart of the solution.
2. When raising a value to a negative power, the sign used to raise to a power (the exponent) cannot immediately precede the negative sign. Use parentheses to separate them.
3. The annual interest rate should be read from a DATA statement. Use −1 to indicate end of data.

Results:

```
WHAT IS THE LOAN AMOUNT?100000
NUMBER OF YEARS?30
NUMBER OF PAYMENTS PER YEAR?12

RATE   PAYMENT

 .12   1028.61
 .15   1264.44
 .18   1507.08
 .21   1753.4

IF YOU WANT TO TRY AGAIN
WITH DIFFERENT AMOUNTS OR TIME,
TYPE 1 FOR YES, 2 FOR NO
?1

WHAT IS THE LOAN AMOUNT?100000
NUMBER OF YEARS?40
NUMBER OF PAYMENTS PER YEAR?12

RATE   PAYMENT

 .12   1008.5
 .15   1253.22
 .18   1501.18
 .21   1750.42

IF YOU WANT TO TRY AGAIN
WITH DIFFERENT AMOUNTS OR TIME,
TYPE 1 FOR YES, 2 FOR NO
?2
```

Figure 4-11 Results of the mortgage program

5 Strings

OBJECTIVES

When you complete this unit, you will be able to:

1. Write LET statements to assign string values to string variables
2. Predict the results of a LET statement assigning a string value to a string variable
3. Write PRINT statements that will display
   a. String constants
   b. String variables
4. Write INPUT statements that will accept string values
5. Write READ and DATA statements that will assign string values to string variables
6. Write IF-THEN statements that will test comparisons of string variables and/or constants
7. Predict the results of IF-THEN statements testing comparisons of string values
8. Code and execute a program to process string values
   a. Given a program with a flowchart
   b. Given a program without a flowchart

INTRODUCTION

We have already discussed numeric constants, numeric variables, and string constants. In this unit we will discuss string variables. We defined a string constant previously as an alphanumeric set of characters whose contents do not change. An alphanumeric character set can contain letters, digits, and special characters (such as ', $, /, &, ?, %), but not quotation marks, because they are used to enclose strings.

What Is a String Variable?

A string variable is a symbol that represents a string value that can be changed.

Using Strings

In general anything that can be done to a numeric variable can be done to a string variable, except arithmetic operations. Another difference is the way that string variables are named. One fairly common form of a string variable is a letter followed by a dollar sign ($)—for example, B$, C$, F$. Since the methods of handling strings vary among different computers, in this unit we will cover only fundamental operations that apply to most systems. You should consult your manufacturer's reference manual for particulars about your system.

We have previously used string constants only in PRINT statements, to print headings or messages; the alphanumeric characters in the string constants were enclosed in quotation marks and could not be changed. Now you will learn to use string variables in statements other than PRINT statements. This will give you more flexibility in programming, because alphanumeric characters assigned to string variables *can* be changed. As a result, you can do anything to string variables that you can do to numeric variables, except arithmetic operations.

Some computers require a DIM ("dimension") statement to reserve storage for strings longer than one character. We will assume that a proper DIM statement is present if it is required. We will not show it, however, in our illustrations. You should check whether it is required on your computer and include it in your program, if it is. Since most computers allow at least 15 characters per string, we will not use any string longer than 15 characters. Check your computer manual to see how many characters may be assigned to a string variable. When choosing names for strings, we will use variable names like E$, consisting of a letter followed by $. This method is fairly common in most computers. You should check for variations for your computer.

Now let's look at some examples of strings in use.

Assigning a String Constant to a String Variable

In Figure 5-1, E$ will be assigned the value of the string constant STOP, which is enclosed within quotation marks. E$ will contain STOP until it is changed by a subsequent LET, READ, or INPUT statement. Remember that the constant to the right of the equals sign must be enclosed within quotation marks.

Line number	Statement name	The string value is assigned to this name	Means "replaced by"	The string constant is enclosed within quotation marks
115	LET	E$	=	"STOP"

(*"Let the contents of E$ be replaced by 'STOP'*)

Figure 5-1 LET statement assigning a string constant to a string variable

Assigning One String Variable to Another String Variable

In Figure 5-2 you can see Q$ being assigned the value of the string variable E$. For example, if E$ contains STOP, Q$ would now also contain STOP.

Line number	Statement name	The string value is assigned to this name	Means "replaced by"	String variable
115	LET	Q$	=	E$

(*"Let the contents of Q$ be replaced by the contents of E$"*)

Figure 5-2 LET statement assigning the value of one string variable to another string variable

Reading a String Constant

Study Figure 5-3.

The variable B$ in READ statement 130 will be assigned the string value JANE, which is enclosed within quotation marks in DATA statement 140. Both numeric and string data can appear in DATA statements. However, it is important that the types of variable names in the READ statement be arranged to correspond to the type of data as it appears in the DATA statement. This is necessary so that, when a string variable is read in the READ statement, the data pointer will be set to a string value in the DATA statement. You will see examples of this later.

Line number	Statement name	The string value from the DATA statement will be assigned to this name
130	READ	B$
140	DATA	"JANE"

("Read the string constant 'JANE' from the DATA statement and assign it to B$")

Figure 5-3   READ and DATA statements assigning a string constant to a string variable

Inputting a String Constant

Study Figure 5-4.

In this figure the INPUT statement behaves as it did when we used it for numeric values. When the statement is executed, a question mark is displayed and the user types a string value, which is assigned to the variable C$. If only one string is entered per INPUT statement, the user does not need to enclose the string in quotes. If more than one string is entered in a single INPUT statement, the user should enclose each string value within quotation marks. You will see examples of this in later illustrations. You can mix numeric and string variables in the same INPUT statement. As with READ and DATA statements, however, the value entered must match the type of variable named in the INPUT statement.

Line number	Statement name	The value entered from the keyboard will be assigned to this name
160	INPUT	C$

("Display a ? signaling the user to enter a string constant from the keyboard, which will be assigned to C$")

Figure 5-4   INPUT statement assigning a string constant entered from the keyboard to a string variable

Comparing a String Variable to Another String Variable

Study Figure 5-5.

Here the IF statement tests whether the contents of the variable C$ are equal to E$. If they are equal, the program will branch to line number 300; otherwise, it will go to the next statement in sequence. String values are compared in a slightly different way from that in which numeric values are compared. In numeric comparisons, all digits of the entire value are used in determining if one value is less than, equal to, or greater than another value. When string values are compared, the comparison begins with the leftmost character of each string and continues character by character until a difference (inequality) is found. At that point the comparison is stopped. If no difference is found, the strings are equal.

For example, in Figure 5-5 under C$ write JACK; under E$ write STOP. Now begin at the left, comparing one character at a time. The first character of each string J and S is different; therefore, the comparison stops. Since the condition being tested is equality, the condition is not true and the branch to line 300 will not occur. In later illustrations you will see how characters can be tested for high or low conditions.

Line number		String variable or constant	Relation or condition being tested	String variable or constant		Branch to this line number if condition is met
195	IF	C$	=	E$	THEN	300

Statement name spans the String variable / Relation / String variable columns.

("If the contents of C$ equal the contents of E$ then go to Line 300, otherwise go to the next line")

Figure 5-5   IF statement comparing contents of one string variable to the contents of another string variable

Comparing One String Variable to a String Constant

Study Figure 5-6.

The contents of the string variable C$ are compared with string constant KEN, which is enclosed within quotes. Assume that C$ contains the string JACK. Since the first letter, J, of C$ differs from the first letter of K, the constant, comparison stops. The branch to line 240 will not occur, because the two strings are not equal.

Line number		String variable or constant	Relation or condition being tested	String variable or constant		Branch to this line number if condition is met
200	IF	C$	=	"KEN"	THEN	240

Statement name spans the String variable / Relation / String variable columns.

("If the contents of C$ equal 'KEN', then go to line 240; otherwise go to the next line.")

Figure 5-6   IF statement comparing contents of a string variable with a string constant

Line number	Statement name	The string constant appearing within quotation marks will be displayed
155	PRINT	"ENTER THE FIRST NAMES OF YOUR FAVORITE COUPLE"

("Display the words 'ENTER THE FIRST NAMES OF YOUR FAVORITE COUPLE'")

Figure 5-7   PRINT statement displaying a string constant

Displaying a String Constant

Study Figure 5-7 on the preceding page.

This is an example of something that you have done many times before—displaying a string constant that is enclosed within quotes within a PRINT statement.

Displaying String Variables and Constants on the Same Line

Figure 5-8 is an example of something that you haven't done before.

In this example, the PRINT statement displays the contents of two variables, C$ and D$, mixed with string constants on the same line. One point to note about printing strings is that a semicolon following a string variable or a string constant leaves no space before printing the next value. The comma does leave space. In this example, therefore, the word AND is both preceded and followed by a blank space within quotes. Blank spaces are considered string characters, and they occupy one space each. Thus the word AND will be separated from the contents of C$ and D$ by one blank on both sides. Similarly the phrase WENT UP THE HILL is preceded by a blank to separate it from the contents of D$.

Line number	Statement name	Contents of string variable and string constants that will be displayed
210	PRINT	C$; " AND "; D$; " WENT UP THE HILL."

("Display the contents of C$ and D$ separated by the word 'AND' and followed by 'WENT UP THE HILL' on the same line")

Figure 5-8 PRINT statement displaying contents of string variables and constants on the same line

Using Strings in a Complete Program

In Figure 5-9 read the REMARK statements in lines 10 through 30, which describe what the program will do. This program is designed to give you a brief look at strings in a complete program.

Look at flowchart symbol 118–120 on page 84, where values are assigned to E$ and A$. At symbol 130–140, a value is assigned to B$ in the READ statement. In the program this is accomplished by lines 118 through 140, at the encircled 1. E$ is assigned STOP and A$ DICK in lines 118 and 120, in LET statements. B$ is assigned a value of JANE as a result of the READ and DATA statements in lines 130 and 140. The values of E$, A$, and B$ remain unchanged throughout the program.

Now look at flowchart symbol 155–170, which calls for the input of the first names of a favorite couple as C$ and D$. In the program, at the encircled 2, lines 155 through 170 request the input of the first names of the user's favorite couple as C$ and D$. Look at the first encircled 2 in section A of the results. JACK is entered as C$ and JILL as D$. In the flowchart at symbol 175–190, A$ and B$ are printed along with a message. In the program, at the encircled 3, lines 175–190 print the contents of A$, the message SAID LOOK, LOOK, and then the contents of B$. Examine the

```
10 REM A PROGRAM THAT ALLOWS A PERSON TO INPUT THE
20 REM FIRST NAMES OF A FAVORITE COUPLE. THE FIRST NAME OF EACH
30 REM WILL BE TESTED AND A PARTICULAR MESSAGE WILL BE PRINTED.
50 REM ******************** LEGEND ********************
60 REM   A$    BOY'S NAME      B$    GIRL'S NAME
70 REM   C$    BOY'S NAME      D$    GIRL'S NAME
80 REM   E$    STOP CODE
90 REM
100 REM ************** PROGRAM STARTS HERE **************
```

Figure 5-9 Using strings in a complete program

```
   ⎧ 118 LET E$="STOP"
   │ 120 LET A$="DICK"
 ①⎨ 130 READ B$
   ⎩ 140 DATA "JANE"
   ⎧ 155 PRINT "ENTER THE FIRST NAMES OF YOUR FAVORITE COUPLE."
 ②⎨ 160 INPUT C$
   ⎩ 170 INPUT D$
 ③⎧ 175 PRINT
   ⎩ 190 PRINT A$;" SAID, LOOK,LOOK ";B$
   ⎧ 195 IF C$=E$ THEN 300
 ④⎨ 200 IF C$="KEN" THEN 240
   ⎩ 205 IF C$ <> "JACK" THEN 270
 ⑤⎧ 210 PRINT C$;" AND ";D$;" WENT UP THE HILL."
   ⎩ 220 PRINT
     230 GO TO 155
     240 PRINT C$; "THINKS"; D$"IS A DOLL."
     250 PRINT
     260 GO TO 155
     270 PRINT "ME "; C$; "YOU "; D$; "!"
     275 PRINT
     280 GO TO 155
     300 PRINT "THE PEOPLE WANT US TO ";C$;" ";D$;"."
     310 PRINT B$;" SAID, OH SHUT UP ";A$,A$
     999 END
```

Program

```
   ⎧ ENTER THE FIRST NAMES OF YOUR FAVORITE COUPLE.  ⎫
 ②⎨ ?JACK ←——— C$                                   ⎬ Ⓐ
   ⎩ ?JILL ←——— D$                                   ⎭

 ③ A$ ——→ DICK SAID, LOOK,LOOK JANE ←——— B$
 ⑤ C$ ——→ JACK AND JILL WENT UP THE HILL.
                         ↑
                        D$
```

```
   ⎧ ENTER THE FIRST NAMES OF YOUR FAVORITE COUPLE.  ⎫
 ②⎨ ?KEN                                            ⎬ Ⓑ
   ⎩ ?BARBIE                                         │
                                                     │
     DICK SAID, LOOK,LOOK JANE                       │
     KEN THINKS BARBIE IS A DOLL.                    ⎭
```

```
   ⎧ ENTER THE FIRST NAMES OF YOUR FAVORITE COUPLE.  ⎫
 ②⎨ ?TARZAN                                          ⎬ Ⓒ
   ⎩ ?JANE                                           │
                                                     │
     DICK SAID, LOOK,LOOK JANE                       │
     ME TARZAN YOU JANE!                             ⎭
```

```
   ⎧ ENTER THE FIRST NAMES OF YOUR FAVORITE COUPLE.  ⎫
 ②⎨ ?STOP                                            ⎬ Ⓓ
   ⎩ ?STOP                                           │
                                                     │
     DICK SAID, LOOK,LOOK JANE                       │
     THE PEOPLE WANT US TO STOP STOP.                │
     JANE SAID, OH SHUT UP DICK DICK                 ⎭
```

Results

Figure 5-9 Continued

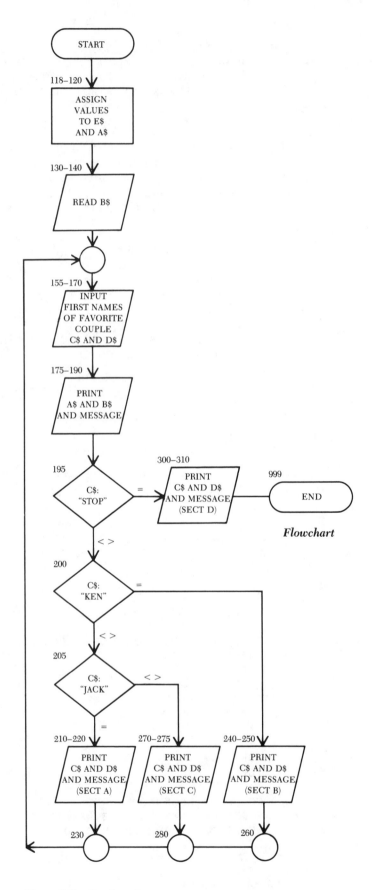

Figure 5-9   Continued

results in section A at the encircled 3. You see this printed as DICK SAID, LOOK, LOOK, JANE. DICK is A$ and JANE is B$. The contents of this line will be repeated throughout the program, because A$ and B$ do not change. The contents of the next line, however, will change throughout the program. This change will be based on the contents of C$, which was input as one of the names of the favorite couple. In the program at the encircled 4 (lines 195 through 205), the IF statements decide what action will be taken based on the contents of C$.

Look back at flowchart symbol 195. This is a decision symbol comparing the contents of C$ with STOP. If this does equal STOP, the branch to the right leads to symbol 300–310, which says to print the contents of C$ and D$, the favorite couple, along with a message, and end the program. Since C$ does not equal STOP because it contains JACK, we don't take this branch. Instead, at symbol 195, we follow the downward branch (the not-equal branch) to decision symbol 200, which compares C$ to KEN. If C$ does equal KEN, the branch to the right leads to symbol 240–250, which prints C$, D$, and a message. Again C$ does not equal the appropriate name, so we take the downward branch from 200 to decision symbol 205. Symbol 205 compares C$ with JACK. If C$ is not equal to JACK, the branch to the right leads to symbol 270–275 to print C$, D$, and a message; but in this instance C$ does equal JACK, so at decision symbol 205 we take the downward equal branch to symbol 210–220 and print C$, D$, and a message.

In the program at the encircled 4, examine statements 195, 200, and 205.

These are the IF statements that test C$ to determine which of the various messages will be printed along with C$ and D$. In this case, since C$ is equal to JACK, none of the conditions of the IF statements is true, so we arrive at line 210, which prints C$, D$, and the message WENT UP THE HILL. Line 220 causes a blank line to be printed, and line 230 branches back to line 155 to input the names of another couple.

Look at the encircled 5 in section A of the results. C$ (which is JACK) and D$ (which is JILL) are printed as JACK AND JILL WENT UP THE HILL. Below that a message is printed, requesting the names of another couple. Look back at the flowchart, just below symbol 210–220. Once C$, D$, and the message are printed, the flow goes back to symbol 155–170 to input the first names of another couple. Then the flow goes to symbol 175–190, where A$, B$, and a message are printed; the decision regarding the contents of C$ is repeated again. C$, D$, and a particular message are printed based on the contents of C$, unless C$ equals STOP.

Once C$, D$, and the message are printed, the program always branches back to symbol 155–170 to input the names of another couple, and the entire process is repeated again. If C$ does equal STOP at symbol 195, C$, D$, and the message are printed at symbol 300–310, and the program ends.

Later, you might want to examine the results and the program further.

Strings and LET Statements

Incorrect Uses of Strings with LET Statements

In Figure 5-10 we will ask you to correct some errors.

At encircled item 1, describe the error in lines 10 and 20 in the empty boxes to the right.

You should have said that the quotation marks are missing around the strings at the right of the equals sign. This is not allowed on most systems.

Look at encircled item 2 and describe the error in statement 30.

You should have said that a string constant is being assigned to a numeric variable name.

Now look at encircled item 3 and describe any errors in the partial program (lines 40 through 90).

You should have said that we can't perform arithmetic operations on string variables or constants.

Describe error

```
   10 LET Z$=RHENSTROM PHILPOT
①  20 LET Y$=2

②  30 LET Y="YES"

   40 LET X=2      ⎫    Assume statements have been
   50 LET W$="2"   ⎭ ← executed in lines 60 through 90
③  60 LET Y$=W$+X
   70 LET Y$=W$+2
   80 LET Y$="2"-"2"
   90 LET Y$=X+"2"
```

① [   ]

② [   ]

③ [   ]

Note: Assume appropriate DIM statements, if required.

Figure 5-10   Some incorrect uses of strings with LET statements

Additional Examples of Strings with LET Statements

In Figure 5-11 lines 10 through 90 give you additional examples of string values and LET statements. We will work some of the examples now, and let you finish the remainder as part of the Application Exercises.

Look at line 10. Enter the contents Y$ in the appropriate number of spaces to the right.

You should have entered Y in space 1, E in space 2, and S in space 3.

Do the same at line 20. Use small b to represent a blank space.

You should have entered a blank in space 1, Y in space 2, E in space 3, and S in space 4.

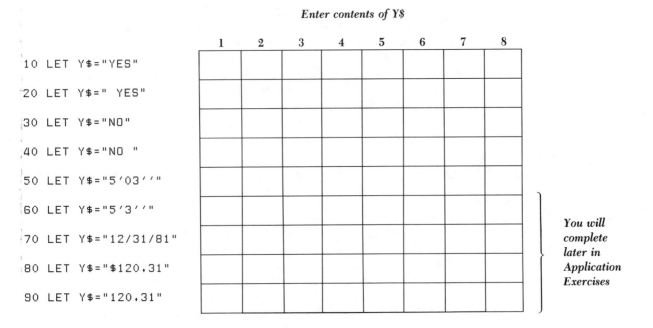

Enter contents of Y$

```
10 LET Y$="YES"

20 LET Y$=" YES"

30 LET Y$="NO"

40 LET Y$="NO "

50 LET Y$="5'03''"

60 LET Y$="5'3''"

70 LET Y$="12/31/81"

80 LET Y$="$120.31"

90 LET Y$="120.31"
```

	1	2	3	4	5	6	7	8

You will complete later in Application Exercises

Note: Assume appropriate DIM statements, if required.

Figure 5-11   Additional examples of LET statements and strings

Now compare the contents of Y$ from line 20 with the contents of Y$ from line 10. Notice that the characters in space 1 are different: a Y in one case and a blank in the other. You might think that both contain YES and are, therefore, logically the same, but technically they are not the same, and that is how the computer treats them.

Fill in the spaces to the right of lines 30 and 40.

Opposite line 30 you should have entered NO in spaces 1 and 2. Opposite line 40 you should have entered NO and a blank in spaces 1, 2, and 3. The string in line 30 has no characters in space 3. This is called a *null character*. The string in line 40 has a blank in space 3. Thus these two strings are different, because of the trailing blank space in line 40. However, since some computers do not use blank spaces for comparison purposes, you should check to see how they are handled on your computer.

Now fill in the spaces to the right of line 50. In spaces 1 through 6 you should have entered: 5′03″. Notice that two apostrophes are used to simulate quotation marks. Quotation marks are not allowed in strings, because they are used to enclose strings. We will ask you to complete lines 60 through 90 as part of the Application Exercises.

Strings and READ/DATA Statements

Additional Examples of Strings with READ and DATA Statements

In Figure 5-12 you will become familiar with the movement of the data pointer with both string and numeric data. The movement of the pointer is the same for both types of data. The following suggestion will make it easier to follow these examples. Each time a variable is read, you should circle the variable name in the READ statement and circle the item of data that was read from the DATA statement.

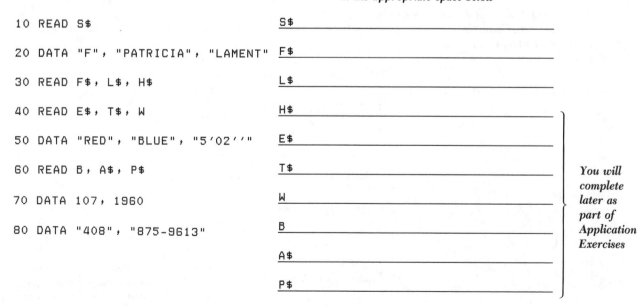

Enter contents of variables in the appropriate space below

```
10 READ S$

20 DATA "F", "PATRICIA", "LAMENT"

30 READ F$, L$, H$

40 READ E$, T$, W

50 DATA "RED", "BLUE", "5'02''"

60 READ B, A$, P$

70 DATA 107, 1960

80 DATA "408", "875-9613"
```

S$ _____

F$ _____

L$ _____

H$ _____

E$ _____

T$ _____

W _____

B _____

A$ _____

P$ _____

You will complete later as part of Application Exercises

Note: Assume appropriate DIM statement, if required.

Figure 5-12 Additional examples of READ and DATA statements with strings

In line 10 the variable S$ is read, and the data pointer points at the first data item in line 20, the letter F within quotes. Circle both the S$ and the F. In the space to the right, beside S$, enter the letter F. The pointer will move to the next data item in line 20, the string PATRICIA within quotes. Look at statement 30, the next READ statement. The next variable to be read is F$. Since the pointer is located at PATRICIA in line 20, PATRICIA will become the contents of F$. Enter PATRICIA in the space beside F$, and note that the pointer is at the string LAMENT. Now enter the contents of the next variable to be read, in the appropriate space to the right. You should have entered LAMENT beside L$, because that is the new variable read in line 30.

Note that the pointer is now in line 50 at the string RED, and the next variable to be read in line 30 is H$. Circle RED and H$. We will ask you to complete the entries in the figure as part of the Application Exercises.

Strings and INPUT Statements

Additional Examples of Strings with INPUT Statements

Look at Figure 5-13. At line 10 INPUT C$ causes a question mark to be displayed. Following the question mark is what the user typed, the letters JACK. Since only one variable was requested in the INPUT statement, it is not necessary to enclose

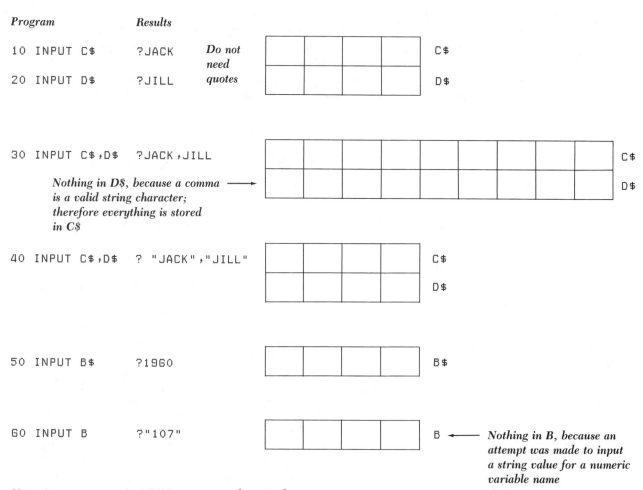

Note: Assume appropriate DIM statements, if required.

Figure 5-13   Additional examples of INPUT statements and strings

JACK within quotes. Therefore, in the boxes for C$, enter the letters JACK. Now in line 20, assuming INPUT D$ is executed, enter the contents of D$ in the boxes at the right.

You should have entered JILL.

At line 30 we have something slightly different. Two string variables, C$ and D$, are to be input in one INPUT statement. When this occurs with numeric variables, the user simply enters each of the variables separated by a comma. However, since the comma is a valid string character in string variables, it is entered as part of the contents of C$, followed by the letters JILL. So in the boxes for C$ at the right of line 30, enter JACK,JILL. Note that D$ contains nothing, because the computer is still waiting for input (everything was entered under C$).

In line 40 the same kind of input is requested. But this time each of the two strings, JACK and JILL, is enclosed within a separate set of quotes and separated by a comma. In the boxes to the right of line 40, enter the contents of C$ and D$ when line 40 is executed.

You should have entered JACK in C$ and JILL in D$.

In line 50 enter the contents of B$ based on the input shown.

You should have entered 1960 in B$; quotes are not required.

In line 60 note the results of executing INPUT B on the input shown. An error message would result. B contains nothing, because the 107 within quotes is a string and is being assigned to B, a numeric variable.

Strings and IF Statements

Collating Hierarchy

When comparing string values character by character in IF statements, it is important to know which character has a higher or lower value, unless you are checking for an equal condition. Two of the most commonly used coding systems used in computers, ASCII and EBCDIC, are shown in Figure 5-14. The letters ASCII, pronounced "as-kee," stand for American Standard Code for Information Interchange. The letters EBCDIC, pronounced "eb-see-dic," stand for Extended Binary Coded Decimal Interchange Code.

In Figure 5-14 we show the lowest-ranking character at the top and the highest-ranking character at the bottom for both coding systems. This is not a complete listing of all special characters. Check your computer manufacturer's reference manual for the particular codes used on your computer and a more complete list of characters.

In this *Programming Essentials* text, we will use ASCII rather than EBCDIC as the basis for comparisons. This hierarchy is sometimes referred to as a *collating sequence*. Note under the ASCII column that the lowest-ranking character is the null character, which stands for no character at all. The next lowest is a space or blank character. Following these are some special characters, such as the dollar sign, ampersand (&), apostrophe, comma, and dash. The next highest are numbers 0 through 9, with 0 ranking lowest and 9 highest. The next higher-ranking characters are the uppercase letters of the alphabet, with A ranking lowest and Z highest. Finally, the highest-ranking characters are the lowercase letters a through z. We will not use lowercase letters in any illustrations, exercises, or problems in this *Programming Essentials* text.

You will find this chart useful when you work on some of the later exercises and problems. Remember, *we will use ASCII* in this book.

Comparison ranking	ASCII character	EBCDIC character
Lowest	Null (no character) Space (blank) $ (dollar sign) & (ampersand or "and" sign) ' (apostrophe) , (comma) — (dash or minus)	Null (no character) Space (blank) & (ampersand or "and" sign) $ (dollar sign) — (dash or minus) , (comma) ' (apostrophe)
	0 ↓ 9 Numerals	a ↓ z Lowercase letters and numerals
	A ↓ Z Uppercase letters	A ↓ Z Uppercase letters
Highest	a ↓ z Lowercase letters	0 ↓ 9 Numerals

Note: See your computer manufacturer's reference manual for the particular code used on your computer and a more complete list of character rankings.

In this *Programming Essentials* text, *ASCII will be used* as the basis for comparisons.

Figure 5-14 Collating hierarchy of selected ASCII and EBCDIC characters

Additional Examples of Strings with IF Statements

Figure 5-15 will give you some practice in comparing various string values in IF statements.

Look at line 10. It tests Y$ to see whether it is equal to YES. Follow the arrow from Y$ in the IF statement to the top two blocks on the right to find the contents of Y$. The blocks contain NO. Now follow the arrow from the string constant YES in the IF statement to the bottom three blocks on the right and note that the contents align under Y$.

The comparison begins from left to right. The first character, Y, in the constant YES is greater than the first character, N, in Y$, thereby making them unequal. Therefore, the comparison stops at this point, and the constant YES is greater. As a result, the equal condition being tested in the IF statement is false, and the program will not branch to statement 100. Instead it will continue to the next statement in sequence.

Look at line 20. When the contents of Y$ in the top two blocks are compared with the contents of the constant NO in the bottom two blocks, the two are found to be equal. Thus the equal condition being tested is true, so the program branches to statement 200. We will ask you to complete lines 30 through 90 as part of the Application Exercises.

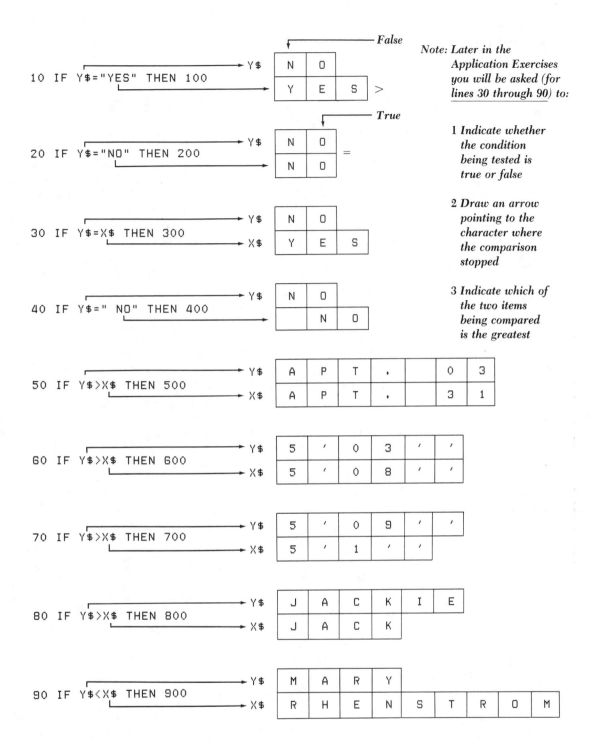

Note: Later in the
Application Exercises
you will be asked (for
lines 30 through 90) to:

1 Indicate whether
the condition
being tested is
true or false

2 Draw an arrow
pointing to the
character where
the comparison
stopped

3 Indicate which of
the two items
being compared
is the greatest

Note: Assume appropriate DIM statements, if required. Comparison begins with the first
character of each string and continues from left to right until an unequal condition is
detected. Comparison stops at that point.

Figure 5-15   Additional examples of IF statements and strings

Strings and PRINT Statements

Additional Examples of Strings with PRINT Statements

In Figure 5-16 you can see various examples showing how to leave space between string characters.

In lines 10 through 20, string constants are assigned to string variables F$, L$, and H$. None of them has extra blank spaces within the quotation marks. In line 25 the numeric constant 107 is assigned to the numeric variable W. Lines 30 through 39, labeled "output without spaces," are PRINT statements that create the output to the right of the program. Note that, in the first line, which reads PATRI-CIALAMENTHASREDHAIR, this all runs together without spaces. This happens because, in line 30 of the program, F$, L$, the constant HAS (the word "has"), H$, and the constant HAIR are separated by only semicolons, and the constants do not contain blank spaces. Remember that a semicolon following a string value leaves no space between a string and the next value. The second line of output is also run together except for the value of 107, which has spaces around it.

Look at line 35 in the program. Both the constant AND and the constant WEIGHS are followed by semicolons; therefore, no spaces appear before the next value is printed. You might wonder about W in the PRINT statement. It is also followed by a semicolon, but the output doesn't run together with the other output. Since it is a numeric variable, it allows space for the sign preceding the 1 in 107. The semicolon following W allows the standard close spacing for numeric values.

Let's see how we can allow for spaces when dealing with strings. Lines 40 through 55 assign values to F$, L$, H$, and E$. In line 45 note that the string constant being assigned to L$ has a blank space as a last character, and the string constant being assigned to H$ has a blank space as a leading character.

Now look at line 60. Each element of the PRINT statement is followed by a semicolon, but they are separated by spaces in the printed output. The first space in

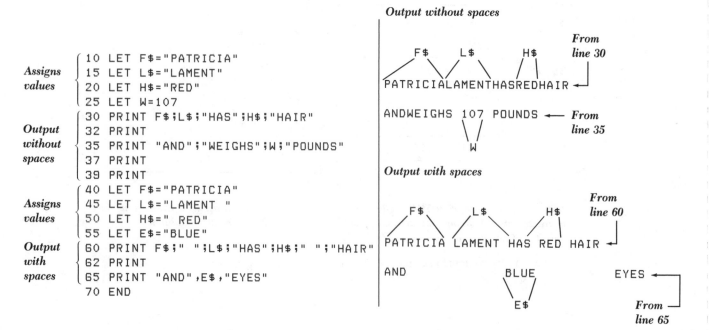

Figure 5-16   Additional examples of PRINT statements and strings

the output between PATRICIA and LAMENT is caused by the blank string constant between F$ and L$, in the PRINT statement in line 60. The next space in the output, between LAMENT and HAS, is caused by the trailing blank space that is part of L$. The space between HAS and RED is caused by the leading blank space that is part of H$. The space between RED and HAIR is caused by the PRINT statement in line 60, since the blank string constant follows the variable name H$. Line 62 causes a blank line to print. Line 65 uses commas as separators to cause spaces between the output of the words AND, BLUE, and EYES. So you can see that there are many ways to cause spaces between string values in printed output.

Finding a Date

In Figure 5-17 read the description of the program in REMARK statements 10 through 45 and in the legends of REMARK statements 63 through 90.

In this program we will concentrate primarily on examining the printed results (Figure 5-18) and the flowchart (Figure 5-19), with only occasional reference to the program. Later you can examine the program in more detail.

Look at flowchart symbol 108–109 in Figure 5-19, which displays a message requesting information from the user—that is, the person seeking the date. Symbol 110–120 calls for the input of the current year as Y. Look at the displayed results at the encircled 1 in Figure 5-18 to see the first line displayed. Next look at the line at the encircled 2, the request for the current year. Following the question mark, the user enters 1984, which is labeled Y.

Look at the results at the encircled 3, where you see several lines requesting the user's specifications for a date. After the question mark in the line for MALE or FEMALE, the user types F, which is labeled G$. In the line for hair color, the user types BLONDE, which is labeled I$. In the next line, for tallest height, the input is 5′09′′, labeled C$; and in the following line, the shortest height is 5′00′′, labeled D$. Now look at the flowchart symbol 130–205, which corresponds to what you have just seen in the results as the input of the user's specifications for a date.

Symbol 210 in the flowchart calls for the sex code, S$, to be read for one of the potential dates. The data for the potential date is located in DATA statements in program lines 920–936. Look at line 920. Each line of data contains specifications for one of the dates. The variable name for each specification is shown above the first DATA statement in line 920. The first specification in line 920 is F, labeled S$ for sex code. The next, PATRICIA, is labeled F$ for first name; then LAMENT, labeled L$ for last name; RED, labeled H$ for hair color; BLUE, labeled E$ for color of eyes; 5′2′′, labeled T$ for height; 107, labeled W for weight; 1960, labeled B for birthdate; 408, labeled A$ for area code; and last, 875–9613, labeled P$ for phone number. Notice that all variables are strings, except for weight (W) and birthdate (B), which are numeric.

Now look at symbol 212 in the flowchart. S$, which has just been read as F for female, is now tested to see whether it equals E, which would indicate that the end of data has been reached. Since S$ doesn't equal E, the program proceeds to symbol 215, which calls for the remainder of the data in the DATA statement to be read.

The next five symbols are decision symbols comparing the data for the potential date in the DATA statement with the corresponding specifications input from the user seeking a date. With the exception of symbol 224, if any specification is not met, the program branches left to connector symbol 1 that leads back to symbol 210, which reads the data about another potential date and then goes through the same process again.

The program tries to match the DATA statement information with the user's input specifications. In our example the user specified blonde hair, which was input

```
10 REM A PROGRAM THAT ALLOWS A PERSON (DATER) SEEKING A DATE (DATEE)
20 REM TO INPUT DESIRED SPECIFICATIONS REGARDING SEX, HAIR COLOR,
30 REM AND UPPER AND LOWER HEIGHT LIMITS. IT WILL THEN SEARCH A FILE
40 REM OF POTENTIAL DATEES IN DATA STATEMENTS AND PRINT OUT DATA
45 REM ABOUT ANYONE WHO FITS SPECIFICATIONS.
50 REM ************** LEGEND ***************
63 REM Y$ YES/NO CODE
64 REM
65 REM ***** CODES FOR POTENTIAL DATES *****
67 REM A  AGE (Y-B)   Y  CURRENT YEAR   B  YEAR OF BIRTH
68 REM A$   AREA CODE          F$   FIRST NAME
69 REM  E$  COLOR EYES        H$   COLOR HAIR
70 REM L$  LAST NAME         P$  PHONE NO.
72 REM  S$  SEX               T$   HEIGHT
74 REM W  WEIGHT
75 REM ***** CODES FOR DATE SPECIFICATIONS *****
76 REM C$  TALLEST HEIGHT    D$  SHORTEST HEIGHT
78 REM G$  SEX               I$  COLOR HAIR
90 REM
100 REM ************** PROGRAM STARTS HERE ***************
108 PRINT "TO FIND A DATE,PLEASE ENTER THE FOLLOWING INFORMATION."
109 PRINT
110 PRINT "ENTER CURRENT YEAR (EG. 1984) ";
120 INPUT Y
130 PRINT "ENTER YOUR SPECIFICATIONS FOR A DATE"
140 PRINT "MALE OR FEMALE ( M OR F) ";
150 INPUT G$
160 PRINT "HAIR COLOR (BLONDE,BROWN,BLACK,RED,ANY) ";
170 INPUT I$
180 PRINT "TALLEST ACCEPTABLE HEIGHT(NEAREST INCH EG. 5'07'') ";
190 INPUT C$
200 PRINT "SHORTEST ACCEPTABLE HEIGHT ";
205 INPUT D$
210 READ S$
212 IF S$="E" THEN 800
215 READ F$,L$,H$,E$,T$,W,B,A$,P$
220 IF S$ <> G$ THEN 210
224 IF I$="ANY" THEN 240
230 IF H$ <> I$ THEN 210
240 IF T$>C$ THEN 210
250 IF T$<D$ THEN 210
260 LET A=Y-B
265 PRINT
270 PRINT "HOW ABOUT "F$;" ";L$;"? ";A$;" ";P$;" AGE ";A
280 PRINT T$;" EYES OF ";E$;" WEIGHING ";W;" POUNDS."
300 GO TO 210


800 PRINT
810 PRINT "NONE OF THE REMAINING PEOPLE IN OUR FILE MEET YOUR SPECIFICATIONS"
820 PRINT "DO YOU WANT TO TRY AGAIN ( YES OR NO ) ";
830 INPUT Y$
840 IF Y$="NO" THEN 900
850 RESTORE
860 GO TO 130
900 PRINT "GOOD BYE AND GOOD LUCK."
```

Figure 5-17 Program for finding a date

```
          S$        F$          L$         H$       E$         T$        W      B     A$       P$
920 DATA "F","PATRICIA","LAMENT","RED","BLUE","5'02''",107,1960,"408","875-9613"
922 DATA "F","PAMELA","ZUBLINKSKI","BROWN","GREEN","5'09''",135,1950,"408","213-2205"
924 DATA "M","WILLIAM","WILLIAMS","BROWN","GREEN","5'09''",135,1965,"408","213-2205"
926 DATA "M","REGINALD","ZAMBINI","RED","GREEN","5'10''",160,1955,"415","525-3891"
928 DATA "F","DOROTHY","OZ","BLACK","HAZEL","4'10''",105,1952,"916","862-9217"
930 DATA "F","JANICE","ADAMS","GRAY","BROWN","5'10''",110,1961,"408","321-5122"
932 DATA "M","TIMOTHY","ZORICH","AUBURN","GREEN","5'02''",118,1963,"916","421-9512"
934 DATA "M","LEOPOLD","KELLY","BLONDE","BLUE","5'11''",160,1951,"916","967-3312"
936 DATA "E"
999 END
```

Figure 5-17 Continued

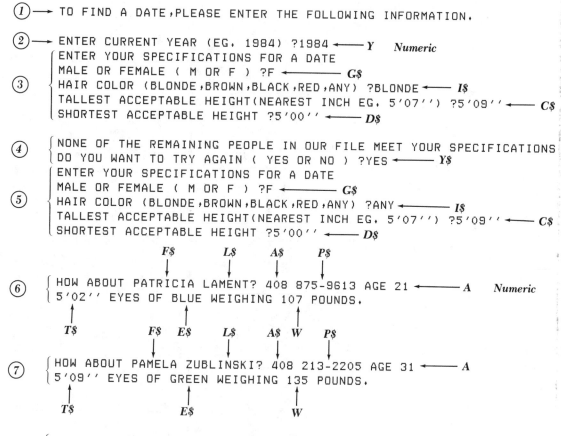

Figure 5-18 Results of program for finding a date

as I$, and the hair color of the first person in the DATA statement is RED, which was read as H$. Look at symbol 224 in the flowchart. I$, which equals BLONDE, is compared with ANY, which would indicate that the person seeking the date is not concerned about hair color. Since these are not equal, we go to symbol 230, where H$ (which equals RED, the potential date's hair color) is compared with I$, which is

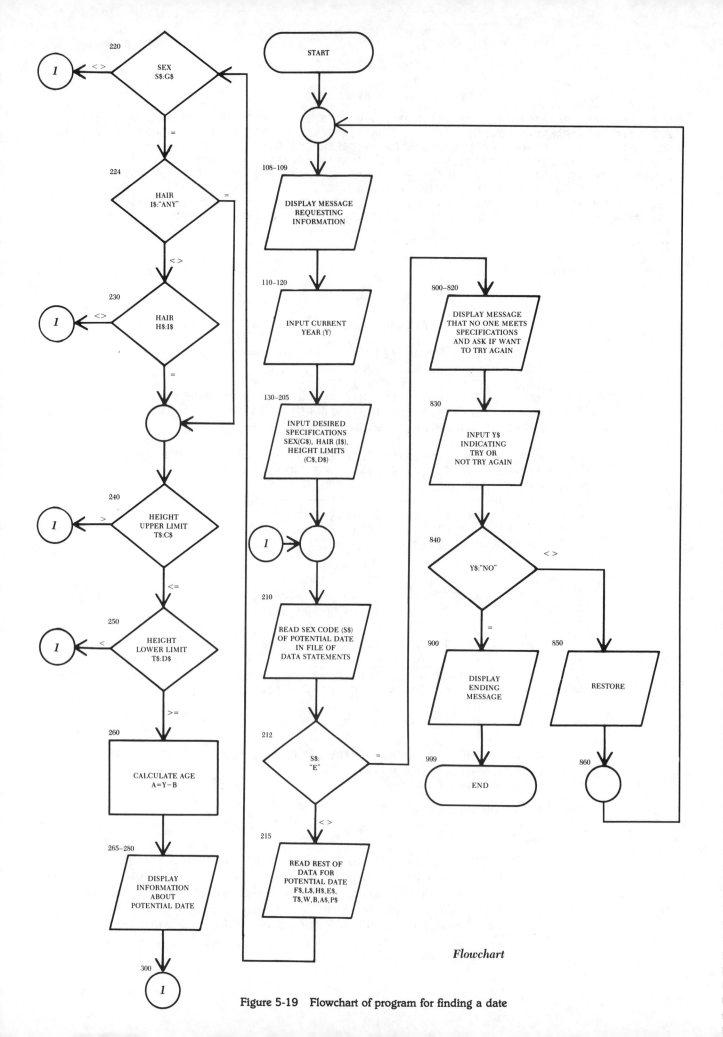

Flowchart

Figure 5-19 Flowchart of program for finding a date

BLONDE, the color specified by the user. Since they are not equal, the program branches back to the READ symbol 210 to read another DATA statement for another potential date.

Based on our first input specifications, none of the DATA statements contains anyone who meets all the specifications. So the last DATA statement is read; it contains an E for sex code S$. Therefore, at symbol 212 in the flowchart, S$ equals the letter E and flow branches to symbol 800–820. This causes a message to be displayed stating that no one meets the specifications. Symbol 830 calls for the user to input YES or NO for Y$, indicating whether the user wants to try again. You can see this in the printed results at the encircled 4.

In the flowchart again, symbol 840 tests Y$. If Y$ equals NO, an ending message is displayed. Otherwise, symbol 850 restores the DATA statement pointer to the first item of data in the DATA statement with the lowest line number. The flow then branches back to symbol 108–109 to begin again by asking the user to input new information—shown in our example in the results at the encircled number 5. This branching back is accomplished through the use of a GO TO statement.

This time data that matches the user's specifications is found, and all conditions in the decision symbols are successfully met. So in the flowchart, after the last decision symbol 250, we take the downward branch to symbol 260, which calculates the person's age (A) by subtracting the potential date's year of birth (B) from the current year (Y). Because of this arithmetic operation, these values must be numeric. The flow then goes to the next symbol (265–280); this displays the information about the potential date and then branches back to symbol 210 to read another person's DATA statement to see whether it meets the specifications. In our example, two people's DATA statements meet the specifications. The displayed results can be seen at the encircled 6 and 7. Finally, at the encircled 8, the user indicates that he or she does not want to try again. The program displays the ending message shown at the encircled 9.

PROGRAMMING TECHNIQUES

1. Displaying strings close together without running them together, by including blank spaces between strings:

```
50 PRINT "MY NAME IS ";F$;" ";L$
```
Blank space between strings ⎯⎯⎯⎯⎯⎯⎯⎯⎯
```
210 PRINT C$;" AND ";D$;" WENT UP THE HILL"
```

2. Using apostrophes to give the appearance of quotation marks within a string:

```
60 PRINT "5' 2'' EYES OF BLUE"
```
⎯⎯ *Apostrophes*

DEBUGGING AIDS

ERROR	CAUSE	CORRECTION
10 LET A="JOHN"	Assigns string value to numeric variable name	10 LET A$="JOHN"
20 LET G$=120	Assigns numeric value to string variable name	20 LET G$="120"
50 LET S$=A$-B$	Attempting arithmetic operations on string values	50 LET S=A-B
60 READ F$,L$ 70 DATA "JOHN",SMITH	Missing quotes around string value	60 READ F$,L$ 70 DATA "JOHN","SMITH"
80 READ F,L 90 DATA "JOHN","SMITH"	Reading string data with numeric variable name	80 READ F$,L$ 90 DATA "JOHN","SMITH"
10 INPUT F$,L$ RUN ? JOHN SMITH	Missing quotes around two strings entered by user	10 INPUT F$,L$ RUN ?"JOHN","SMITH"
10 PRINT "ANSWER Y OR N"; 20 INPUT A RUN ANSWER Y OR N ? Y	Using numeric variable name (A) for string input data (Y or N)	10 PRINT "ANSWER Y OR N"; 20 INPUT A$ RUN ANSWER Y OR N ? Y
30 IF A$=Y THEN 80	Missing quotes around the string constant	30 IF A$="Y" THEN 80
40 IF A="Y" THEN 90	Comparing a numeric variable to a string constant	40 IF A$="Y" THEN 90
50 PRINT F$;L$ RUN JOHNDOE	Two strings run together	50 PRINT F$;" ";L$ RUN JOHN DOE

REFERENCE

STATEMENT SUMMARY

ASSIGNMENT STATEMENT	GENERAL FORM
The string constant(s) or string variable(s) to the right of the equals sign replaces the variable to the left of the equals sign; if a string constant appears to the right of the equals sign, it must be enclosed in quotes	LET string variable = string constant or string variable *Examples:* 115 LET E$="STOP" 120 LET Q$=E$ *Flowchart symbol:*

```
┌─────────┐
│         │
│  Q$←E$  │
│         │
└─────────┘
```

PRINT STATEMENT	GENERAL FORM
The string constant(s) or string variable(s) to the right of the word PRINT are displayed	PRINT string constant(s), string variable(s), or expression to be displayed *Example:* `210 PRINT "HELLO ";A$` *Flowchart symbol:* PRINT

INPUT STATEMENT	GENERAL FORM

Inputting string data is very similar to inputting numeric data, as discussed in a previous unit; as a result, we will focus here only on implications that relate to strings: if a single string variable is input in one INPUT statement, the value typed by the user can (but, need not be) enclosed in quotes; however, if *two or more variables* are input *in one INPUT* statement, the values typed by the user *must be* enclosed in quotes	INPUT string variable name(s)
	
	Examples:
	
	`160 INPUT C$`
	`170 INPUT B$,G$`
	
	Flowchart symbol:
	
	INPUT C$

READ/DATA STATEMENTS	GENERAL FORM

Reading string data is very similar to reading numeric data, as discussed in a previous unit; as a result, we will focus here only on implications that relate to strings: a string value in a DATA statement must be enclosed within quotes; both string and numeric data can be read in the same READ statement; however, you must take care to ensure that the type of variable (string or numeric) is the same as the type of value in the corresponding position in the DATA statement	READ variable name(s)
	
	Examples:
	
	`10 READ B$`
	`20 DATA "JANE"`
	`30 READ F$,L$,W,Y`
	`40 DATA "JOHN","DOE",150,1984`
	
	Flowchart symbol:
	
	READ B$

IF-THEN STATEMENT	GENERAL FORM

Testing string data is very similar to testing numeric data, as discussed in a previous unit; as a result, we will focus here only on implications that relate to strings being tested in IF-THEN statements: string comparisons follow a given hierarchy (see Figure 5-14); string constants must be enclosed in quotes	IF. . . THEN
	
	Examples:
	
	`195 IF C$=E$ THEN 300`
	`200 IF A$="YES" THEN 240`
	
	Flowchart symbol:
	
	C$: E$

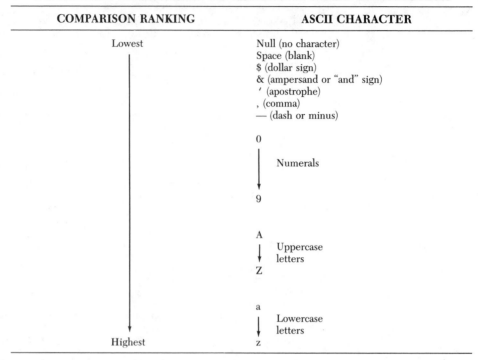

COLLATING HIERARCHY OF SELECTED ASCII CHARACTERS

COMPARISON RANKING	ASCII CHARACTER
Lowest	Null (no character)
	Space (blank)
	$ (dollar sign)
	& (ampersand or "and" sign)
	' (apostrophe)
	, (comma)
	— (dash or minus)
	0
	Numerals
	9
	A
	Uppercase letters
	Z
	a
	Lowercase letters
Highest	z

Note: See your computer manufacturer's reference manual for the particular code used on your computer and a more complete list of character rankings.

APPLICATION EXERCISES

Assume appropriate DIM statements when required.

1. Complete the entries in Figure 5-11.
2. Complete the entries in Figure 5-12.
3. Complete the entries in Figure 5-15. For each line number:
   a. Indicate whether the condition being tested is true or false
   b. If the two terms are equal, enter =
   c. If the two terms are not equal, indicate which is greater and draw an arrow pointing to the position where comparison stopped

Describe errors in the following statements in each area shown:

Errors

4. `10 LET A="JOHN"`

5. `20 LET G$=120`

6. `30 LET A$="50"`
   `40 LET O$="25"`
   `50 LET S$=A$-O$`

7. `60 READ S$,F$,L$,W,P$`
   `70 DATA "M","JOHN",SMITH,107,213-9613`

Enter the statement number to which each program would transfer control:

8. `10 IF "1984 BC"<="1984 AD" THEN 200` _____
    `20 ............`
9. `30 IF "2001 AD">"1984 AD" THEN 300` _____
    `40 ............`
10. `50 IF "JOHN">"JOHN" THEN 600` _____
    `60 ............`
11. `70 IF " JOHNNY">"JOHN" THEN 700` _____
    `80 ............`

In the following program show what statement 200 will print each time it is executed. Assume proper DIM statements, if required on your computer.

12. _____
13. _____
14. _____
15. _____

```
20 READ A$
30 LET B$="1200 3 RD ST"
40 READ C$
49 IF C$="END OF DATA" THEN 80
50 IF A$<B$ THEN 70
60 IF A$<C$ THEN 100
65 LET D$=A$
67 GO TO 200
70 IF B$<C$ THEN 100
80 LET D$=B$
90 GO TO 200
100 LET D$=C$
200 PRINT D$
205 IF C$="END OF DATA" THEN 999
210 GO TO 40
300 DATA "1200 T ST."
310 DATA "1200 T AVE."
320 DATA "1200 B ST."
330 DATA "1200 W AVE."
340 DATA "END OF DATA"
999 END
```

Answers to Application Exercises

1. (From Figure 5-11)

	1	2	3	4	5	6	7	8
10 LET Y$="YES"	Y	E	S					
20 LET Y$=" YES"		Y	E	S				
30 LET Y$="NO"	N	O						
40 LET Y$="NO "	N	O						
50 LET Y$="5'03''"	5	'	0	3	'	'		
60 LET Y$="5'3''"	5	'	3	'	'			
70 LET Y$="12/31/81"	1	2	/	3	1	/	8	1
80 LET Y$="$120.31"	$	1	2	0	.	3	1	
90 LET Y$="120.31"	1	2	0	.	3	1		

2. (From Figure 5-12)

```
10 READ S$
20 DATA "F","PATRICIA","LAMENT"


30 READ F$,L$,H$
40 READ E$,T$,W
50 DATA "RED","BLUE","5'02''"


60 READ B,A$,P$
70 DATA 107,1960,"408","875-9613"
```

S$	F
F$	PATRICIA
L$	LAMENT
H$	RED
E$	BLUE
T$	5'02''
W	107
B	1960
A$	408
P$	875-9613

3. (From Figure 5-15)

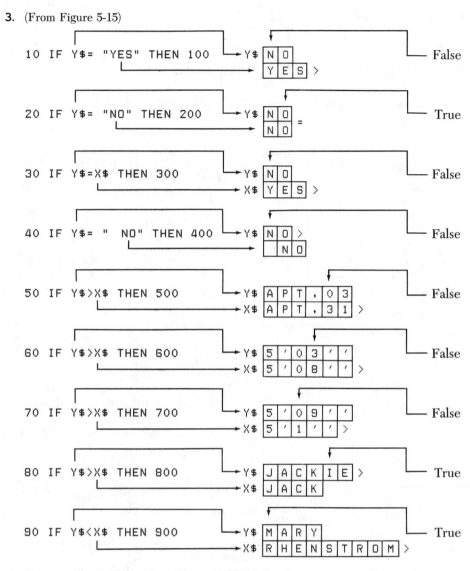

4. Assigns string value to numeric variable name
5. No quotation marks around 120
6. Attempts arithmetic operation on string values
7. Quotation marks missing around SMITH and 213-9613
8. 20
9. 300
10. 60
11. 80
12. 1200 T ST.
13. 1200 T ST.
14. 1200 W AVE.
15. 1200 3RD ST.

PROGRAMMING PROBLEMS

5-1. Program for Personalized Dating Letter

Given the following data on prospective dates (datees):

S E X	FIRST NAME	LAST NAME	HAIR COLOR	EYE COLOR	HEIGHT	WEIGHT	YEAR OF BIRTH	AREA CODE	PHONE
F	PATRICIA	LAMENT	RED	BLUE	5'02"	107	1960	408	875-9613
F	PAMELA	ZUBLINSKI	BROWN	GREEN	5'09"	135	1950	408	213-2205
M	WILLIAM	WILLIAMS	BROWN	GREEN	5'09"	135	1965	408	213-2205
M	REGINALD	ZAMBINI	RED	GREEN	5'10"	160	1955	415	525-3891
F	DOROTHY	OZ	BLACK	HAZEL	4'10"	105	1952	916	862-9217
F	JANICE	ADAMS	GRAY	BROWN	5'10"	110	1961	408	321-5122
M	TIMOTHY	ZORICH	AUBURN	GREEN	5'02"	118	1963	916	421-9512
M	LEOPOLD	KELLY	BLONDE	BLUE	5'11"	160	1951	916	967-3312
E	(When this is recognized, it signals the end of datee data)								

Given the following data on the person seeking a date (dater):

Age—25; height—5'08"; first name—MORLEY; last name—LUMPWOOD; area code—415; phone—948-4503

Write a program that will allow the person seeking a date (dater) to write a letter to a prospective date (datee). The program should permit the following variables to be inserted into the text of the letter:

1. Input by dater:
   a. Dater's data
   b. Opening salutation, closing phrase, date of letter, first and last name of datee
2. Read from DATA statement:
   a. Datee's data
3. Various messages based on datee's data:
   a. Height: "THE SAME HEIGHT AS I AM"
               or
         "SLIGHTLY TALLER THAN I AM"
               or
         "SLIGHTLY SHORTER THAN I AM"
   b. Sex: "MEN" or "WOMEN"
   c. Age: "MY AGE"
               or
         "YOUNGER THAN I AM"
               or
         "OLDER THAN I AM"

Each time a new letter is to be written, the dater must input the information in item 1b.

Programming tips:

1. Draw a flowchart of the solution.
2. The first eight DATA statements should contain information about the datees. The last DATA statement should contain a code of E in place of the code for sex. When this is recognized, it signals the end of datee data. No other data about the datee is required in the last DATA statement.
3. To print the letter, refer to the underlined portions of the sample output to determine where the variable information should be inserted. *Your letter, however, should not contain underlining.*
4. Once the letter is printed, the pointer must be restored to the beginning of the datee data before a new letter can be started.
5. Both the year of the letter and the datee's year of birth should be entered as numeric variables, since these will be used in calculating the datee's age.
6. Don't forget to include a DIM statement if your computer requires it.

Results:

```
TO WRITE A DATING LETTER,PLEASE ENTER
THE FOLLOWING ABOUT YOURSELF:
AGE ?25
HEIGHT(EG. 5'09'') ?5'08''
FIRST NAME ?MORLEY
LAST NAME ?LUMPWOOD
AREA CODE ?415
PHONE NUMBER ?948-4503
ENTER OPENING SALUTATION ?DEAR
ENTER CLOSING PHRASE ?SINCERELY
ENTER DATE OF LETTER.
MONTH ?MAY
DAY ?30
YEAR ?1984
ENTER THE FIRST AND LAST NAME OF THE PERSON TO WHOM
THE LETTER WILL BE ADDRESSED.
(EACH IN QUOTATION MARKS AND SEPARATED BY A COMMA)
?"PAMELA","ZUBLINSKI"
```

```
                                    MAY 30, 1984
DEAR PAMELA,

     I HAVE BEEN LOOKING FORWARD TO MEETING YOU EVER SINCE
I READ YOUR DESCRIPTION. GREEN EYES AND BROWN
HAIR IS ONE OF MY FAVORITE COMBINATIONS. I ALSO FEEL
LUCKY TO MEET SOMEONE SO PHYSICALLY COMPATIBLE. AT
5'09'' YOU ARE SLIGHTLY TALLER THAN I AM. FURTHERMORE,
I HAVE ALWAYS BEEN FASCINATED BY WOMEN WHO ARE OLDER THAN I AM.
     IF YOU ARE INTERESTED IN THE POSSIBILITY OF SEEING
EACH OTHER, CALL ME AT 415 948-4503.

                                    SINCERELY,


                                    MORLEY LUMPWOOD
```

Results are continued on next page.

Figure 5-20   Program results for personalized dating letter

```
DO YOU WANT TO WRITE TO ANOTHER PERSON(YES OR NO) ?YES
ENTER OPENING SALUTATION ?DEAREST
ENTER CLOSING PHRASE ?HOPEFULLY
ENTER DATE OF LETTER,
MONTH ?JUNE
DAY ?7
YEAR ?1984
ENTER THE FIRST AND LAST NAME OF THE PERSON TO WHOM
THE LETTER WILL BE ADDRESSED,
(EACH IN QUOTATION MARKS AND SEPARATED BY A COMMA)
?"PATRICIA","LAMENT"
```

                                        JUNE 7, 1984
DEAREST PATRICIA,

      I HAVE BEEN LOOKING FORWARD TO MEETING YOU EVER SINCE
I READ YOUR DESCRIPTION, BLUE EYES AND RED
HAIR IS ONE OF MY FAVORITE COMBINATIONS, I ALSO FEEL
LUCKY TO MEET SOMEONE SO PHYSICALLY COMPATIBLE, AT
5'02'' YOU ARE SLIGHTLY SHORTER THAN I AM, FURTHERMORE,
I HAVE ALWAYS BEEN FASCINATED BY WOMEN WHO ARE YOUNGER THAN I AM,
      IF YOU ARE INTERESTED IN THE POSSIBILITY OF SEEING
EACH OTHER, CALL ME AT 415 948-4503,

                        HOPEFULLY,

                        MORLEY LUMPWOOD

DO YOU WANT TO WRITE TO ANOTHER PERSON(YES OR NO) ?NO

Figure 5-20   Continued

5-2. Program for Personalized Sales Letter

Given the following data on prospective customers:

FIRST NAME	LAST NAME	STREET	CITY	STATE	ZIP CODE
JIMMY	KENNEDY	1200 EVA AVE.	LOS ALTOS	CALIF.	94022
TEDDY	CARTER	12 SAN JUAN COURT	LOS ALTOS	CALIF.	94022
RONNIE	FORD	1230 BUBB ROAD	CUPERTINO	CALIF.	95014

END (when this is recognized, it signals the end of customer data)

Given the following data on a sales company:

Company name—HOLIDAY SALES; phone—213-996-4917;
salesperson name—RHENSTROM PHILPOT

Write a program that will allow a salesperson to write a personalized sales letter to selected customers. The program should permit the following variables to be inserted in the standard text of the letter:

1. Input by salesperson:
   a. Company name, phone number, and salesperson name
   b. Date of letter, product name, holiday name, closing phrase, and first and last names of potential customer
2. Read from DATA statements: Customer name and address data

We are assuming that each family has children and the letter is to be addressed to the wife. Each time a letter is to be written, the salesperson must input all the information in item 1b.

Your printed output should include two letters and match the output shown in Figure 5-22.

Programming tips:

1. The first three DATA statements should contain customer data. The fourth should contain the word END in place of the first name. When this is recognized, it signals the end of customer data. No last name or address data is required in the last DATA statement.
2. To print the letter, refer to the underlined portions of the sample output to determine where the variable information should be inserted. *Your letter, however, should not contain underlining.*
3. Once the letter is printed, the pointer must be restored to the beginning of the customer data before a new letter can be started.
4. Don't forget to include a DIM statement if your computer requires it.
5. Use the flowchart in Figure 5-21 as a general guide in developing your program.

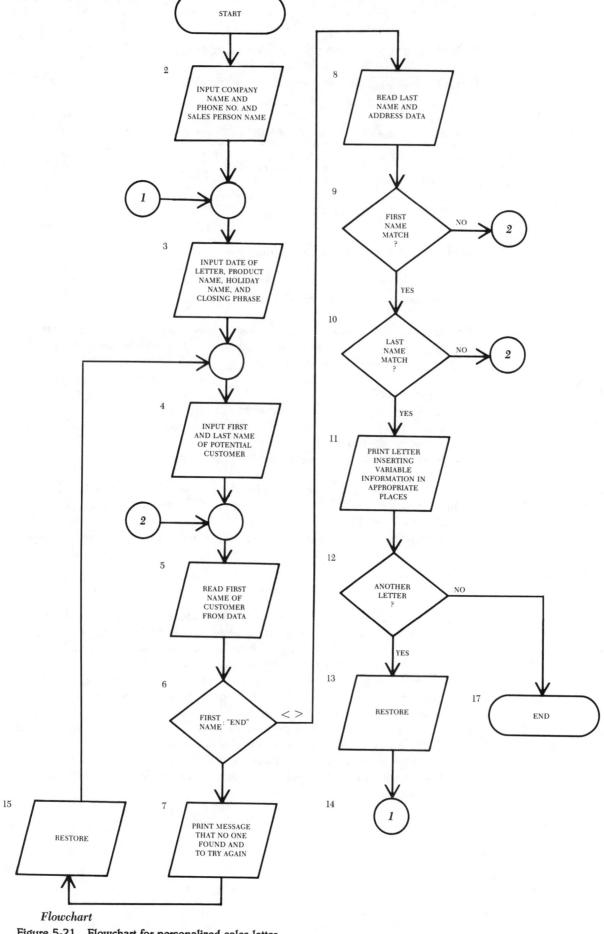

Flowchart

Figure 5-21 Flowchart for personalized sales letter

Results:

```
WELCOME TO PERSONALIZED LETTER WRITING.
PLEASE ENTER THE FOLLOWING ABOUT YOUR COMPANY:
COMPANY NAME ?HOLIDAY SALES
PHONE(INCLUDE AREA CODE) ?213 996-4917
SALESPERSON NAME ?RHENSTROM PHILPOT
PLEASE ENTER THE FOLLOWING ABOUT THIS PARTICULAR LETTER:
DATE OF LETTER ?NOVEMBER 15, 1984
PRODUCT NAME ?TURKEY
NAME OF HOLIDAY ?THANKSGIVING
CLOSING PHRASE ?HAVE A NICE
CUSTOMER FIRST AND LAST NAME(EACH IN SEPARATE QUOTES
AND SEPARATED FROM EACH OTHER BY A COMMA.
?"TEDDY","CARTER"


                                        NOVEMBER 15, 1984
DEAR MRS. CARTER,

     WELL IT'S THAT TIME OF YEAR AGAIN.
I HAVE BEEN TAKING A LOT OF ORDERS FOR TURKEY
IN YOUR NEIGHBORHOOD AROUND 12 SAN JUAN COURT.
KNOWING THE WAY YOU TAKE CARE OF MR. CARTER
AND ALL THE LITTLE CARTERS, I THOUGHT
YOU OF ALL PEOPLE WANT TO HAVE PLENTY OF
TURKEY ON HAND WHEN THANKSGIVING ROLLS AROUND.
     IF YOU HAVEN'T CHECKED THE PRICES OF TURKEY
IN STORES THROUGHOUT LOS ALTOS RECENTLY, I THINK
YOU WILL FIND CONSIDERABLE SAVINGS WHEN BUYING
DIRECTLY FROM US AT HOLIDAY SALES. PLEASE DO
YOURSELF AND YOUR FAMILY A FAVOR MRS. CARTER
AND GIVE US A CALL AT 213 996-4917.

                         HAVE A NICE THANKSGIVING,


                         RHENSTROM PHILPOT
                         YOUR FRIEND AT HOLIDAY SALES

----------------------------------------------------------

TEAR ALONG DOTTED LINE
```

Results are continued on next page.

Figure 5-22   Program results for personalized sales letter

```
WOULD YOU LIKE TO HAVE ANOTHER LETTER TYPED?
ENTER YES OR NO ?YES
PLEASE ENTER THE FOLLOWING ABOUT THIS PARTICULAR LETTER:
DATE OF LETTER ?DECEMBER 1, 1984
PRODUCT NAME ?TINSEL
NAME OF HOLIDAY ?CHRISTMAS
CLOSING PHRASE ?MERRY
CUSTOMER FIRST AND LAST NAME(EACH IN SEPARATE QUOTES
AND SEPARATED FROM EACH OTHER BY A COMMA.
?"RONNIE","FORD"


                                    DECEMBER 1, 1984
DEAR MRS. FORD,

     WELL IT'S THAT TIME OF YEAR AGAIN.
I HAVE BEEN TAKING A LOT OF ORDERS FOR TINSEL
IN YOUR NEIGHBORHOOD AROUND 1230 BUBB ROAD.
KNOWING THE WAY YOU TAKE CARE OF MR. FORD
AND ALL THE LITTLE FORDS, I THOUGHT
YOU OF ALL PEOPLE WANT TO HAVE PLENTY OF
TINSEL ON HAND WHEN CHRISTMAS ROLLS AROUND.
     IF YOU HAVEN'T CHECKED THE PRICES OF TINSEL
IN STORES THROUGHOUT CUPERTINO RECENTLY, I THINK
YOU WILL FIND CONSIDERABLE SAVINGS WHEN BUYING
DIRECTLY FROM US AT HOLIDAY SALES. PLEASE DO
YOURSELF AND YOUR FAMILY A FAVOR MRS. FORD
AND GIVE US A CALL AT 213 996-4917.

                              MERRY CHRISTMAS,


                              RHENSTROM PHILPOT
                              YOUR FRIEND AT HOLIDAY SALES


-----------------------------------------------------------

TEAR ALONG DOTTED LINE
WOULD YOU LIKE TO HAVE ANOTHER LETTER TYPED?
ENTER YES OR NO ?NO
```

Figure 5-22 Continued

6 BASIC Built-In Functions

OBJECTIVES

When you complete this unit, you will be able to:

1. Write a BASIC statement that uses one or more of the following BASIC built-in functions for a given problem
   a. General functions—absolute value, random number, square root, tabulation, truncation
   b. Trigonometric functions—arc tangent, cosine, sine, tangent
2. Code and execute a BASIC solution to a problem requiring the use of the following BASIC built-in functions:
   a. Given a program with a flowchart
   b. Given a program without a flowchart

INTRODUCTION

What Is a BASIC Built-In Function?

A BASIC built-in function is a set of instructions preprogrammed for a BASIC system that may be easily used by a programmer by simply referencing the function.

Using BASIC Built-in Functions

Certain computing operations are required on a routine basis. In this unit we will introduce you to some common functions that are available in most versions of BASIC.

This unit introduces BASIC built-in functions that are preprogrammed for your BASIC system. We will not discuss all functions in this unit, but when you learn to use the ones introduced here, you will be able to handle the other functions when the situation demands.

Sample BASIC Built-in Function

All BASIC built-in functions work in a similar way. As a general illustration, we have chosen the absolute-value function in Figure 6-1.

Line 10 is a LET statement that says: "Calculate the absolute value of the variable A and assign it to the variable S." ABS is the function name. The value it

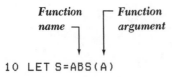

("Calculate the absolute value of the variable A and assign it to S")

Figure 6-1   BASIC built-in function

must operate on—that is, the function argument—is enclosed within parentheses following the function name. In this case the argument is the variable A. The absolute-value function always delivers a positive value. Thus, whether the value of A is +3.5 or −3.5, S is assigned a value of +3.5. The argument of most functions can be any valid BASIC expression—a variable, a constant, a BASIC function, or a combination of these.

Some functions have certain limitations; we will note these as we encounter them. All functions return a single value regardless of the form of the argument and rank above exponentiation in the priority of operations. Let's examine some other functions.

General BASIC Built-in Functions

Figure 6-2 summarizes some BASIC built-in functions. The first column describes the function, the second column gives the form of the function, and the third column illustrates the function in use.

| | Form | | |
| | Function Name | (Argu- ment) | |
Description			**Illustration**
Absolute value Returns the absolute value of the argument (the argument without regard to sign—thus the returned value is always positive)	ABS(A)		10 LET S=ABS(3.5) (S is 3.5) 20 LET S=ABS(-3.5) (S is 3.5)
Truncation Drops the fractional part of the argument and returns an integer (whole number) that is less than the argument	INT(A)		30 LET W=INT(3.5) (W is 3) 40 LET W=INT(-3.5) (W is −4)
Square root Returns the square root of the argument	SQR(A)		50 LET W=SQR(25) (W is 5)
Tabulation Moves the current print position to the column specified in the argument; used in the PRINT statement	TAB(A)		60 PRINT TAB(10);SQR(W) (The square root of W would print in print position 10)
Random number Returns a decimal value between 0 and 1; not all versions of BASIC require an argument or use it in the same way (discussed in more detail in this unit)	RND(A)		70 LET W=RND(0) (W would be between 0 and 1; for example, .000001 to .999999) (*Note:* We used zero as an argument to get a different set of random numbers each time; it may be different on your computer)

Figure 6-2   Some general BASIC built-in functions

Absolute-Value Function (ABS)

The first function in the table is the absolute-value function. We have just discussed it, so here we will only point out its form in the second column; this form will be common to all the functions. The function name ABS is followed by A within parentheses. The A represents any valid BASIC expression as an argument; that is, a variable, a constant, a BASIC function, or a combination of these. The argument will be evaluated and reduced to a single value, and the function will be performed on that single value. Once the function is performed, the result will be a single value. The nature of the result depends on the function. In the absolute-value function, the result will be positive regardless of the sign of the original argument.

Truncation Function (INT)

Read the description in Figure 6-2.

Now look at line 30 in the illustration column. Since the argument of the INT function is 3.5, the nearest integer (whole number) less than the argument is 3. Thus, when the fraction .5 is dropped, the value 3 is returned by the INT function and assigned to W in this example. Now look at line 40, where the argument is −3.5. In this case the nearest integer lower than −3.5 is −4, because −4 is lower than −3. So when the fraction .5 is dropped, −4 is the value assigned to W. The INT function does not round numbers; it drops fractions regardless of how big or small the fraction is.

Square-Root Function (SQR)

This function returns the square root of the argument. Make a note under the form column that the argument cannot be a negative number.

The illustration shows an argument of 25 for the SQR function; thus the value returned is 5.

Tabulation Function (TAB)

This function can be useful in aligning the printed output. Read the description.

The number of print positions across the page or display screen varies, depending on the version of BASIC and the computer being used.

A fairly common number of print positions is 72, so we will use that number in our discussion. These 72 positions are numbered beginning with 0 and ending with 71. Thus, print position 0 is the first position, print position 1 is the second, and print position 71 is the seventy-second position. This might seem confusing at first, but for now just be aware that there are 72 positions. If you want to begin printing in one of these positions, the TAB function can be used in the PRINT statement.

Look at the illustration. Following the word PRINT in line 60 is the function name TAB, followed by the argument 10 in parentheses. The TAB function would move the current print position to position 10. Next, a semicolon appears, followed by the variable W. This means that the value for W would begin printing in print position 10. We will bring out other aspects of the TAB function in later examples, but one important point should be noted here. You cannot tabulate backward. For example, assume that in the process of printing several items on the same line you have caused the current print position to be at position 30 which is beyond 35. When a TAB function with an argument of 25 is encountered, the TAB function will be ignored or on some computers it will print at position 25 of the next line. Using the TAB function will probably involve trial and error to align things properly, so don't get discouraged.

Random-Number Function (RND)

Read the description and examine the illustration.

Sometimes, such as when programming computer games, it is desirable to generate random numbers. Generating random numbers means that no number will appear more often than another: each number has an equal chance of occurring. We will not discuss the details of the series of random numbers here, but will merely show how numbers can be generated. Unfortunately, the method for generating random numbers varies slightly among different makes of computers. Be sure to learn how your computer system works; it should be similar, but not necessarily identical, to the method we have used.

In the illustration, line 70 assigns a random number between 0 and 1 to the variable W. This is accomplished by the RND function name, followed by an argument 0 within parentheses. On our computer the argument of 0 will cause a different sequence of random numbers to be generated each time the program is executed. On some systems a RANDOMIZE statement must be used; on other computers an argument of 1 is required; some computers have still other requirements for generating a different series of numbers each time. Find out what your computer system requires.

You might occasionally want to produce the same sequence of numbers each time the program is executed—for example, in testing your program. This method varies too, so learn how it's done on your computer. (Rarely will you want to deal with numbers in the range between 0 and 1.) Later in this unit we will show you a technique for using the RND function to generate numbers in various ranges.

Trigonometric Functions

The four functions shown in Figure 6-3 are all trigonometric functions. Not everyone will use these, but those who do will find the descriptions and illustrations adequate, so we will not discuss them further.

| | Form | | |
Description	Function Name	(Argu-ment)	Illustration
Sine Returns the sine of the argument angle, which must be in radians (15 degrees equals 0.2611799 radians)	SIN(A)		80 LET W=SIN(.261799) (W is .258819) See note 1 below
Cosine Returns the cosine of the argument angle, which must be in radians	COS(A)		90 LET W=COS(.261799) (W is .965926) See note 1 below
Tangent Returns the tangent of the argument angle, which must be in radians	TAN(A)		100 LET W=TAN(.261799) (W is .267949) See note 1 below
Arc tangent Returns the angle in radians whose tangent is the argument	ATN(A)		110 LET W=ATN(.267949) (W is .261799) See note 2 below

Note 1: The illustrations for the SIN, COS, and TAN functions are based on a 15-degree angle, which equals 0.261799 in radians.
Note 2: The illustration is based on the arc tangent of a 15-degree angle, which is 0.267949.

Figure 6-3   Some trigonometric BASIC built-in functions

Using TAB, ABS, INT, and SQR

In Figure 6-4 read the remarks in program lines 10 through 80.

Flowchart symbol 110–160 says to print headings. Program lines 110 through 160 do this. Look at line 110. The PRINT statement uses the TAB function with an

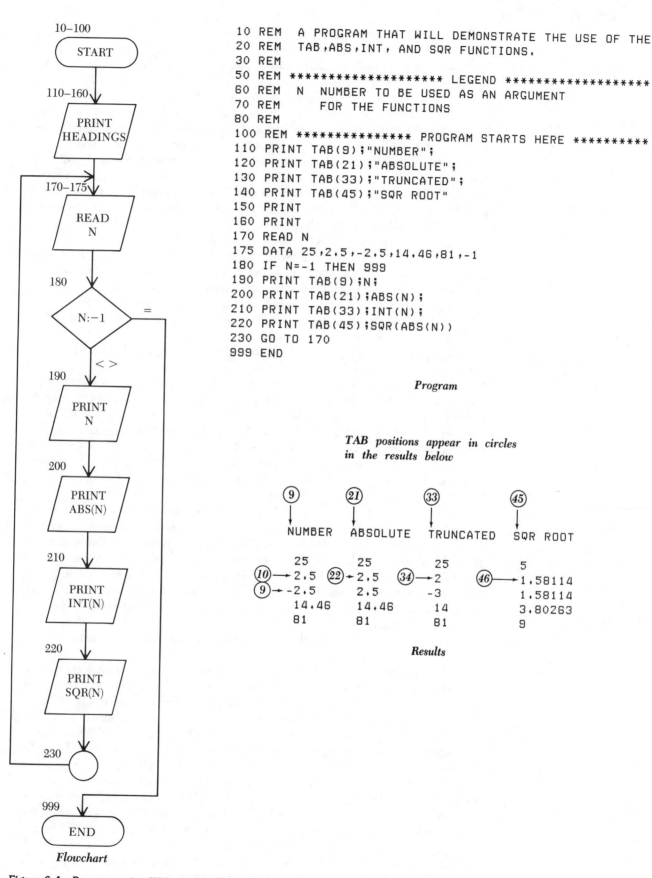

```
10 REM   A PROGRAM THAT WILL DEMONSTRATE THE USE OF THE
20 REM   TAB,ABS,INT, AND SQR FUNCTIONS.
30 REM
50 REM ******************* LEGEND ******************
60 REM   N  NUMBER TO BE USED AS AN ARGUMENT
70 REM      FOR THE FUNCTIONS
80 REM
100 REM ************** PROGRAM STARTS HERE **********
110 PRINT TAB(9);"NUMBER";
120 PRINT TAB(21);"ABSOLUTE";
130 PRINT TAB(33);"TRUNCATED";
140 PRINT TAB(45);"SQR ROOT"
150 PRINT
160 PRINT
170 READ N
175 DATA 25,2.5,-2.5,14.46,81,-1
180 IF N=-1 THEN 999
190 PRINT TAB(9);N;
200 PRINT TAB(21);ABS(N);
210 PRINT TAB(33);INT(N);
220 PRINT TAB(45);SQR(ABS(N))
230 GO TO 170
999 END
```

Program

TAB positions appear in circles in the results below

Flowchart labels:
10–100 START
110–160 PRINT HEADINGS
170–175 READ N
180 N:−1
190 PRINT N
200 PRINT ABS(N)
210 PRINT INT(N)
220 PRINT SQR(N)
230
999 END

Flowchart

Figure 6-4 Program using TAB, ABS, INT, and SQR built-in functions

argument of 9. This means that the current print position is print position 9; thus the word NUMBER following the semicolon will begin printing there. In the results TAB position 9 is encircled above the N in NUMBER in the heading. The A in ABSOLUTE is at TAB position 21, the T in TRUNCATED is at TAB position 33, and the S in SQR ROOT is at TAB position 45.

Line 110 in the program ends with a semicolon; therefore, the next character to be printed will appear on the same line as the word NUMBER. Line 120, the next PRINT statement, says to tab to print position 21 and print the word ABSOLUTE. This also ends with a semicolon, so the next PRINT statement (line 130) will cause the word TRUNCATED to be printed on the same line, beginning at print position 33. Similarly, in line 140 the words SQR ROOT will print on the same line at TAB position 45. The PRINT statements in lines 150 and 160 cause extra blank lines between the heading line and the printed data.

Line 170 says to read N. Various values of N are contained in the DATA statement in line 175; the last value is -1. In line 180, N is checked and, if it is equal to -1, the program branches to the END statement at line 999. Otherwise the program continues to the PRINT statements in lines 190 through 220, which print N, the absolute value of N, the truncated value of N, and the square root of the absolute value of N—all on the same line. Line 230 branches the program back to line 170 to read another value of N, and the process begins again.

Let's take a look at more results produced by this program. Look at the second line of printing after the heading in the results.

It begins with the number 2.5. To the left of the 2 in 2.5 you can see a blank at TAB position 9. To the left of the next number on the line is a blank in position 21; the next number on the line is a blank in position 33; and, finally, to the left of the square root is a blank in position 45. Now look at the third line of printing after the heading, which begins with the number -2.5. The minus sign is at TAB position 9.

In the program, at line 190, the PRINT statement says to tab to print position 9 and print the value of N that was read from the DATA statement. Check the second line of the results to see where the value of N is printed.

On the second line the value of N is 2.5, but notice that it is printed beginning in print position 10 rather than 9. This occurs because one print position is reserved to the left of the number for the sign. Since 2.5 is positive, the plus sign is not printed. In the line below, however, the minus sign for the value of N (-2.5) is printed in print position 9. This type of spacing applies to all values printed. Minus signs for negative values will be printed in the print position specified by the TAB function. Positive values will print one position to the right of the position specified by the TAB function.

Now let's look at the third line of the results after the heading to see how the various functions operate.

The first printed value is the value of N, read from the DATA statement as -2.5. The next value, 2.5, is printed as a result of line 200 in the program, which says to print ABS (N)—that is, the absolute value of the argument N. Since N is -2.5, the absolute value is 2.5 because the ABS function always returns a positive value. The next value, -3, is printed as a result of line 210, which says to print INT(N)—that is, the truncated value of the argument N. Since N is -2.5, the INT function drops the fractional part of the number (.5) and then returns a whole number that is less than the argument. This might sound tricky at first with a negative number, because it is. So don't give up! The argument is -2.5. The two whole numbers with values above and below it are -2 and -3. Since -3 is less than -2, the INT function returns the value of -3. Look at the line above, the truncated value of the positive number 2.5. The two whole numbers above and below it are 3 and 2. Since 2 is less than 3, the INT function returns the value of 2. No rounding occurs. The fraction is simply truncated—that is, dropped. You might want to experiment with this later.

Now look at line 220 of the program.

It says to PRINT SQR(ABS(N)). We are interested in getting the square root of N; however, since arguments of square-root functions must be positive, we use the ABS or absolute-value function to ensure that the value of N used by the SQR function will not be negative. The result is printed as the last value in the third line of the results after the heading. Because of the ABS function, the square root of negative 2.5 is the same as the value printed above it, which is the square root of positive 2.5.

Using SIN, COS, and TAN

Read the REMARK statements in lines 10 through 90 of Figure 6-5.

This program is very similar to the previous program, but here we demonstrate

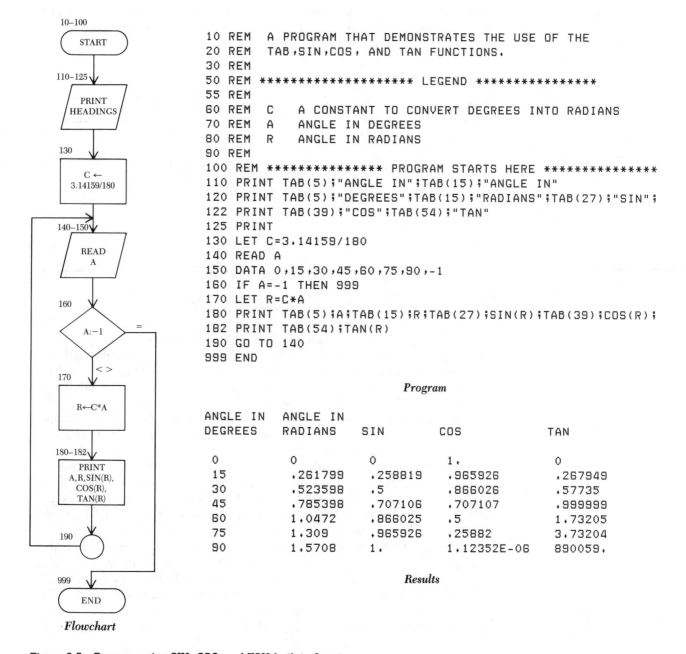

```
10 REM   A PROGRAM THAT DEMONSTRATES THE USE OF THE
20 REM   TAB,SIN,COS, AND TAN FUNCTIONS.
30 REM
50 REM ****************** LEGEND ***************
55 REM
60 REM   C   A CONSTANT TO CONVERT DEGREES INTO RADIANS
70 REM   A   ANGLE IN DEGREES
80 REM   R   ANGLE IN RADIANS
90 REM
100 REM ************** PROGRAM STARTS HERE **************
110 PRINT TAB(5);"ANGLE IN";TAB(15);"ANGLE IN"
120 PRINT TAB(5);"DEGREES";TAB(15);"RADIANS";TAB(27);"SIN";
122 PRINT TAB(39);"COS";TAB(54);"TAN"
125 PRINT
130 LET C=3.14159/180
140 READ A
150 DATA 0,15,30,45,60,75,90,-1
160 IF A=-1 THEN 999
170 LET R=C*A
180 PRINT TAB(5);A;TAB(15);R;TAB(27);SIN(R);TAB(39);COS(R);
182 PRINT TAB(54);TAN(R)
190 GO TO 140
999 END
```

Program

ANGLE IN DEGREES	ANGLE IN RADIANS	SIN	COS	TAN
0	0	0	1.	0
15	.261799	.258819	.965926	.267949
30	.523598	.5	.866026	.57735
45	.785398	.707106	.707107	.999999
60	1.0472	.866025	.5	1.73205
75	1.309	.965926	.25882	3.73204
90	1.5708	1.	1.12352E-06	890059.

Results

Flowchart

Figure 6-5 Program using SIN, COS, and TAN built-in functions

three trigonometric functions: sine, cosine, and tangent. Since these functions require an argument in radians rather than degrees, lines 130 and 170 are used to convert degrees into radians. Many of you will have no use for these functions, so we will not discuss them further. Those who plan to use them can examine this figure further at their convenience.

Rounding Positive Numbers

Many times while programming you will calculate values that you will want to round to the nearest larger number. In Figure 6-6 we present a generalized equation to round a positive value to any given number of decimal places. You do not need to understand all the details of this equation now, because you will see examples of its use in the remainder of this unit.

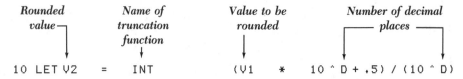

Figure 6-6   Equation for rounding positive numbers

Rounding to a Fixed Number of Decimal Places

To see the rounding equation in use, look at Figure 6-7 and read the REMARK statements in lines 10 through 100.

To understand how this program works, look at the results.

The first line asks the user to enter the desired number of decimal places for gross pay. In this case, 2 is entered. Lines 110 and 120 accomplish this in the program. D, as you have seen, has a value of 2; this will be used throughout the rest of the program. In the next statement, line 130, the hourly rate of pay is R, and it is read from the DATA statement in line 135. R takes on the value of 3.658; this will be used throughout the rest of the program. Lines 139 and 142 provide for inputting the number of hours worked as H. In line 145 the IF statement checks to see whether the H is a −1. If it is, the program branches to the END statement, because −1 indicates that there are no more hours to be entered.

Look at the second line of printing in the results. The number 40.8 is entered as the number of hours for H. In program line 150, the hours (H) are multiplied by the hourly rate of pay (R) and the result is assigned to V1, which represents the gross pay before rounding. In line 160 the rounding equation is used to round V1 and the rounded results are assigned to V2, the gross pay after rounding. Lines 200 and 210 print both V1 and V2. Now look at the third line in the results, where the unrounded gross pay (V1) is printed as 149.246. Then look at the fourth line, where the rounded pay (V2) is printed as 149.25. In the program, line 230 sends control back to line 139, which requests that the number of hours be entered or, if there are none, −1. This loop is repeated three more times in the results until −1 is entered in the last line and the program is terminated. A flowchart for this program is located on page 120.

```
10 REM   A PROGRAM USING THE TRUNCATION FUNCTION (INT) IN A FORMULA TO ROUND
20 REM   VALUES TO A DESIRED NUMBER OF DECIMAL PLACES.
50 REM ****************** LEGEND **************
55 REM
60 REM   D    NUMBER OF DECIMAL PLACES REQUESTED BY USER
70 REM   R    HOURLY RATE OF PAY
80 REM   H    NUMBER OF HOURS WORKED
90 REM   V1   GROSS PAY (UNROUNDED)
95 REM   V2   GROSS PAY (ROUNDED)
97 REM
100 REM ************** PROGRAM STARTS HERE **************
110 PRINT "ENTER THE NUMBER OF DECIMAL PLACES YOU WANT IN GROSS PAY ";
120 INPUT D
130 READ R
135 DATA 3.658
137 PRINT
139 PRINT "ENTER THE NUMBER OF HOURS. IF NONE,TYPE -1 ";
142 INPUT H
145 IF H=-1 THEN 999
150 LET V1=H*R
160 LET V2=INT(V1*10 ^ D+.5)/(10 ^ D)
200 PRINT TAB(5);"UNROUNDED PAY IS ";V1
210 PRINT TAB(5);"ROUNDED PAY IS    ";V2
220 PRINT
230 GO TO 139
999 END
```

Program

```
ENTER THE NUMBER OF DECIMAL PLACES YOU WANT IN GROSS PAY ?2 ←— (D)

ENTER THE NUMBER OF HOURS. IF NONE,TYPE -1 ?40.8 ←— (H)
     UNROUNDED PAY IS   149.246 ←— (V1)
     ROUNDED PAY IS     149.25 ←— (V2)

ENTER THE NUMBER OF HOURS. IF NONE,TYPE -1 ?30.4
     UNROUNDED PAY IS   111.203
     ROUNDED PAY IS     111.2

ENTER THE NUMBER OF HOURS. IF NONE,TYPE -1 ?40
     UNROUNDED PAY IS   146.32
     ROUNDED PAY IS     146.32

ENTER THE NUMBER OF HOURS. IF NONE,TYPE -1 ?42.
     UNROUNDED PAY IS   153.636
     ROUNDED PAY IS     153.64

ENTER THE NUMBER OF HOURS. IF NONE,TYPE -1 ?-1
```

Results

Figure 6-7   Rounding positive numbers to a fixed number of decimal places

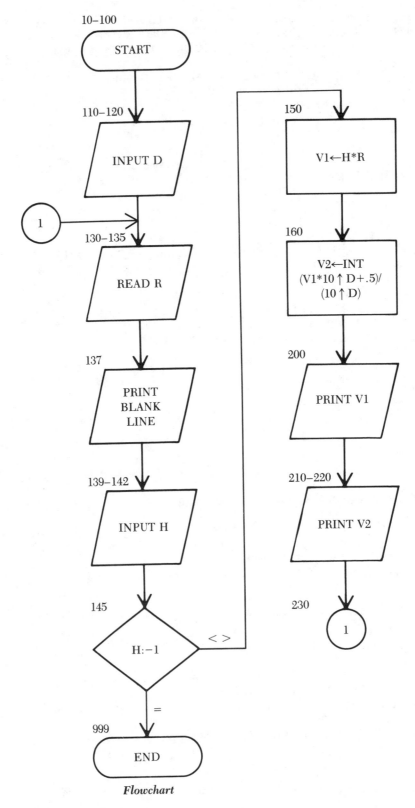

Flowchart

Figure 6-7   Continued

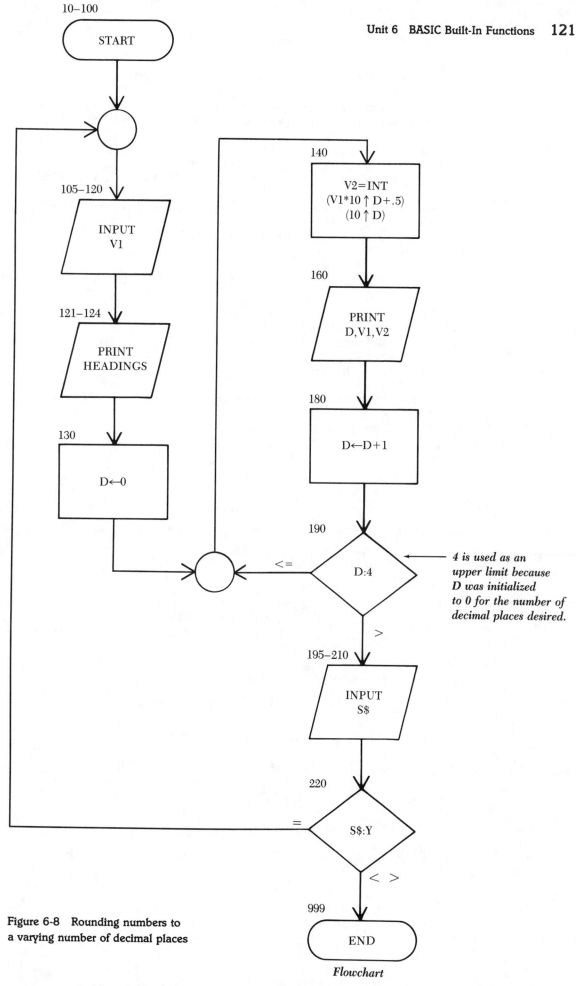

Figure 6-8   Rounding numbers to
a varying number of decimal places

Flowchart

```
10 REM   A PROGRAM THAT SHOWS ROUNDING A NUMBER
20 REM   WITH 0,1,2,3, AND 4 DECIMAL PLACES
30 REM   USING THE EQUATION V2=INT ( V1 * 10 ^ D + .5 ) / ( 10 ^ D )
50 REM ******************** LEGEND **************
60 REM   V1    NUMBER (UNROUNDED)
65 REM   V2    NUMBER (ROUNDED)
70 REM   D     DESIRED NUMBER OF DECIMAL PLACES
80 REM   S$    CODE FOR CONTINUING OR TERMINATING PROGRAM
90 REM
100 REM *************** PROGRAM STARTS HERE **************
105 PRINT
110 PRINT "ENTER THE NUMBER YOU WANT ROUNDED ";
120 INPUT V1
121 PRINT
122 PRINT TAB(5);"DEC. PLACES";TAB(20);"UNROUNDED";TAB(33);"ROUNDED"
124 PRINT
130 LET D=0
140 LET V2=INT(V1*10 ^ D+.5)/(10 ^ D)
160 PRINT TAB(9);D;TAB(20);V1;TAB(33);V2
180 LET D=D+1
190 IF D<=4 THEN 140
195 PRINT
200 PRINT "DO YOU WANT ANOTHER NUMBER ROUNDED(TYPE Y OR N ) ";
210 INPUT S$
220 IF S$="Y" THEN 105
99 END
```

Program

```
ENTER THE NUMBER YOU WANT ROUNDED ?4.78921 ←── (V1)

    DEC. PLACES     UNROUNDED     ROUNDED ←── (V2)

        0           4.78921       5
        1           4.78921       4.8
        2           4.78921       4.79
        3           4.78921       4.789
        4           4.78921       4.7892

DO YOU WANT ANOTHER NUMBER ROUNDED(TYPE Y OR N ) ?Y

ENTER THE NUMBER YOU WANT ROUNDED ?3.45678

    DEC. PLACES     UNROUNDED     ROUNDED

        0           3.45678       3
        1           3.45678       3.5
        2           3.45678       3.46
        3           3.45678       3.457
        4           3.45678       3.4568

DO YOU WANT ANOTHER NUMBER ROUNDED(TYPE Y OR N ) ?N
```

Results

Rounding to a Varying Number of Decimal Places

Look at the program in Figure 6-8 and read REMARK statements 10 through 80.

The purpose of this program is to show you how a number looks when it is rounded to various decimal places, ranging from none to four. We are using most of the same variable names that we used in the previous example: V1 is the unrounded amount, V2 is the rounded amount, and D is the number of decimal places.

The first line of the results says to enter the number you want to be rounded. Following the question mark, you can see that 4.78921 was entered for V1, the unrounded amount. Next you see the printed heading. So far we have described what has been accomplished by lines 105 through 124 in the program. Look at line 130 in the program. In this program we don't let the user enter a value for the number of decimal places. Instead, in line 130, we assign D an initial value of 0. So the first time we come to line 140 to calculate the rounded number, the calculated value assigned to V2 will have no decimal places. Line 160 prints V1 (the unrounded number) and V2 (the rounded number) on the same line. Line 180 adds one to D, so that the next time V2 is calculated, it will have one more decimal place.

Line 190 checks D to see if it is less than or equal to 4. If it is, the program branches to line 140 to calculate another value of V2 with an additional decimal place. If D is greater than 4, the program does not branch back, because we do not want the number rounded to any more than four decimal places. So the program continues on to statements 195 through 220, which ask whether another number is to be rounded. If Y is entered (indicating another number is to be rounded), the program branches back to statement 105 and the whole process is repeated. If not, the program stops. In the results you will see that we do want another number, 3.45678, to be rounded. Later you might want to study these examples of rounding and the effect of using different numbers of decimal places. Also you might find the flowchart helpful in your further study.

Random-Number Function

As we mentioned earlier, the RND function will generate a number between 0 and 1. In line 10 of Figure 6-9, N will be assigned a value between and including 0.000000 and 0.999999.

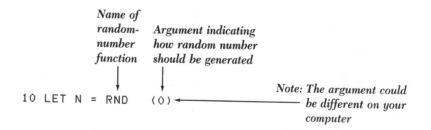

("*Generate a number greater than 0 and less than 1*")

Figure 6-9   Random number function

Generating Random Numbers Between But Not Including 0 and 1

In Figure 6-10, read the remarks in lines 10 through 70.

As you can see, the purpose of this program is to generate a number within a range of numbers between 0 and 1.

Look at flowchart symbol 110–125. N is input as the desired number of random numbers that the user wants generated. In the first line of the results, you can see that 10 is entered as the value of N.

In the flowchart at symbol 130, the count, C, is initialized as 0. After printing the heading in symbol 140–150, we enter the first step of the loop at symbol 160–165,

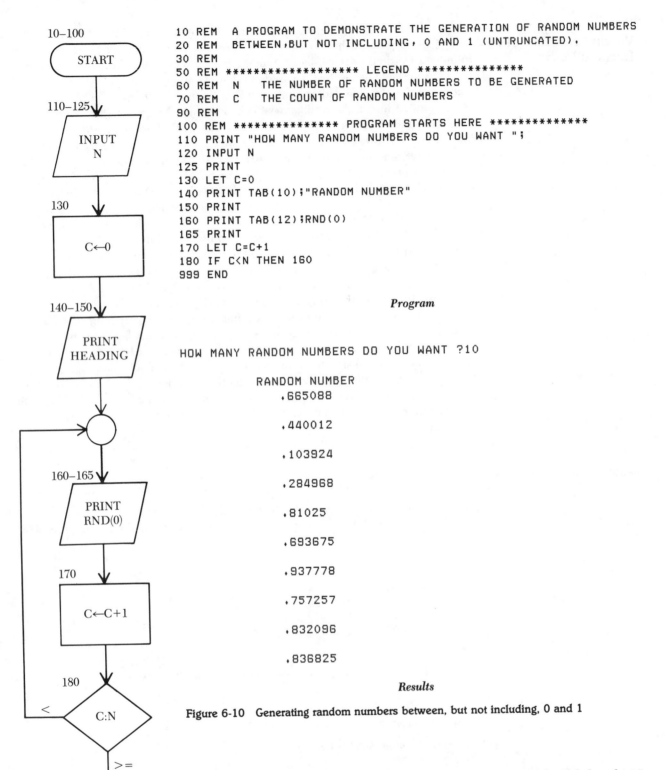

```
10–100
      ( START )

110–125
      / INPUT  /
      /   N    /

130
      |        |
      |  C←0   |
      |        |

140–150
      / PRINT    /
      / HEADING  /

           ( O )

160–165
      / PRINT   /
      / RND(0)  /

170
      |        |
      | C←C+1  |
      |        |

180
   <  < C:N >
         >=

999
      ( END )

      Flowchart
```

```
10 REM   A PROGRAM TO DEMONSTRATE THE GENERATION OF RANDOM NUMBERS
20 REM   BETWEEN,BUT NOT INCLUDING, 0 AND 1 (UNTRUNCATED).
30 REM
50 REM ***************** LEGEND **************
60 REM  N   THE NUMBER OF RANDOM NUMBERS TO BE GENERATED
70 REM  C   THE COUNT OF RANDOM NUMBERS
90 REM
100 REM ************** PROGRAM STARTS HERE *************
110 PRINT "HOW MANY RANDOM NUMBERS DO YOU WANT ";
120 INPUT N
125 PRINT
130 LET C=0
140 PRINT TAB(10);"RANDOM NUMBER"
150 PRINT
160 PRINT TAB(12);RND(0)
165 PRINT
170 LET C=C+1
180 IF C<N THEN 160
999 END
```

Program

```
HOW MANY RANDOM NUMBERS DO YOU WANT ?10

          RANDOM NUMBER
           .665088

           .440012

           .103924

           .284968

           .81025

           .693675

           .937778

           .757257

           .832096

           .836825
```

Results

Figure 6-10   Generating random numbers between, but not including, 0 and 1

which says to print a random number. Line 160 in the program accomplishes this. It is a PRINT statement with a TAB function and a RND function.

Look at the first random number in the results. It is .665088. In flowchart symbol 170, the count (C) is increased by 1, and then in symbol 180 it is compared to N, the desired number of random numbers. If the count (C) is less than N, which in this case is 10, the flowchart branches back to symbol 160–165 to print another random number.

Look at the results and the list of ten numbers that resulted from this particular execution of the program. This is not the most useful form of random numbers. See Figure 6-11 to find a generalized way of creating random numbers between and including other limits.

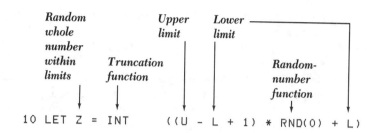

("*Generate a random whole number that can include but can be no higher than U or lower than L and assign it to Z*")

Figure 6-11 Equation for generating random whole numbers between and including various limits

Generating Random Whole Numbers Between and Including Various Limits

In Figure 6-11 the expression to the right of the equals sign will generate a random integer (a whole number) between and including two limits U (the upper limit) and L (the lower limit). For example, if U has a value of 2 and L has a value of 1, then Z will be assigned a value between and including 1 and 2. If U has a value of 50 and L has a value of 40, then Z can be any value between and including 40 and 50. A program illustrating this appears in Figure 6-12; read the remarks in lines 10 through 88.

Rather than following the flowchart all the way, first you will look at parts of the program and the results they produce. Look at lines 110 through 200 in the program in Figure 6-12.

They produce the first three lines of output in the results. In the first line of results, the desired number of random numbers is requested. Following the question mark, a 20 is entered by the user as the value of N. In the next line, 1 is entered for the lowest number, L. In the third line, 2 is entered for the highest number, U. This program is similar to the previous program, since the user inputs the desired number of random numbers as N, and this is compared with count C to determine when that number is reached. However, this program differs from the previous one in two major areas: (1) the type of random numbers generated, and (2) the use of a variable as an argument for the TAB function.

First, let's examine the types of random numbers. Look at line 220 in the program in Figure 6-12. After the message within quotes and the semicolon, the variable L appears, then a semicolon, the word AND in quotes, a semicolon, and the variable U. In the results, this produces the fourth line of printing as specified; the range of random whole numbers can be between and including 1 (L) and 2 (U). Going back to line 240 in the program: T is the variable used as an argument for the TAB function, and it is initialized to a value of 1.

At line 250, Z is assigned a random whole number within the range of U and L, as a result of using the generalized expression in the previous figure (Figure 6-11). Line 260 prints Z at TAB position T, which is print position 1 for the first value. The semicolon following Z will cause the next value of Z to be printed on the same line. Line 270 adds 8 to the value of T, so the new value of Z will be printed eight spaces to the right of the previous one. Line 280 controls how many values of Z will be printed on the same line. We have arbitrarily chosen to print only five values per line. So in line 280 the TAB variable T is compared with 33; if T is less than or equal to 33, we branch to line 300, where the count C is increased by 1. In line 310, C is compared with N, the desired number of random numbers. If C is less than N, the program branches back to line 250 to generate another random number.

Let's see what happens after five values have been printed on one line. By this time the TAB variable T will have a value of 41, since progressive increments of 8 occur from 1 to 9 to 17 to 25 to 33 for the first five values, and then to 41. In line 280, therefore, there is no branch, because T is no longer less than 33. Line 285 is executed next.

Previously we used the kind of PRINT statement in line 285 to skip a line by printing a blank line. Here its effect is different. Recall that in line 260 the PRINT statement ended in a semicolon. This caused each subsequent execution of the PRINT statement to display results on the same line, so we had five values printed across the page. Now we want the next five values to print on the next line. The PRINT statement in line 285 cancels out the effect of the semicolon by causing a carriage return and line feed. The next time a PRINT statement (particularly the PRINT statement in line 260) is executed, it will print on a new line. In line 240 the TAB variable is reset to 1, so the first value on the next line will print at the beginning of the line. The entire process of printing up to five values per line is repeated until the desired number of random numbers has been generated. The user is then given the opportunity, as a result of lines 340 through 360, to request more random numbers in the program. Later you might want to examine the flowchart and the program in detail.

Guessing Game

Figures 6-13, 6-14, and 6-15 all illustrate the guessing game. Read the remarks in lines 10 through 90 in the program in Figure 6-14 on page 131.

As you can see, this program will generate a random number between limits selected by the user. The user is then permitted up to five chances to guess the number. Before looking at either the flowchart or the program, we are going to have you examine the results in Figure 6-15 on page 132. You'll be able to follow the program just by examining the output. To help you associate the results with the flowchart and the program later, we have drawn brackets around various parts and lettered them. This identification technique is used in both the flowchart and the program. For discussion purposes, assume that you are the user running the program. Now examine the results in Figure 6-15 (page 132).

Read the part of the results with the encircled a. The program tells you what it can do and what you are allowed to do.

The next part, with the encircled b, asks you to enter low and high limits for the number that the program will choose.

At the part with the encircled c, the program confirms your limits by printing them.

Next read the section with the encircled d. This section asks you to enter your guess, and when you are too low, too high, or correct, it gives you an appropriate message. In the section with the encircled e, you are told to type a Y if you want to guess another number; otherwise, type an N. In this case you type T instead of Y or N, an error message is printed, and you are allowed to type Y or N again. You then type Y and in the next section, with the encircled b, you enter your new low and high limits. The sections with the encircled c through e are repeated again. Read these sections.

When the program asks whether you want to guess a new number this time, you answer with an N and the computer prints the ending message in the section with the encircled f. Here you can see fairly clearly what the program is doing. You can return to these illustrations later and study the program and flowchart in detail. This will be especially helpful to you in preparing for the second programming problem in this unit.

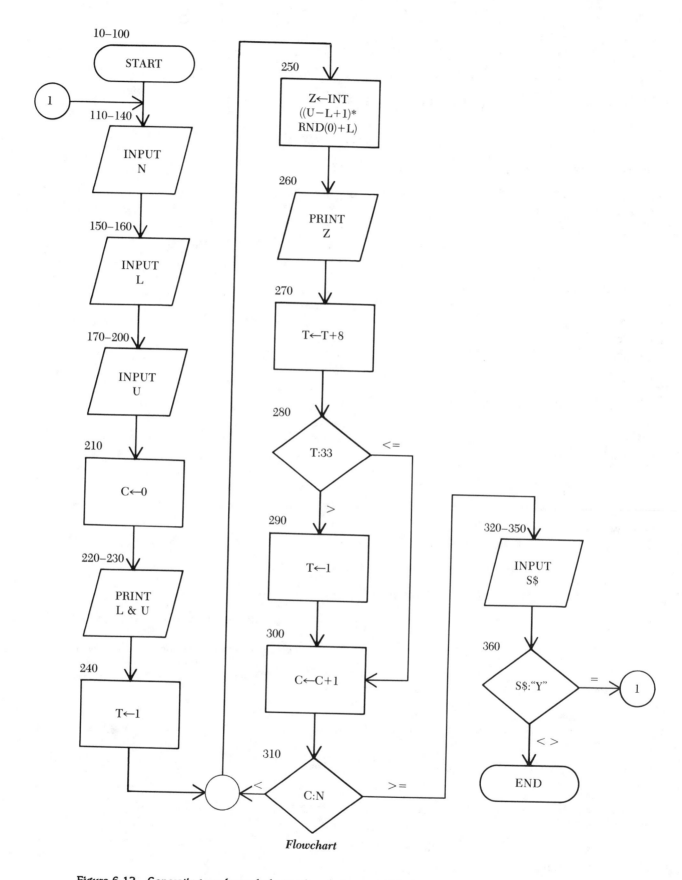

Figure 6-12   Generating random whole numbers between and including limits

```
10 REM  A PROGRAM TO GENERATE RANDOM WHOLE NUMBERS
20 REM   BETWEEN AND INCLUDING VARIOUS LIMITS.
50 REM ****************** LEGEND ******************
60 REM  N    THE NUMBER OF RANDOM NUMBERS TO BE GENERATED
70 REM  C    THE COUNT OF RANDOM NUMBERS
75 REM  U    UPPER LIMIT FOR RANDOM NUMBER
80 REM  L    LOWER LIMIT FOR RANDOM NUMBER
85 REM  Z    RANDOM NUMBER (TRUNCATED)
87 REM  T    VARIABLE FOR TAB FUNCTION ARGUMENT
88 REM  S$   CODE FOR CONTINUING OR ENDING PROGRAM
100 REM ************** PROGRAM STARTS HERE **************
110 PRINT
120 PRINT
130 PRINT "HOW MANY RANDOM NUMBERS DO YOU WANT ";
140 INPUT N
150 PRINT "ENTER THE LOWEST RANDOM NUMBER YOU WANT ";
160 INPUT L
170 PRINT "ENTER THE HIGHEST RANDOM NUMBER YOU WANT ";
180 INPUT U
200 PRINT
210 LET C=0
220 PRINT TAB(1);"RANDOM WHOLE NUMBERS BETWEEN AND INCLUDING";L;"AND";U
230 PRINT
240 LET T=1
250 LET Z=INT((U-L+1)*RND(0)+L)
260 PRINT TAB(T);Z;
270 LET T=T+8
280 IF T<=33 THEN 300
285 PRINT
290 LET T=1
300 LET C=C+1
310 IF C <N THEN 250
320 PRINT
330 PRINT
340 PRINT "DO YOU WANT MORE RANDOM NUMBERS( TYPE Y OR N) ";
350 INPUT S$
360 IF S$="Y" THEN 110
999 END
```

Program

```
HOW MANY RANDOM NUMBERS DO YOU WANT ?20  ◄─────  (N)

ENTER THE LOWEST RANDOM NUMBER YOU WANT ?1  ◄─── (L)

ENTER THE HIGHEST RANDOM NUMBER YOU WANT ?2  ◄─── (U)

                                           (L)      (U)
                                            ↓        ↓
RANDOM WHOLE NUMBERS BETWEEN AND INCLUDING 1    AND 2

   1       2       2       2       1 ⎫
   1       1       1       2       1 ⎬  ◄─ (Z)  ◄───────
   2       1       1       2       1 ⎪
   1       2       2       1       1 ⎭
```

Remember, since these are random numbers, you may get different combinations of numbers, but they all should be within the proper limits.

```
DO YOU WANT MORE RANDOM NUMBERS( TYPE Y OR N) ?Y

HOW MANY RANDOM NUMBERS DO YOU WANT ?15
ENTER THE LOWEST RANDOM NUMBER YOU WANT ?40
ENTER THE HIGHEST RANDOM NUMBER YOU WANT ?50

RANDOM WHOLE NUMBERS BETWEEN AND INCLUDING 40    AND 50

   43      41      49      46      41
   48      45      50      49      42
   41      47      42      50      44

DO YOU WANT MORE RANDOM NUMBERS( TYPE Y OR N) ?N
```

Results

Figure 6-12 Continued

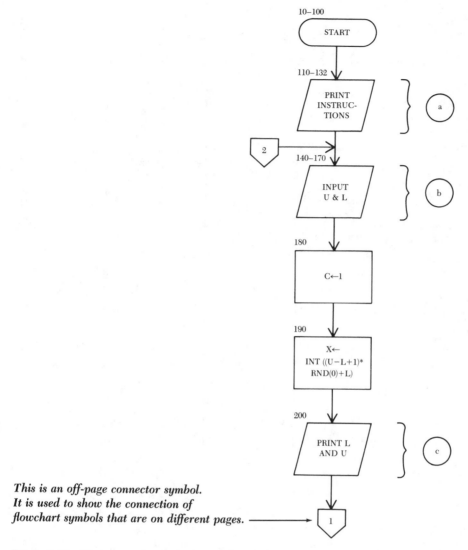

This is an off-page connector symbol.
It is used to show the connection of
flowchart symbols that are on different pages.

Figure 6-13   Flowchart of guessing game for whole numbers between and including various limits

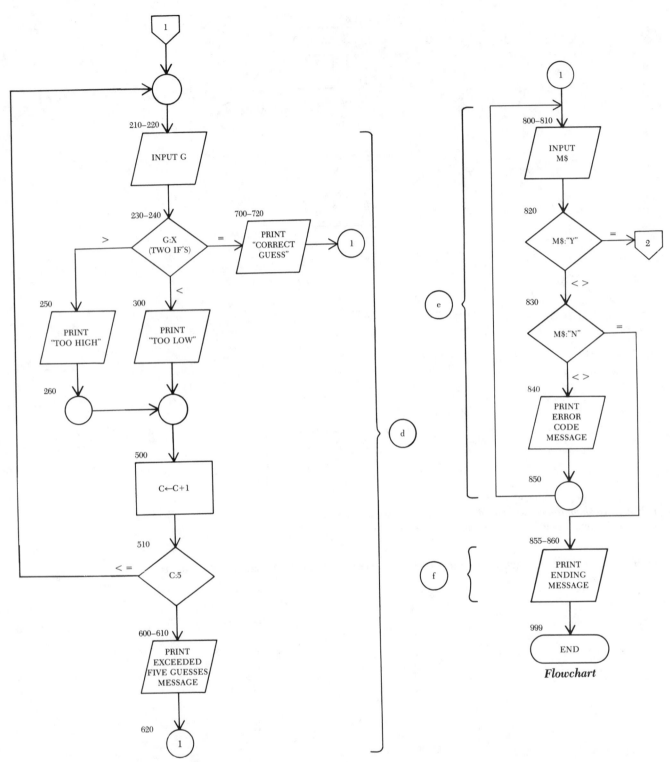

Figure 6-13   Continued

```
         10 REM   A PROGRAM THAT ALLOWS THE USER TO GUESS A NUMBER
         20 REM   THAT IS RANDOMLY SELECTED BY THE COMPUTER.
         30 REM   THE USER SELECTS THE UPPER AND LOWER LIMITS AND IS
         40 REM   ALLOWED MAXIMUM OF FIVE GUESSES.
         50 REM ****************** LEGEND ***************
         54 REM   C      COUNT OF THE NUMBER OF GUESSES
         56 REM   L      LOWER LIMIT FOR RANDOM NUMBER
         58 REM   U      UPPER LIMIT FOR RANDOM NUMBER
         60 REM   X      RANDOM WHOLE NUMBER
         62 REM   G      GUESS MADE BY USER
         64 REM   M$     USER'S CODE FOR CONTINUING OR ENDING THE PROGRAM
         90 REM
        100 REM ************** PROGRAM STARTS HERE ************
        110 PRINT "THIS PROGRAM ALLOWS YOU A MAXIMUM OF FIVE CHANCES"
        112 PRINT "TO GUESS A RANDOM WHOLE NUMBER THAT IS MADE UP BY"
  (a)   114 PRINT "THE COMPUTER."
        120 PRINT "YOU MAY SET THE UPPER AND LOWER LIMITS."
        130 PRINT "OKAY LET'S GO!"
        132 PRINT
        140 PRINT
        142 PRINT "ENTER THE LOWEST NUMBER YOU WOULD WANT ";
  (b)   150 INPUT L
        160 PRINT "ENTER THE HIGHEST NUMBER YOU WOULD WANT ";
        170 INPUT U
        180 LET C=1
        190 LET X=INT((U-L+1)*RND(0)+L)
  (c) → 200 PRINT "THE NUMBER CAN BE BETWEEN AND INCLUDING ";L;"AND";U
        210 PRINT "ENTER YOUR GUESS NUMBER ";C;
        220 INPUT G
        230 IF G=X THEN 700
        240 IF G<X THEN 300
        250 PRINT "YOU ARE TOO HIGH."
        260 GO TO 500
        300 PRINT "YOU ARE TOO LOW."
  (d)   500 LET C=C+1
        510 IF C<=5 THEN 210
        600 PRINT
        605 PRINT "SORRY YOU HAVE USED UP YOUR FIVE GUESSES."
        610 PRINT "THE NUMBER WAS ";X
        620 GO TO 800
        700 PRINT
        710 PRINT "CONGRATULATIONS YOU GUESSED THE CORRECT "
        720 PRINT "NUMBER IN ";C;"GUESS(ES)."
        800 PRINT
        805 PRINT "IF YOU WANT TO GUESS A NEW NUMBER,"
        807 PRINT "ENTER Y FOR YES OR N FOR NO ";
  (e)   810 INPUT M$
        820 IF M$="Y" THEN 140
        830 IF M$="N" THEN 855
        840 PRINT "YOU DID NOT ENTER A Y OR AN N ."
        850 GO TO 800
  (f)   855 PRINT
        860 PRINT "THANKS FOR PLAYING, GOOD BYE."
        999 END
```

Figure 6-14 Program for guessing game

(a) {
THIS PROGRAM ALLOWS YOU A MAXIMUM OF FIVE CHANCES
TO GUESS A RANDOM WHOLE NUMBER THAT IS MADE UP BY
THE COMPUTER.
YOU MAY SET THE UPPER AND LOWER LIMITS.
OKAY LET'S GO!

(b) {
ENTER THE LOWEST NUMBER YOU WOULD WANT ?1
ENTER THE HIGHEST NUMBER YOU WOULD WANT ?10

(c) { THE NUMBER CAN BE BETWEEN AND INCLUDING 1   AND 10

(d) {
ENTER YOUR GUESS NUMBER 1   ?5
YOU ARE TOO LOW.
ENTER YOUR GUESS NUMBER 2   ?8

CONGRATULATIONS YOU GUESSED THE CORRECT
NUMBER IN 2   GUESS(ES).

(e) {
IF YOU WANT TO GUESS A NEW NUMBER,
ENTER Y FOR YES OR N FOR NO ?T ←—————— *Did not input Y or N*
YOU DID NOT ENTER A Y OR AN N.   *so you*
                                                    get a chance to

(e) {
IF YOU WANT TO GUESS A NEW NUMBER, ←——— *enter again*
ENTER Y FOR YES OR N FOR NO ?Y

(b) {
ENTER THE LOWEST NUMBER YOU WOULD WANT ?25
ENTER THE HIGHEST NUMBER YOU WOULD WANT ?30

(c) { THE NUMBER CAN BE BETWEEN AND INCLUDING 25 AND 30

(d) {
ENTER YOUR GUESS NUMBER 1   ?27
YOU ARE TOO LOW.
ENTER YOUR GUESS NUMBER 2   ?29

CONGRATULATIONS YOU GUESSED THE CORRECT
NUMBER IN 2   GUESS(ES).

(e) {
IF YOU WANT TO GUESS A NEW NUMBER,
ENTER Y FOR YES OR N FOR NO ?N

(f) { THANKS FOR PLAYING. GOOD BYE.

Figure 6-15   Results of guessing game

PROGRAMMING TECHNIQUES

1. Equation for rounding positive numbers:

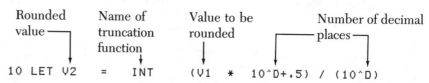

2. Equation for generating random whole numbers between and including various limits:

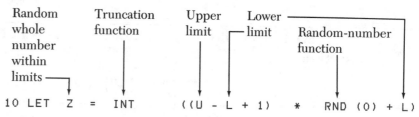

3. Using the absolute-value function to avoid having to calculate the square root of a negative number:

```
10 LET S=SQR(ABS(N))
```

DEBUGGING AIDS

ERROR	CAUSE	CORRECTION
10 LET X=-25 20 LET R=SQR(X)	Calculating the square root of a negative number	10 LET X=-25 20 LET R=SQR(ABS(X))

REFERENCE

SOME GENERAL BASIC BUILT-IN FUNCTIONS

DESCRIPTION	FORM		ILLUSTRATION
	Function Name	**(Argument)**	
Absolute value Returns the absolute value of the argument (the argument without regard to sign, thus the returned value is always positive)	ABS(A)		10 LET S=ABS(3.5) (S is 3.5) 20 LET S=ABS(-3.5) (S is 3.5)
Truncation Drops the fractional part of the argument and returns an integer (whole number) that is less than the argument	INT(A)		30 LET W=INT(3.5) (W is 3) 40 LET W=INT(-3.5) (W is −4)
Square root Returns the square root of the argument: The argument must not be negative.	SQR(A)		50 LET W=SQR(25) (W is 5)
Tabulation Moves the current print position to the column specified in the argument; used in the PRINT statement	TAB(A)		60 PRINT TAB(10); SQR(W) (The square root W would print in print position 10)

REFERENCE

SOME GENERAL BASIC BUILT-IN FUNCTIONS

DESCRIPTION	FORM		ILLUSTRATION
	Function Name	(Argu-ment)	
Random number Returns a decimal value between 0 and 1; not all versions of BASIC require an argument or use it in the same way	RND(A)		70 LET W=RND(0) (W would be between 0 and 1; for example, .000001 to .999999) (*Note:* We used zero as an argument to get a different set of random numbers each time; it might be different on your computer)

SOME TRIGONOMETRIC BASIC BUILT-IN FUNCTIONS

DESCRIPTION	FORM		ILLUSTRATION
	Function Name	(Argu-ment)	
Sine Returns the sine of the argument angle, which must be in radians (15 degrees equals 0.261799 radians)	SIN(A)		80 LET W=SIN(.261799) (W is .258819) See note 1 below
Cosine Returns the cosine of the argument angle, which must be in radians	COS(A)		90 LET W=COS(.261799) (W is .965926) See note 1 below
Tangent Returns the tangent of the argument angle, which must be in radians	TAN(A)		100 LET W=TAN(.261799) (W is .267949) See note 1 below
Arc tangent Returns the angle in radians whose tangent is the argument	ATN(A)		110 LET W=ATN(.267949) (W is .261799) See note 2 below

Note 1: The illustrations for the SIN, COS, and TAN functions are based on a 15-degree angle, which equals 0.261799 in radians.

Note 2: The illustration is based on the arc tangent of a 15-degree angle, which is 0.267949.

PRIORITY OF OPERATIONS FOR BASIC BUILT-IN FUNCTIONS

BASIC built-in functions rank above exponentiation in the priority of operations. If functions are used within other functions, the order of operations is from the innermost to the outermost.

Example:

```
        3rd  2nd  1st        5th 4th
         ↓    ↓    ↓           ↓  ↓
LET V = SQR(INT(ABS(-25.9)))*5^2
```

APPLICATION EXERCISES

1. Write a LET statement for the formula $D = \sqrt{B-4*A*C}$.
   (*Note:* $\sqrt{}$ is the symbol for square root.)

2. Write a LET statement to assign the value of the variable T, truncated to an integer, to the variable T1.

3. Write a single PRINT statement to cause the words "ANNUAL TOTAL" to begin printing in print position 15 and the value of T to begin printing in print position 30.

4. Write a LET statement to cause the square root of the absolute value of G to be assigned to the variable R.

In exercises 5 through 8, enter the value that would be printed in the spaces provided. (*Note: Functions* have the *highest priority* of all arithmetic operations.)

5. `50 PRINT SQR(INT(4.9))` _____
6. `60 PRINT INT(-8.9)` _____
7. `70 PRINT ABS(INT(-68/3))` _____
8. `80 PRINT INT(100*1.4356+.5)/100` _____

9. Using the INT function, write a LET statement to round a value V to three decimal places and assign it to R.

10. Write a LET statement to assign to the variable N a random whole number between and including 15 and 60.

Answers to Application Exercises

1. `10 LET D=SQR(B-4*A*C)`
2. `10 LET T1=INT(T)`
3. `10 PRINT TAB(15);"ANNUAL TOTAL";TAB(30);T`
4. `10 LET R=SQR(ABS(G))`
5. 2
6. −9
7. 23
8. 1.44   (Remember that functions have the highest priority—even higher than division.)
9. `10 LET R=INT(V*10^3+.5)/(10^3)`
10. `10 LET N=INT((60-15+1)*RND(0)+15)`

PROGRAMMING PROBLEMS

6-1. Program for Average, Variance, and Standard Deviation

Write a program that will allow any number of values to be input; calculate their average, variance, and standard deviation; and produce the output illustrated in Figure 6-17.

Programming tips:

1. Use the flowchart in Figure 6-16 as a *general* guide.
2. In symbol 160, $T1=T1+X^2$ is used to calculate the sum of each squared value.
3. Use the equation in Figure 6-6 as a general guide for rounding in symbol 190 in the flowchart.
4. If you assign the rounded values to a different variable name (such as A1 for A and V1 for V), don't use T1 for T; T1 is already being used as the sum of the squares, so use T2.
5. Use the TAB function when printing in symbol 200.
6. Determine TAB positions for numeric values in a trial run before assigning TAB positions as headings.

Symbol definitions:

N = Number of values
D = Number of decimal places in output
T = Sum of values
T1 = Sum of each value squared
C = Count of the input values
X = Value
A = Average of values
V = Variance

$$\frac{\left(T1 - \left(\frac{T^2}{N}\right)\right)}{(N-1)}$$

S = Standard deviation (take square root of V)
G\$ = Continue program code (Y or N)

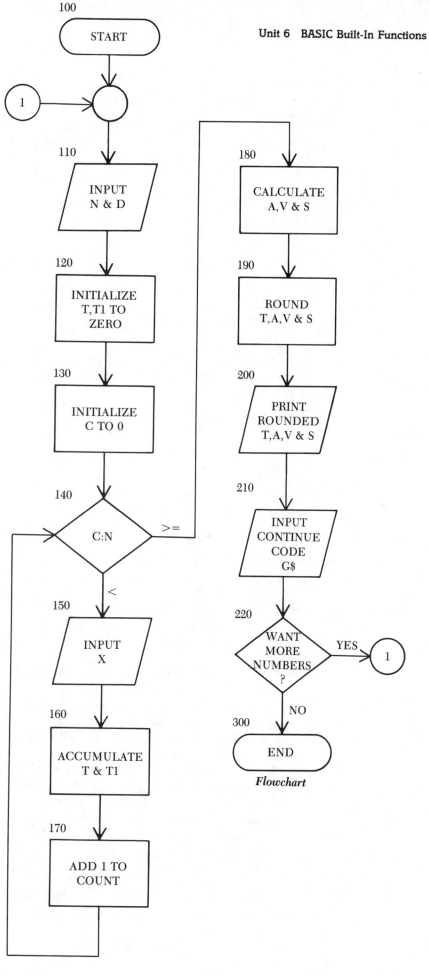

Figure 6-16   Flowchart of
program for average, variance,
and standard deviation

```
HOW MANY NUMBERS ?5
HOW MANY DECIMAL PLACES DO YOU WANT
IN THE ROUNDED OUTPUT ?1
THIS PROGRAM WILL FIND THE SUM,AVERAGE,VARIANCE,
AND STANDARD DEVIATION OF THE FOLLOWING NUMBERS
PLEASE ENTER THE NUMBERS,
?125.16
?122.53
?110.18
?112.59
?106.13

              SUM          MEAN         VARIANCE        STD DEV
             576.6         115.3          66.8            8.2


IF YOU WANT TO TRY MORE NUMBERS,TYPE Y, IF YOU DON'T TYPE N ?Y
HOW MANY NUMBERS ?8
HOW MANY DECIMAL PLACES DO YOU WANT
IN THE ROUNDED OUTPUT ?2
THIS PROGRAM WILL FIND THE SUM,AVERAGE,VARIANCE,
AND STANDARD DEVIATION OF THE FOLLOWING NUMBERS
PLEASE ENTER THE NUMBERS,
?83.789
?65.3271
?40.6390
?123.548
?190.45
?200.678
?100.407
?102.456

              SUM          MEAN         VARIANCE        STD DEV
            907.29        113.41        3203.96          56.6


IF YOU WANT TO TRY MORE NUMBERS,TYPE Y, IF YOU DON'T TYPE N ?N
```

Figure 6-17   Results of program for average, variance, and standard deviation

6-2. Program for Coin-Flipping Simulation

Write a program using random numbers to simulate a coin-flipping game between the computer and a human player. Your program should produce the output illustrated in Figure 6-18 and perform the following:

1. Generate a random number representing heads (1) or tails (2).
2. Allow the player to input a guess whether heads or tails was flipped. The computer should then compare the guess to the random number generated.
3. Display the results of the flip, indicating who won.
4. Keep a count of the total number of times:
   a. Heads were flipped
   b. Tails were flipped
   c. The player won
   d. The computer won
5. Allow the player to stop the game by typing −1 instead of guessing 1 or 2.
6. Print the various totals at the end of play.

Programming tips:

1. Draw a flowchart of the solution.
2. Refer to the equation in Figure 6-11 for generating a random number. Check your manufacturer's reference manual to determine what argument you should use to get a different set of numbers each time and whether you need to use a special statement such as RANDOMIZE.
3. Use the TAB function to print the various totals and their headings; experiment by printing the totals before printing the headings.
4. Use variables as arguments for the TAB function. Thus if you want to change TAB positions, you can merely change the variable value and not have to retype the entire PRINT statement.
5. Experiment by displaying the total values with different TAB settings and notice how they are displayed. After the TAB positions for the values have been determined, set the TAB positions for headings.
6. The numbers that the computer flipped in the results shown in Figure 6-18 will probably not match the numbers in your results. Remember that the computer's numbers are random numbers. Therefore, to determine if your program is correct, check your totals against the results of each flip to see if they add up correctly.
7. The total "ones" and "twos" are those flipped by the computer.

Results:

```
I SIMULATE FLIPPING ONE COIN FOR HEADS OR
TAILS BY USING A RANDOM NUMBER GENERATOR,

YOU CAN COMPETE WITH ME BY GUESSING WHAT
I HAVE FLIPPED
AFTER I FLIP,ENTER YOUR GUESS
WHEN YOU SEE THE    ? TYPE 1 FOR HEADS, OR
2 FOR TAILS, WHEN YOU WANT TO STOP TYPE -1,

OKAY I'VE FLIPPED,ENTER YOUR GUESS, ?2
MY NUMBER WAS  2       YOURS WAS   2
YOU WIN THAT ONE,


OKAY I'VE FLIPPED,ENTER YOUR GUESS, ?1
MY NUMBER WAS  1       YOURS WAS   1
YOU WIN THAT ONE,


OKAY I'VE FLIPPED,ENTER YOUR GUESS, ?2
MY NUMBER WAS  1       YOURS WAS   2
I WON THAT ONE,


OKAY I'VE FLIPPED,ENTER YOUR GUESS, ?1
MY NUMBER WAS  1       YOURS WAS   1
YOU WIN THAT ONE,


OKAY I'VE FLIPPED,ENTER YOUR GUESS, ?-1


THANKS FOR PLAYING WITH ME
THE FINAL TOTALS ARE:

YOUR TOTAL WINS    MY TOTAL WINS
      3                    1

TOTAL ONES         TOTAL TWOS
      3                    1
```

Figure 6-18 Results of program for coin-flipping simulation

7 Looping

OBJECTIVES

When you complete this unit, you will be able to:

1. Write a FOR statement and a NEXT statement:
   a. For a given problem with a flowchart
   b. For a given problem without a flowchart
2. Predict the sequence of statements to be executed, given a computer program containing a FOR statement and a NEXT statement
3. Code and execute a BASIC solution using a FOR statement and a NEXT statement, given a problem that requires looping

INTRODUCTION

What Are FOR and NEXT Statements?

The FOR and NEXT statements cause one or more statements within their range to be executed a specified number of times. The range refers to the set of statements to be executed as a result of the FOR and NEXT statements. The FOR and NEXT statements and the statements within their range are often referred to collectively as a *loop*.

Using FOR and NEXT Statements

The FOR and NEXT statements are used to control the number of times that the statements within their range are executed.

The FOR and NEXT statements are also used to alter program control. The FOR statement and its associated NEXT statement repeat the execution of a set of BASIC statements a specified number of times; this is often referred to as a *FOR-NEXT loop*. The FOR-NEXT statements keep track of the number of times that a set of program statements is executed and provide for transfer out of this loop after the specified number has been reached.

FOR and NEXT Statements

In Figure 7-1, example 1, the word FOR appears in statement 10 and the word NEXT appears in statement 50. This represents the range of the FOR and NEXT statements. The NEXT statement is usually the last statement to be executed in the sequence. The computer will execute all statements from the one following the FOR statement through the associated NEXT statement, unless an IF-THEN or GO TO statement alters the sequence. This entire set of statements is referred to as a FOR-NEXT loop.

Following the word FOR in statement 10 is an assignment statement. To the left of the equals sign in this statement appears what is commonly called the *FOR variable*, which can be any numeric variable (J in this case). This is also referred to as an *index variable* or simply a *counter*. To the right of the equals sign is the initial (or first) value of this FOR variable. This example sets the initial value of the FOR variable J to 1. The initial value is followed by the word TO and then a test value. The test value, 15 in this illustration, is used to end the loop. It is followed by the word STEP and the value 5. Thus the STEP value 5 will be added to the FOR variable each time the loop is executed. If the word STEP and this last value are not written, the value is assumed to be 1. Therefore, when a programmer wants the STEP value to be 1, he or she can omit the word STEP and the 1 at the end of the FOR statement.

Statement 50, the last statement in the loop, contains the word NEXT followed by J. The J indicates that this is the last statement associated with the FOR statement whose FOR variable is J. Some versions of BASIC do not require a variable in the NEXT statement, but we recommend that you always use it so that the end of the loop can be easily identified.

The FOR and NEXT statements direct the program to execute all statements beginning with the FOR statement, statement 10, and ending with the NEXT statement, statement 50. These statements assign a 1 to the FOR variable J and direct the program to execute every instruction between that FOR statement and the NEXT statement, until J (incremented by 5 each time) is greater than the test value, which is 15. This loop is thus executed three times. The FOR variable has a value of 1 during the first loop, 6 during the second, and 11 during the third. When the program attempts to execute the fourth loop, the FOR variable is 16, so the test value is exceeded. Therefore, control of the program then goes to the statement following statement 50, NEXT J, in the program. This program went through the loop three times, and the value of J was incremented by 5 each time.

The test value and the STEP value have been shown as positive whole numbers. They can also be negative numbers, fractional numbers, or variables. Fractional numbers follow the same rules as whole numbers. If a STEP value is negative, control passes to the statement following the NEXT statement when the FOR variable has a value *less than* the test value, rather than *greater than* as in all other cases. We will illustrate this later in the unit.

To the right of the FOR-NEXT loop are the flowchart symbols that we will be using to represent the FOR and NEXT statements. Symbol 10 is a combination of two triangles and a diamond. The triangle above and to the left of the diamond shows the assignment of the initial value 1 to the FOR variable J. The diamond shows a comparison of the FOR variable J with the test value 15. The triangle below the diamond shows the addition of the STEP value 5 to the FOR variable. Look at the diamond again: As long as the FOR variable is less than or equal to the test value, the downward exit is taken and control passes back to the FOR statement each time the NEXT statement is executed. When the FOR variable is greater than the test value, the exit to the right is taken and control passes to the statement following the NEXT statement.

The symbol for the NEXT statement, symbol 50, is a circle indicating that this is the last statement in the loop. Control passes from the NEXT symbol back to the part of the FOR symbol that increments the FOR variable before it is compared with the test value.

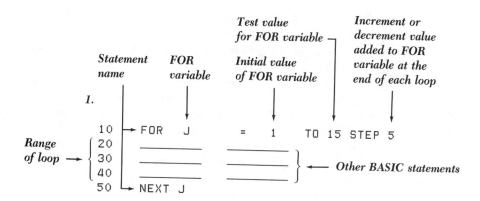

1.

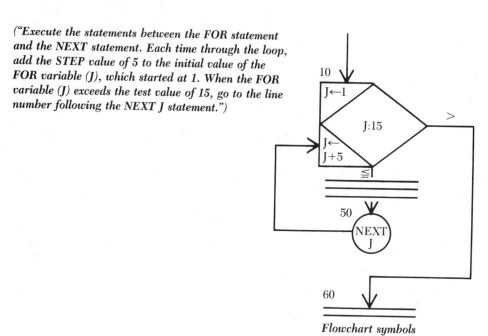

("Execute the statements between the FOR statement and the NEXT statement. Each time through the loop, add the STEP value of 5 to the initial value of the FOR variable (J), which started at 1. When the FOR variable (J) exceeds the test value of 15, go to the line number following the NEXT J statement.")

Flowchart symbols

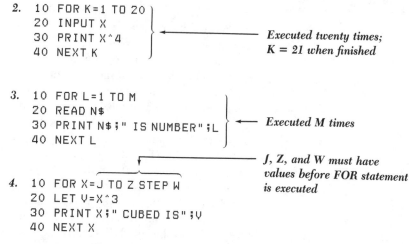

```
2.   10 FOR K=1 TO 20
     20 INPUT X
     30 PRINT X^4
     40 NEXT K
```
Executed twenty times; K = 21 when finished

```
3.   10 FOR L=1 TO M
     20 READ N$
     30 PRINT N$;" IS NUMBER";L
     40 NEXT L
```
Executed M times

J, Z, and W must have values before FOR statement is executed

```
4.   10 FOR X=J TO Z STEP W
     20 LET V=X^3
     30 PRINT X;" CUBED IS";V
     40 NEXT X
```

Figure 7-1 **FOR and NEXT** statements

Example 2 in Figure 7-1 illustrates the form of the FOR statement without a STEP value. This statement directs the program to execute all statements within the range of the FOR-NEXT statements, beginning with a value of 1 for K, with an increment of 1 (because the STEP value is omitted) until the test value of 20 is exceeded. The loop will execute twenty times. It is important to remember that the loop continues until the FOR variable *exceeds* the test value, not until it *equals* the test value—in other words, the loop continues until K has a value of 21.

In example 3 the test value is represented by the variable M. The test value must be assigned a value before the FOR statement is executed. The value can be assigned in a preceding assignment statement, such as LET M=50. Then 50 would be the test value in the FOR statement. The value can also be assigned by a READ or INPUT statement.

Example 4 illustrates the use of numeric variables for the index, test, and STEP values. This is permissible as long as all variables are assigned values before the loop is executed. The programmer should never change any variables in the FOR statement within the FOR-NEXT loop. Once a FOR statement has been written, the values of the FOR variable (X in this example), the initial value (J), the test value (Z), and the STEP value (W) should not be changed during execution of the FOR-NEXT loop, unless the FOR variable is changed by the FOR statement itself. (The only variable that is ever changed by the FOR statement is the FOR variable.) The final value of the FOR variable after the FOR-NEXT loop has been completed is always *greater* than the test value if the STEP value is *positive*, and always *less* than the test value if the STEP value is *negative*. You must take this into consideration if you plan to use the FOR variable in computations, after the loop has been completed.

In example 4, if the programmer wanted to increment the FOR variable by one-half each time through the loop, the STEP variable W would be assigned a value of 0.5; to increment by one-quarter, the STEP variable would be assigned the value 0.25, and so on. These fractional values are added to the FOR variable until the FOR variable exceeds the test value assigned to Z. If W is assigned a negative value, this value is added to the FOR variable each time through the loop, until the FOR variable is less than the test value assigned to Z.

Summing Numbers

In Figure 7-2 you can see a program and its associated flowchart using an IF-THEN loop to sum odd numbers from 1 to 100. Statement 10 sets the accumulator S to 0. Statement 20 starts the counter C at 1. Statement 30 adds the contents of the counter to the accumulator. Statement 40 adds 2 to the counter, since we want to add every other number—that is, odd numbers only. Statement 50 tests to see whether all numbers have been added. If more numbers are to be added, the loop is repeated by giving control back to statement 30. When all numbers have been added, control passes to statement 60, which prints the total. Then the program stops.

Using the IF-THEN loop to solve this problem is acceptable; however, the FOR-NEXT loop, as illustrated in Figure 7-3, is designed to do it another way. Statement 10 clears the accumulator S to 0 as in the previous program. Statement 20, the FOR statement, sets the FOR variable C to 1, establishes an upper bound (100), and provides an increment of 2—all in one statement, compared to the three statements used in the IF-THEN loop. Statement 30, the accumulator, is the same as that used in the previous program. The FOR-NEXT loop does require an additional statement, statement 40, the NEXT statement to indicate the last statement in the loop.

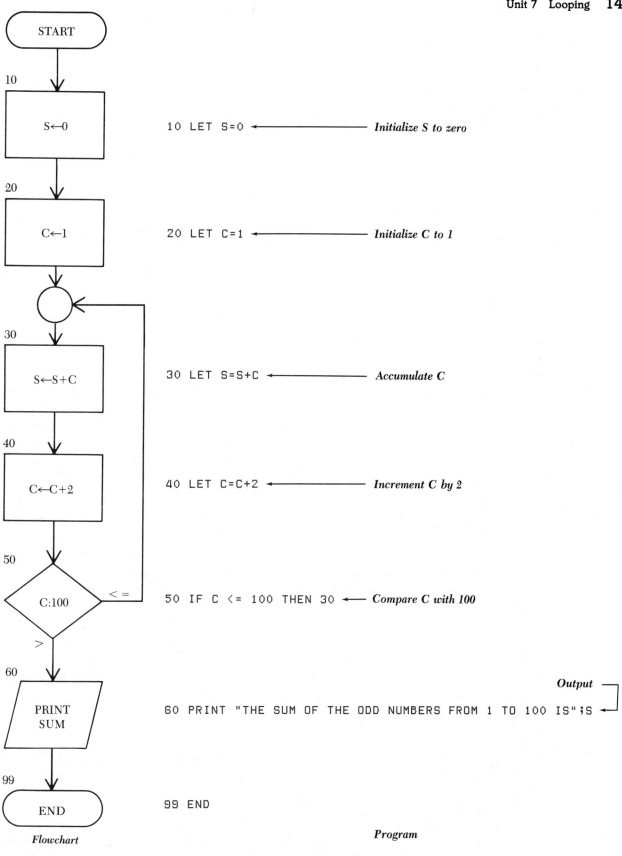

10 LET S=0 ⟵——————— *Initialize S to zero*

20 LET C=1 ⟵——————— *Initialize C to 1*

30 LET S=S+C ⟵——————— **Accumulate C**

40 LET C=C+2 ⟵——————— *Increment C by 2*

50 IF C <= 100 THEN 30 ⟵—— *Compare C with 100*

Output ⟶

60 PRINT "THE SUM OF THE ODD NUMBERS FROM 1 TO 100 IS";S ⟵

99 END

Flowchart

Figure 7-2 Summing numbers with the IF-THEN statement

Program

THE SUM OF THE ODD NUMBERS FROM 1 TO 100 IS 2500

Results

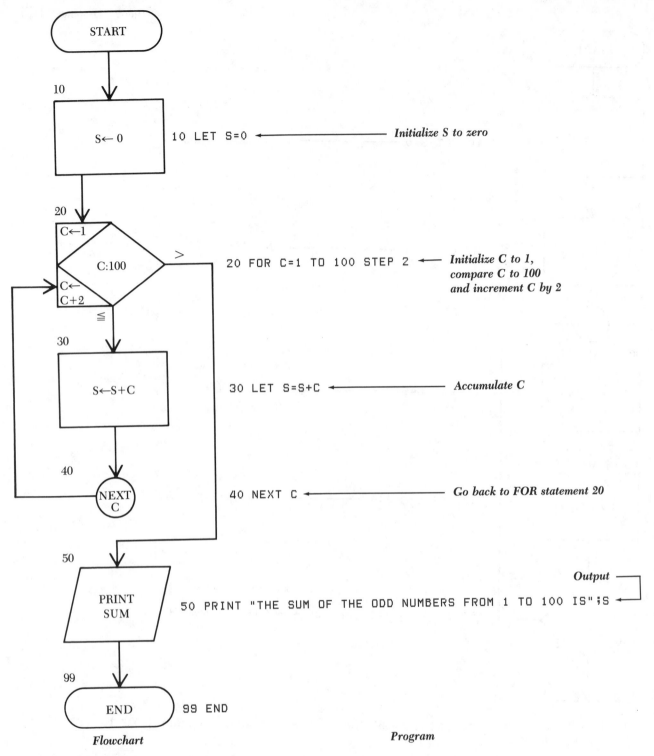

```
10 LET S=0          ← Initialize S to zero

20 FOR C=1 TO 100 STEP 2  ← Initialize C to 1,
                             compare C to 100
                             and increment C by 2

30 LET S=S+C        ← Accumulate C

40 NEXT C           ← Go back to FOR statement 20

                                           Output ─┐
50 PRINT "THE SUM OF THE ODD NUMBERS FROM 1 TO 100 IS";S ←

99 END
```

Flowchart   *Program*

Figure 7-3 Summing
numbers with the FOR-NEXT
loop

THE SUM OF THE ODD NUMBERS FROM 1 TO 100 IS 2500

Results

Although the program containing the FOR-NEXT loop is only one statement shorter than the program using the IF-THEN loop, it is preferable, because it makes writing the program easier—thus reducing errors—and it enables others to understand the program logic more easily.

Averaging Values

Figure 7-4 illustrates the use of FOR and NEXT statements for averaging values. These values and the number of values to be totaled and averaged are input from the keyboard.

The flowchart begins as usual with the start symbol. Symbol 110 initializes S to 0. Symbol 120–130 represents the keyboard input specifying the number of values to be averaged. Symbol 140 indicates the beginning of a FOR-NEXT loop. In the upper left corner of the symbol, the FOR variable is initialized to 1. The diamond illustrates how the value of K is compared with the test value of N each time the FOR statement is executed. If this test indicates that the value of K is less than or equal to the value of N, the downward branch is taken. If it is greater, the branch to the right is taken.

Look at the FOR statement in the program. This directs the program to execute all statements from the FOR statement through statement 180, the NEXT K statement. It initializes the value of K to 1, and it establishes a test value (N), the value entered from the first keyboard input. Look again at symbol 140. Until the value of K exceeds the value of N, symbol 150–160 will be executed. This input symbol begins accepting the values (V) to be added, one at a time, each time the FOR-NEXT loop is executed. Symbol 170 is used to accumulate the values in S so that they can be averaged later in the program.

Look at the BASIC programming for this loop. The loop ends at line 180 with the NEXT K statement. Control repeatedly passes from the NEXT statement back to the FOR statement until the FOR variable exceeds the test value, N. Now look at symbol 190 in the flowchart. When K is greater than N, control passes to symbol 190, which finds the average of the values. The count and average are written, and the program ends.

In the program, when the FOR variable exceeds the test value, control passes to the statement following the FOR-NEXT loop, which in this case is the assignment statement used to find the average.

Decrementing with a FOR Statement

Figure 7-5 is a flowchart of a program that will obtain the sum of all numbers between 1 and an input value. This program illustrates decrementing in a FOR-NEXT loop.

Symbol 20 clears the accumulator, T, to 0. Input symbol 30 represents the assignment of the initial value, N; this is to be the largest value included in the sum. To sum the numbers from 150 to 1, 150 would be input and assigned to N. If we wanted to sum the numbers between 5000 and 1, we would input 5000. In the FOR symbol, D will be assigned whatever is input as an initial value. The FOR variable, D, is then reduced by 1 each time the loop is executed. D is compared with the test value 1 each time through the loop. When D is less than 1, control passes to the output symbol following the NEXT symbol to print the contents of the accumulator. Then the program stops.

If the input value of N had been 150, D would also have the assigned value of 150 when initialized in the FOR symbol. So, the first time through the loop, 150 would be added to T in symbol 50. The next time through the loop, D would be reduced by 1 as shown in the FOR symbol; so 149 would be added to T, then 148, then 147, and so on, until all numbers from 150 to 1 had been added.

At the conclusion of this unit, write a BASIC program from this flowchart in the space provided. A suggested solution is given in the Answers to Application Exercises.

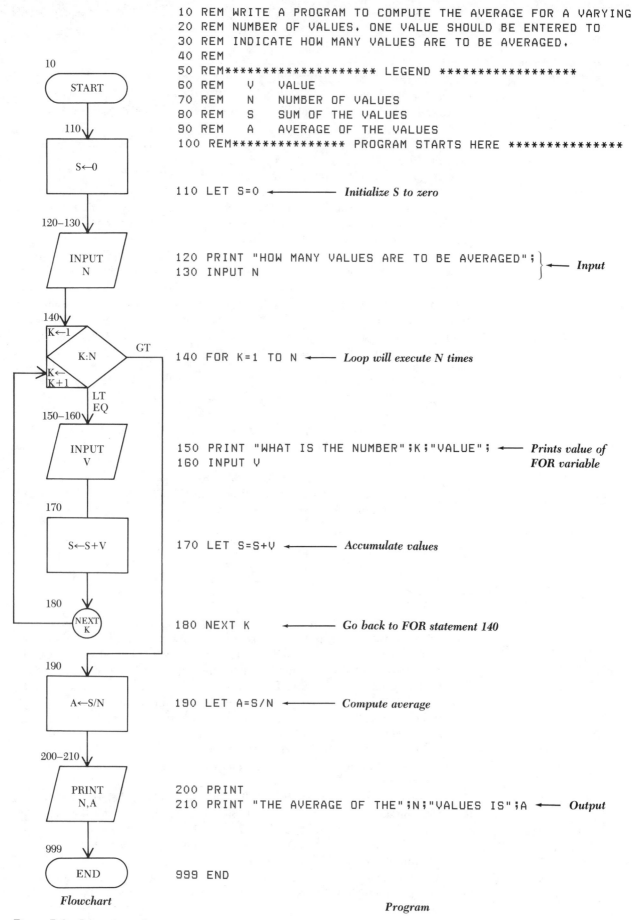

```
10 REM WRITE A PROGRAM TO COMPUTE THE AVERAGE FOR A VARYING
20 REM NUMBER OF VALUES. ONE VALUE SHOULD BE ENTERED TO
30 REM INDICATE HOW MANY VALUES ARE TO BE AVERAGED.
40 REM
50 REM******************* LEGEND ******************
60 REM    V    VALUE
70 REM    N    NUMBER OF VALUES
80 REM    S    SUM OF THE VALUES
90 REM    A    AVERAGE OF THE VALUES
100 REM************** PROGRAM STARTS HERE **************


110 LET S=0 ◄─────── Initialize S to zero


120 PRINT "HOW MANY VALUES ARE TO BE AVERAGED"; ◄── Input
130 INPUT N


140 FOR K=1 TO N ◄─── Loop will execute N times


150 PRINT "WHAT IS THE NUMBER";K;"VALUE"; ◄── Prints value of
160 INPUT V                                     FOR variable


170 LET S=S+V ◄─────── Accumulate values


180 NEXT K ◄─────── Go back to FOR statement 140


190 LET A=S/N ◄─────── Compute average


200 PRINT
210 PRINT "THE AVERAGE OF THE";N;"VALUES IS";A ◄── Output


999 END
```

Flowchart

Program

Figure 7-4 Averaging values

```
HOW MANY VALUES ARE TO BE AVERAGED?4
WHAT IS THE NUMBER 1     VALUE?56
WHAT IS THE NUMBER 2     VALUE?89
WHAT IS THE NUMBER 3     VALUE?75
WHAT IS THE NUMBER 4     VALUE?42

THE AVERAGE OF THE 4     VALUES IS 65.5
```

Results

Figure 7-4   Continued

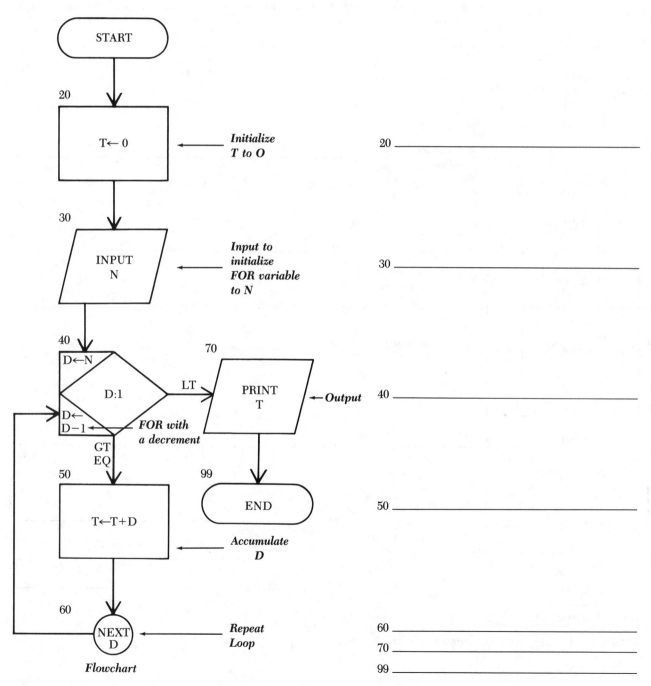

Flowchart

Figure 7-5   Accumulating the numbers from 1 to N

Using a STEP Variable in a FOR Statement

The purpose of the program in Figure 7-6 is to compute the square of every Nth value between 10 and 30 and print these values. Input symbol 20 assigns a value to N. N can represent every value between 10 and 30, or every second value, or every third value, and so on. Look at the FOR symbol (30). X is initialized with the value of 10, the test value is 30, and the increment value is N. Until X exceeds the value of 30, the downward branch is taken. Process symbol 40 computes the square of X, and output symbol 50 prints it. When the test value is exceeded, an exit from the loop occurs.

At the conclusion of this unit, write a BASIC program from this flowchart in the space provided. A suggested solution is given in the Answers to Application Exercises.

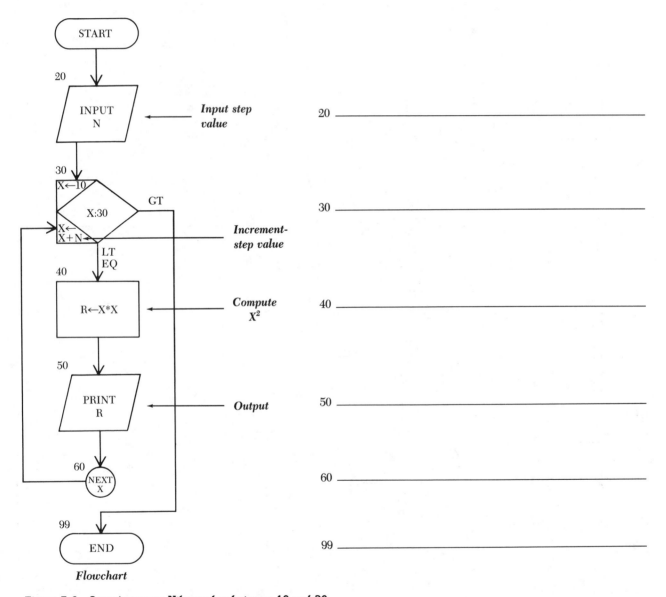

Flowchart

Figure 7-6   Squaring every Nth number between 10 and 30

Using a FOR-NEXT Loop to Calculate an Average

Figure 7-7 shows a flowchart and a partially completed program using a FOR-NEXT loop to accept input and accumulate the number of calories consumed at each noon meal during a five-day period. The average calories for these five days is then computed. We will write the program together. The first symbol (110) after the START symbol initializes the accumulator S to 0. Write the BASIC statement to do this.

The correct statement is 110 LET S=0. Symbol 120 in the flowchart represents the FOR statement. Write the FOR statement using the information in this symbol.

The correct statement is 120 FOR K=1 (to set the FOR variable to 1) TO 5 (the test value, because we want to go through the loop five times). The increment value (STEP 1) can be omitted, because the increment is 1. The FOR loop is executed five times; each time it takes the downward branch to symbol 130–140 in the flowchart. Statements 130 and 140 read the days of the week. Write statements 150, 160, and 170 to display the input request message and to get the input for the variable R. Use the flowchart and the results at the top of page 153 as a guide.

The correct statements are:

```
150 PRINT "HOW MANY CALORIES FOR ";D$;","
160 PRINT "MEAL NUMBER ";K;
170 INPUT R
```

Next, write an assignment statement to accumulate each value of R after it is input, as illustrated in symbol 180.

The correct statement is 180 LET S=S+R. Now write the statement to end the loop at statement 190.

The statement is NEXT K. After the fifth execution of the loop, control passes to symbol 200. Write a statement to compute and print the average, as indicated in symbol 200. Use the last line of the results as a guide.

The correct statement is 200 PRINT "AVERAGE CALORIES=";S/5. Write the last statement to show the normal end of the program.

The last statement should be 999 END.

FOR-NEXT Loop Rules

The exit and entry within FOR-NEXT loops must follow certain rules; these are illustrated in Figure 7-8. Arrow 1 illustrates entering a loop from outside the loop before the FOR statement is executed. This would probably cause incorrect results, because the FOR statement never has a chance to establish the FOR variable, the test value, and the STEP value.

Arrow 2 illustrates another incorrect transfer—that is, transferring from the middle of a FOR-NEXT loop directly to the FOR statement. Transfer to the FOR statement occurs automatically as a result of executing the last statement in the loop, the NEXT statement, and it is the only correct method of getting to the FOR statement from within the loop.

Arrow 3, showing transfer out of a loop, is valid. The value of the FOR variable contains the value computed in the last execution of the FOR statement.

Arrow 4 illustrates how the complete FOR-NEXT loop can be executed again from different parts of the program. When control is transferred back to the FOR statement, this reinitializes the FOR variable in the FOR statement, and the FOR-NEXT loop is again executed the prescribed number of times.

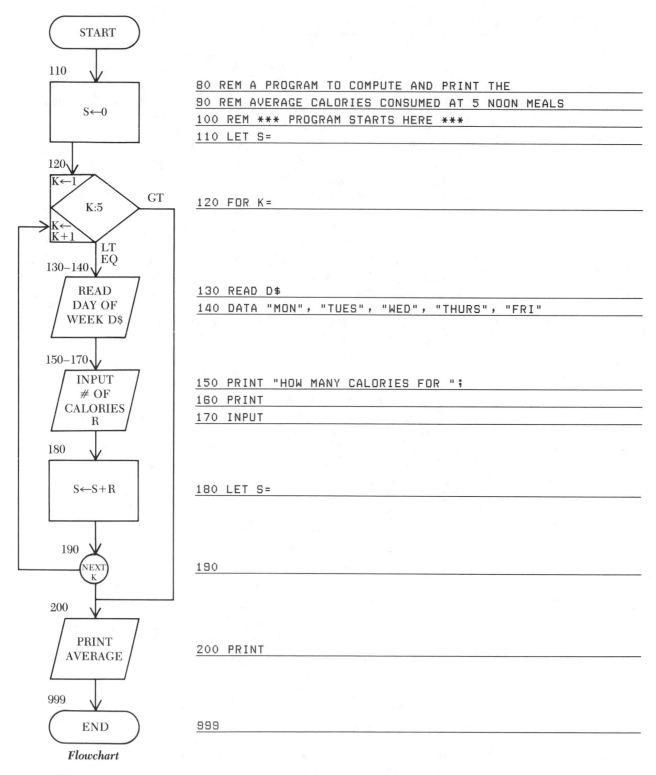

```
80 REM A PROGRAM TO COMPUTE AND PRINT THE
90 REM AVERAGE CALORIES CONSUMED AT 5 NOON MEALS
100 REM *** PROGRAM STARTS HERE ***
110 LET S=

120 FOR K=

130 READ D$
140 DATA "MON", "TUES", "WED", "THURS", "FRI"

150 PRINT "HOW MANY CALORIES FOR ";
160 PRINT
170 INPUT

180 LET S=

190

200 PRINT

999
```

Flowchart

Figure 7-7   Computing an average

```
HOW MANY CALORIES FOR MON,
MEAL NUMBER 1     ?2000
HOW MANY CALORIES FOR TUES,
MEAL NUMBER 2     ?1900
HOW MANY CALORIES FOR WEDN,
MEAL NUMBER 3     ?2100
HOW MANY CALORIES FOR THUR,
MEAL NUMBER 4     ?1900
HOW MANY CALORIES FOR FRI,
MEAL NUMBER 5     ?1800
AVERAGE CALORIES= 1940
```

Results

Figure 7-7 Continued

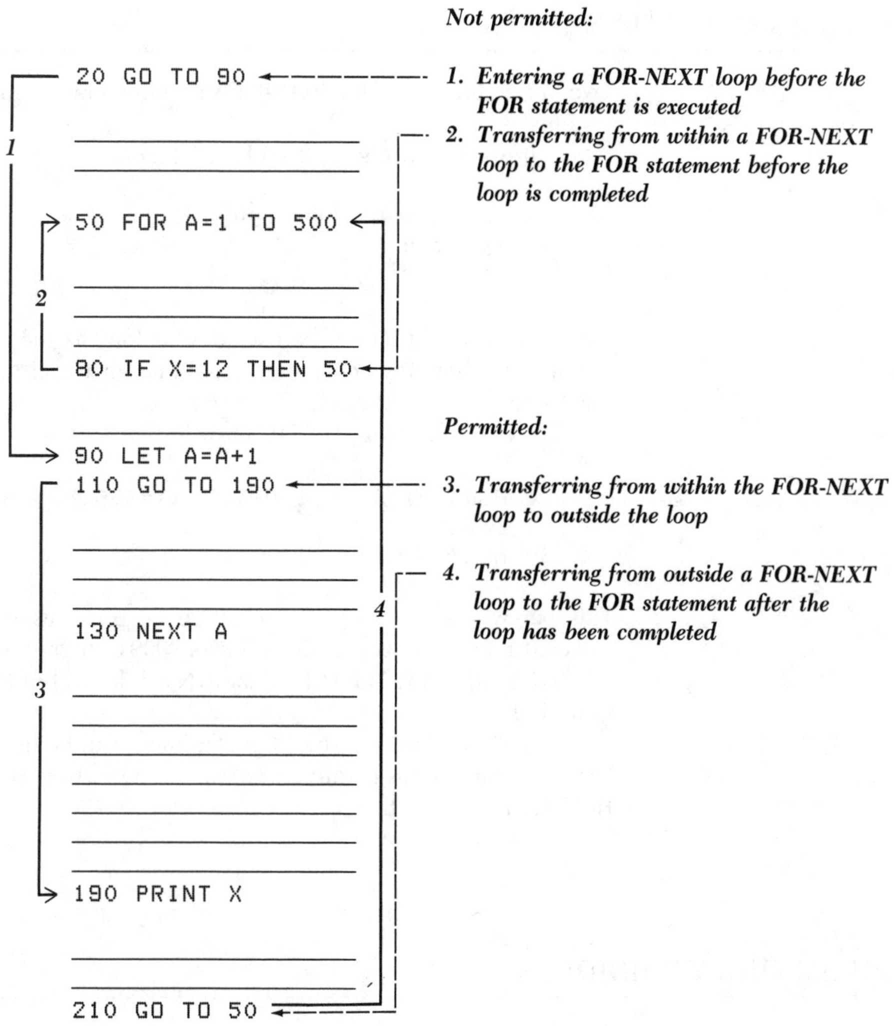

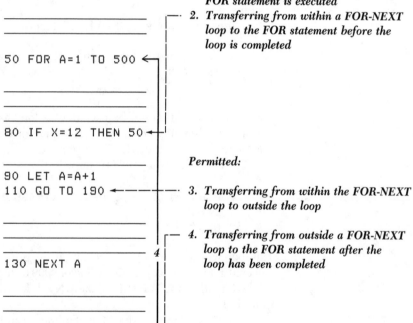

Not permitted:
20 GO TO 90
1. Entering a FOR-NEXT loop before the FOR statement is executed
2. Transferring from within a FOR-NEXT loop to the FOR statement before the loop is completed
1
50 FOR A=1 TO 500
2
80 IF X=12 THEN 50
Permitted:
90 LET A=A+1
110 GO TO 190
3. Transferring from within the FOR-NEXT loop to outside the loop
4. Transferring from outside a FOR-NEXT loop to the FOR statement after the loop has been completed
4
130 NEXT A
3
190 PRINT X
210 GO TO 50

Figure 7-8 FOR-NEXT loop rules

Programmers will sometimes find it useful to have a FOR-NEXT loop within another FOR-NEXT loop, commonly called *nested FOR-NEXT loops*. When this technique is used, the inner loop must be contained within the outer loop. An unlimited number of FOR-NEXT loops can be nested. The only requirement is that each loop be self-contained; the NEXT statement of the innermost FOR-NEXT loop must come before the NEXT statement of any other FOR-NEXT loop. Nested FOR-NEXT loops are commonly used to manipulate arrays; we will cover this topic in detail in a later unit.

Some versions of BASIC permit indention of statements. A programmer can then indent all FOR-NEXT loops. This technique reduces the errors associated with FOR-NEXT loops and also makes it easier for others to follow the program logic.

Other Forms of the FOR-NEXT Loop

Two other forms of the FOR-NEXT statement are available with some BASIC systems.

An example of the FOR-WHILE loop is:

```
10 FOR A=1 WHILE X<9999
20 INPUT X
30 NEXT A
```

This loop will continue to be executed as long as the value of X is less than 9999. When the value of X becomes greater than or equal to 9999, control passes to the statement following the NEXT A statement.

An example of the UNTIL form is:

```
10 FOR A=1 STEP 1 UNTIL X>=9999
20 INPUT X
30 NEXT A
```

This loop will achieve the same results as the previous example—that is, the program will continue in the loop until a value of 9999 or higher is input. A STEP value can be used with either the WHILE or the UNTIL form, but it can be omitted if the STEP value is 1.

These two forms of the FOR statement can be used to exit from a FOR-NEXT loop when a certain condition is true, rather than exiting from the loop with an IF-THEN statement.

PROGRAMMING TECHNIQUES

1. Using a FOR-NEXT loop to accumulate values:

```
10 LET T=0
20 FOR J=1 TO 20
30 INPUT X
40 LET T=T+X
50 NEXT J
```

2. Using a FOR-NEXT loop to average N values:

```
10 LET T=0
20 READ N
30 FOR I=1 TO N
40 INPUT R
50 LET T=T+R
60 NEXT I
70 LET A=T/N
```

3. Using a FOR-NEXT loop to average an unknown number of values (input of 9999 indicates that all values have been input):

```
10 LET T=0
20 FOR D=1 TO 1000
30 INPUT V
40 IF V=9999 THEN 70
50 LET T=T+V
60 NEXT D
70 LET A=T/(D-1)
```

4. Using a FOR-NEXT loop to manipulate every Nth value:

```
10 INPUT N
20 FOR K=1 TO 100 STEP N
30 PRINT 1/K
40 NEXT K
```

5. Using a FOR-NEXT loop to print the incrementing FOR variable within the loop:

```
10 FOR M=1 TO 10
20 PRINT "ENTER VALUE NUMBER"; M
30 INPUT V
40 NEXT M
```

6. Indention of FOR-NEXT loops:

```
10 INPUT N
20 FOR I=1 TO N
30      PRINT I
40 NEXT I
50 END
```

```
10 FOR I=1 TO 10
20   FOR J=1 TO 10
30     FOR K=1 TO 10
40       PRINT I,J,K
50     NEXT K
60   NEXT J
70 NEXT I
```

DEBUGGING AIDS

ERROR	CAUSE	CORRECTION
10 FOR X=1 TO -50 20 PRINT X 30 NEXT X	Loop never executed	(Change test value) 10 FOR X=1 TO 50 20 PRINT X 30 NEXT X
10 READ X,Y 20 FOR W=X TO Y STEP Z 30 PRINT W 40 NEXT W	STEP value not defined	(Define STEP value) 10 READ X,Y,Z 20 FOR W=X TO Y STEP Z 30 PRINT W 40 NEXT W
10 FOR A=1 TO 50 20 LET A=A/2 30 PRINT A 40 NEXT A	Changing the FOR variable; test value or STEP value within a FOR-NEXT loop will give incorrect results	(Assign computation to a variable other than FOR variable) 10 FOR A=1 TO 50 20 LET Z=A/2 30 PRINT Z 40 NEXT A
10 FOR A=1 TO 50 20 PRINT A 30 GO TO 10 40 NEXT A	NEXT statement not executed; FOR variable not incremented. A is reinitialized to 1	(Eliminate GO TO statement) 10 FOR A=1 TO 50 20 PRINT A 30 NEXT A
10 FOR B=1 TO 20 20 PRINT B 30 NEXT B 40 GO TO 20	Branching into middle of FOR-NEXT loop; FOR statement never executed	10 FOR B=1 TO 20 20 PRINT B 30 NEXT B 40 GO TO 10
10 FOR C=1 TO 10 20 FOR R=1 TO 5 30 PRINT C,R 40 NEXT C 50 NEXT R	Inner loop not self-contained; NEXT C precedes NEXT R; loops will not execute	(Interchange NEXT C with NEXT R) 10 FOR C=1 TO 10 20 FOR R=1 TO 5 30 PRINT C,R 40 NEXT R 50 NEXT C
10 LET T=0 20 FOR I=1 TO 10 30 INPUT V 40 LET T=T+V 50 NEXT I 60 PRINT T/I	An incorrect average will result, because FOR variable increments until it exceeds test value	(Use a counter C) 10 LET T=0 20 LET C=0 30 FOR I=1 TO 10 40 INPUT V 50 LET C=C+1 60 LET T=T+V 70 NEXT I 80 PRINT T/C

REFERENCE

FOR-NEXT STATEMENTS	GENERAL FORM

Repeats execution of statements between the FOR and NEXT statements a specified number of times

$$\textbf{FOR} \;\; \text{variable} = \begin{array}{c}\text{initial}\\ \text{value}\\ \text{of FOR}\\ \text{variable}\end{array} \;\; \textbf{TO} \;\; \begin{array}{c}\text{test}\\ \text{value}\end{array} \;\; \textbf{STEP} \;\; \begin{array}{c}\text{increment}\\ \text{value}\end{array}$$

$$\textbf{NEXT} \;\; \begin{array}{c}\text{FOR}\\ \text{variable}\end{array}$$

Example:

```
40 FOR J=3 TO 50 STEP 2

80 NEXT J
```

Flowchart symbol:

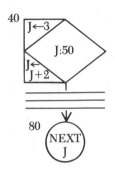

APPLICATION EXERCISES

1. Write a program from the flowchart in Figure 7-5.
2. Write a program from the flowchart in Figure 7-6.
3. Write FOR-NEXT loops to do the following: For every fifth value between and including 7 and 42, square the number, divide the result by 2, add 100 to it, and print the result.
4. Write a program segment to input 50 values and print the square of each value.
5. Write a program segment to read 300 values and count the negative values.
6. Write a program segment to input 10 names; if the name PATTY is input, print HELLO PATTY; otherwise, print nothing.

For exercises 7 and 8, use the work area on the right while stepping through the program at the left.

<u>V</u> <u>I</u> <u>S</u>

```
 5 LET V=0
10 FOR I=2 TO 7 STEP 3
20 LET V=V+I
25 LET S=V^2
30 NEXT I
35 LET S=S+1
40 END
```

7. How many times will this loop be executed? a. 1 b. 2 c. 3 d. 4 e. 5
8. What will be the final value of S? a. 4 b. 5 c. 49 d. 50 e. 126

Assume that the following program has been run. Circle the number of times that each statement is executed, and write the corresponding letter on the line at the left.

			a.	b.	c.	d.	e
9. _____	5 GO TO 30		0	1	4	8	10
10. _____	10 LET A=1.6		0	1	4	8	10
11. _____	20 IF A<0 THEN 45		0	1	4	8	10
12. _____	25 IF A>0 THEN 75		0	1	4	8	10
13. _____	30 FOR I=1 TO 8		0	1	4	8	10
14. _____	40 LET I2=I^2		0	1	4	8	10
15. _____	45 IF I2-16>0 THEN 60		0	1	4	8	10
16. _____	50 GO TO 70		0	1	4	8	10
17. _____	60 LET C=I		0	1	4	8	10
18. _____	70 NEXT I		0	1	4	8	10
19. _____	75 LET K=C+2		0	1	4	8	10
20. _____	80 FOR L=1 TO K		0	1	4	8	10
21. _____	85 LET L2=L+1		0	1	4	8	10
22. _____	90 NEXT L		0	1	4	8	10
23. _____	99 END		0	1	4	8	10

Use the following work areas when stepping through the program.

I   I2   C   K   L   L2

Answers to Application Exercises

```
1. 20 LET T=0
   30 INPUT N
   40 FOR D=N TO 1 STEP -1
   50 LET T=T+D                    (Figure 7-5 solution)
   60 NEXT D
   70 PRINT T
   99 END

2. 20 INPUT N
   30 FOR X=10 TO 30 STEP N
   40 LET R=X*X                    (Figure 7-6 solution)
   50 PRINT R
   60 NEXT X
   99 END
```

```
3. 10 FOR X=7 TO 42 STEP 5
   20 PRINT X^2/2+100
   30 NEXT X

4. 10 FOR A=1 TO 50
   20 INPUT V
   25 PRINT V^2
   30 NEXT A

5. 10 LET C=0
   20 FOR I=1 TO 300
   30 READ X
   40 IF X>=0 THEN 60
   50 LET C=C+1
   60 NEXT I

6. 10 FOR N=1 TO 10
   20 INPUT N$
   30 IF N$<>"PATTY" THEN 50
   40 PRINT "HELLO PATTY"
   50 NEXT N
```

7. b	13. d	19. b
8. d	14. d	20. e
9. b	15. d	21. e
10. a	16. c	22. e
11. a	17. c	23. b
12. a	18. d	

PROGRAMMING PROBLEMS

7-1. Team-Scheduling Program

Given the number of teams that will play in a league, prepare a schedule that will assign an equal number of "home" and "away" games to each team and allow all teams to play the same number of games. No team should be scheduled to play all games on consecutive days.

Programming tips:

1. Use the flowchart in Figure 7-9 as a guide to your solution.
2. The formulas for initializing the day starts are:

   High day start = (no. of teams * no. of teams) − no. of teams + 2
   Low day start = −1

3. To determine whether a number is odd or even:

   INT (number/2) − number/2.

   If the result is zero, the number is even; otherwise, the number is odd.
   (*Note:* INT is a function that removes the decimal portion of a number.)

4. The day number to be printed should be a variable that has been assigned the value of either the low-day or high-day variable.
5. In the results, the visiting team is represented by the FOR variable J; the home team is represented by the team counter variable I.

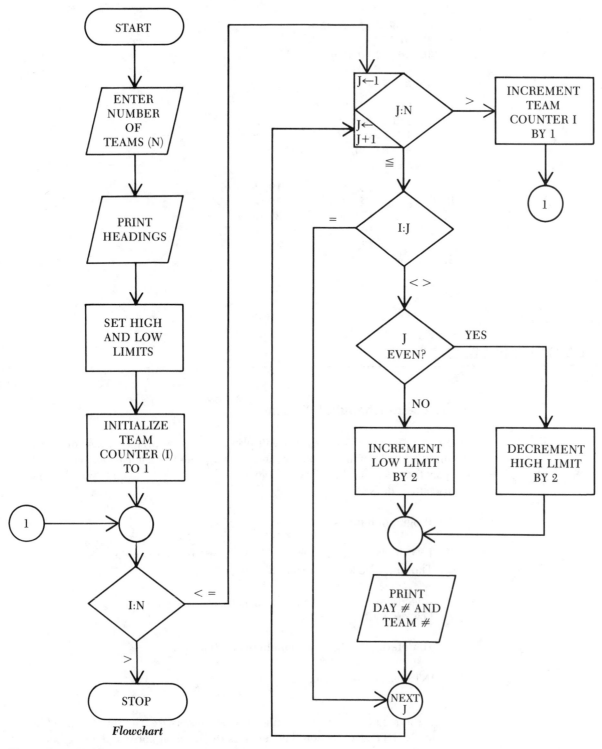

Figure 7-9   Flowchart of the team-scheduling program

```
ENTER THE NUMBER OF TEAMS TO BE SCHEDULED ?6

DAY     VISITOR           HOME
 #         #        VS     #

30         2                1
 1         3                1
28         4                1
 3         5                1
26         6                1
 5         1                2
 7         3                2
24         4                2
 9         5                2
22         6                2
11         1                3
20         2                3
18         4                3
13         5                3
16         6                3
15         1                4
14         2                4
17         3                4
19         5                4
12         6                4
21         1                5
10         2                5
23         3                5
 8         4                5
 6         6                5
25         1                6
 4         2                6
27         3                6
 2         4                6
29         5                6
```

Figure 7-10   Results of the team-scheduling program

7-2. Currency-Exchange Program

Given as input foreign-exchange rates for selected countries, print the value of these currencies in terms of United States dollars.

Programming tips:

1. Draw a flowchart of the solution.
2. Only one FOR-NEXT loop is required. Its initial value, test value, and STEP value can be changed with a READ and a DATA statement.
3. The formula for computing foreign currency in United States dollars is:

US$/FOREIGN EXCHANGE RATE

4. Do not change the initial value, test value, or STEP value within the FOR-NEXT loop.

Results:

```
WHICH TWO CURRENCIES
WOULD YOU LIKE TO EXCHANGE
?"ENGLISH","FRENCH"

WHAT ARE THEIR EXCHANGE RATES
?1.9,.228

US$       ENGLISH      FRENCH

1          .526316      4.38597
2         1.05263       8.77193
3         1.57895      13.1579
4         2.10526      17.5439
5         2.63158      21.9298
6         3.15789      26.3158
7         3.68421      30.7018
8         4.21053      35.0877
9         4.73684      39.4737
10        5.26316      43.8596

100      52.6316      438.596
120      63.1579      526.316
140      73.6842      614.035
160      84.2105      701.754
180      94.7368      789.474
200     105.263       877.193


TRY AGAIN? Y FOR YES, N FOR NO
?Y
WHICH TWO CURRENCIES
WOULD YOU LIKE TO EXCHANGE
?"GERMAN","ITALIAN"

WHAT ARE THEIR EXCHANGE RATES
?.498,.0012

US$       GERMAN       ITALIAN

1         2.00803      833.333
2         4.01606     1666.67
3         6.0241      2500
4         8.03213     3333.33
5        10.0402      4166.67
6        12.0482      5000
7        14.0562      5833.33
8        16.0643      6666.67
9        18.0723      7500
10       20.0803      8333.33

100     200.803      83333.3
120     240.964     100000.
140     281.124     116667.
160     321.285     133333.
180     361.446     150000.
200     401.606     166667.


TRY AGAIN? Y FOR YES, N FOR NO
?N
```

Figure 7-11 Results of the currency-exchange program

8 One-Dimensional Arrays

OBJECTIVES

When you complete this unit, you will be able to:

1. Write a DIM statement, given a description of one or more arrays
2. Write a program that reads data into an array, manipulates its contents, and writes out the array and/or the results of the manipulation:
   a. For a given problem with a flowchart
   b. For a given problem without a flowchart
3. Predict the values resulting from a program that manipulates the contents of an array
4. Code and execute a BASIC solution to a problem that requires reading data into an array, array manipulation, and output

INTRODUCTION

What Is an Array?

An array is a group or list of related items of data that are identified by a single variable name. Data items within the array are referred to as *array elements*. To refer to a particular element in the array, you must specify the array name and the position of the element in the array. For example, assuming that an array named B consists of four elements: to refer to the second element, you would write B(2). The number 2 within parentheses is called a *subscript*. A subscript identifies a particular element in an array and must be enclosed within parentheses immediately following the array name. Before an array can be used, computer storage must be reserved by a dimension (DIM) statement. The DIM statement specifies the name of the array and its maximum size. For example, DIM B(4) reserves four storage positions for an array named B. Some BASIC systems begin arrays at position 0. On such systems, DIM B(4) would reserve five storage positions.

It is often convenient to treat a group of related data items as an array with a single variable name, rather than separately named variables. In this unit we discuss the use of single-dimension arrays.

Types of Arrays

This unit describes how tables or arrays of data are stored and manipulated in computer storage. An array is a group of related values or strings. Two single-dimensional arrays are illustrated in Figure 8-1. One array consists of a simple list or table of sales values for various salespersons, and the other consists of a list of names. A one-dimensional array is sometimes called a *vector*. A two-dimensional array consists of rows and columns and is often referred to as a *matrix*. (We will discuss two-dimensional arrays in a later unit).

Regardless of how many dimensions an array has, it is important to remember that an array is simply a list or table of related (numeric or string) data items, stored in reserved areas of computer storage under the same name. Data items can also be referred to as elements of an array. For our purposes, the main difference between one- and two-dimensional arrays involves the number of subscripts required to refer to them. Subscripts refer to the element number or location of a value within an array. A one-dimensional array requires only one subscript, but a two-dimensional array requires two subscripts.

Array (vector)

Sales rep number	Sales	Name number	Name
1	8500	1	SMITH
2	9000	2	JONES
3	9300	3	BROWN
4	11000	4	ANDREWS

B array   *N\$ array*

Figure 8-1   One-dimensional arrays

Subscripts

Figure 8-2 illustrates subscripting for a one-dimensional array named B, containing four elements. A subscript is used to indicate the element number, or location of a value, in the array. For example, to refer to the third item in the array B, you would write B(3), usually pronounced as "B subscript 3" or "B sub 3." Elements of an array are accessed by using subscripted variables. Before this unit, you had worked with only nonsubscripted variables, so if you wanted to add two variables, A and B, and place the result in the variable S, you wrote LET $S = A + B$.

Any operation you could perform with a nonsubscripted variable you can also perform with a subscripted variable. For example, to add the third and second elements of the B array and place the result in the variable S, you would write the statement shown in statement 10 of Figure 8-2—that is, LET $S = B(3)$, which is 9300, be added to B(2), which is 9000. S would thus have a value of 18300.

Whenever you refer to a value or string within an array, you must use a subscript within parentheses following the array name. Since the subscript indicates a location within the array, it can never be negative. Each location must be identified by a whole number. In many BASIC systems, location 0 is the first position of the array. Since the value of a FOR variable in the FOR-NEXT loop can easily meet the conditions we have just stated, a FOR variable is often used as a subscript to refer to locations within arrays. The program segment in statements 30 through 50 is an example of this usage. In the FOR statement, statement 30, the FOR variable A advances from an initial value of 1 to a final value of 4. Every time the FOR-NEXT loop is executed, A has a different value. A is also used as a subscript for the B array; it refers to a different position of the array every time the statement 40 LET S=S+B(A) is executed.

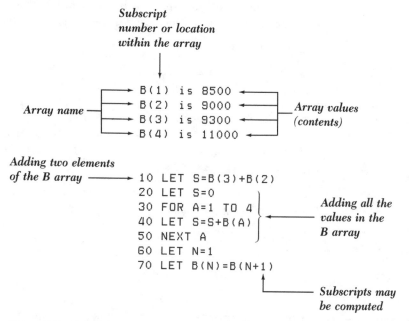

Figure 8-2   Subscripting

Subscript Forms

Subscripts can take several forms. The most common forms that a beginning programmer is likely to use are: first, a single constant, B(3) or B(2), as shown in statement 10 in Figure 8-2; second, a single numeric variable, such as A, as shown in statement 40, where you see B(A); and third, a numeric variable plus or minus a constant, as illustrated in statement 70, LET B(N)=B(N+1). In this last example, N has a value of 1 as a result of statement 60. The contents of the Nth position of the B array (the first position) are replaced by the contents of the Nth+1 position (the second position). A summary of information regarding subscripts is given in the Reference section at the end of this unit.

Defining Arrays

Before using an array in any program, you must specify the name of the array and the maximum number of elements that it can include. The dimension statements illustrated in Figure 8-3 serve this purpose. The first DIM statement in Figure 8-3 begins with the word DIM followed by the array name B. Then indicated within the parentheses is the maximum size of the array—in this case, 4. Actually, five storage locations will be reserved in those BASIC systems where the first location is 0. In the second DIM statement in Figure 8-3, the V$ array has storage positions reserved for 100 string values. Although you can use separate DIM statements for each array, this is not necessary. You can establish more than one array with a single DIM statement, as shown in the third DIM statement in Figure 8-3. However, the array entries must be separated by commas.

Some systems do not require a DIM statement for small arrays of a specific length. We suggest that you use the dimension statement for arrays of any size; the DIM statement should be the first statement in your program, after the remarks section. This might help you to reduce errors when programming with arrays.

Another technique to make programs easier to read is to disregard the 0 position of the array. When this is done, the first element of the array is located at subscript position 1, the second element at subscript position 2, and so on.

Some BASIC systems use brackets rather than parentheses to enclose subscripts. This difference should be disregarded, since their functions are identical.

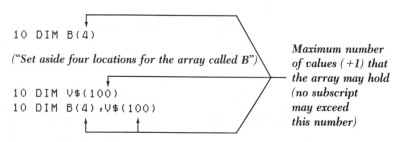

```
10 DIM B(4)

("Set aside four locations for the array called B")

10 DIM V$(100)
10 DIM B(4),V$(100)
```

Maximum number of values (+1) that the array may hold (no subscript may exceed this number)

Figure 8-3   DIM statements

```
10 REM A PROGRAM TO FIND WHAT PERCENTAGE EACH MONTH IS OF THE
20 REM TOTAL YEARLY BUDGET (WITHOUT USING ARRAYS).
30 REM
40 REM
50 REM******************** LEGEND ********************
60 REM    T    TOTAL MONTHS
70 REM
80 REM    M1,M2,M3,M4,M5,M6,M7,M8,M9,M0,N1,N2  EACH OF THE 12 MONTHS
90 REM
100 REM************** PROGRAM STARTS HERE *************
110 READ M1,M2,M3,M4,M5,M6,M7,M8,M9,M0,N1,N2  ◄─────────── Read data
120 DATA 850,900,930,1100,875,960,890,950,925,850,975,1225
130 LET T=M1+M2+M3+M4+M5+M6+M7+M8+M9+M0+N1+N2  ◄─────────── Compute
140 PRINT "MONTH NUMBER  1 IS    ";INT(M1/T*100+.5);"% OF THE TOTAL BUDGET"
150 PRINT "MONTH NUMBER  2 IS    ";INT(M2/T*100+.5);"% OF THE TOTAL BUDGET"
160 PRINT "MONTH NUMBER  3 IS    ";INT(M3/T*100+.5);"% OF THE TOTAL BUDGET"
170 PRINT "MONTH NUMBER  4 IS    ";INT(M4/T*100+.5);"% OF THE TOTAL BUDGET"
180 PRINT "MONTH NUMBER  5 IS    ";INT(M5/T*100+.5);"% OF THE TOTAL BUDGET"
190 PRINT "MONTH NUMBER  6 IS    ";INT(M6/T*100+.5);"% OF THE TOTAL BUDGET"
200 PRINT "MONTH NUMBER  7 IS    ";INT(M7/T*100+.5);"% OF THE TOTAL BUDGET"
210 PRINT "MONTH NUMBER  8 IS    ";INT(M8/T*100+.5);"% OF THE TOTAL BUDGET"
220 PRINT "MONTH NUMBER  9 IS    ";INT(M9/T*100+.5);"% OF THE TOTAL BUDGET"
230 PRINT "MONTH NUMBER 10 IS    ";INT(M0/T*100+.5);"% OF THE TOTAL BUDGET"
240 PRINT "MONTH NUMBER 11 IS    ";INT(N1/T*100+.5);"% OF THE TOTAL BUDGET"
250 PRINT "MONTH NUMBER 12 IS    ";INT(N2/T*100+.5);"% OF THE TOTAL BUDGET"
999 END
```

Output

Program

Figure 8-4   A budget program without an array

```
MONTH NUMBER  1 IS   7   % OF THE TOTAL BUDGET
MONTH NUMBER  2 IS   8   % OF THE TOTAL BUDGET
MONTH NUMBER  3 IS   8   % OF THE TOTAL BUDGET
MONTH NUMBER  4 IS  10   % OF THE TOTAL BUDGET
MONTH NUMBER  5 IS   8   % OF THE TOTAL BUDGET
MONTH NUMBER  6 IS   8   % OF THE TOTAL BUDGET
MONTH NUMBER  7 IS   8   % OF THE TOTAL BUDGET
MONTH NUMBER  8 IS   8   % OF THE TOTAL BUDGET
MONTH NUMBER  9 IS   8   % OF THE TOTAL BUDGET
MONTH NUMBER 10 IS   7   % OF THE TOTAL BUDGET
MONTH NUMBER 11 IS   9   % OF THE TOTAL BUDGET
MONTH NUMBER 12 IS  11   % OF THE TOTAL BUDGET
```

Results

Figure 8-4   Continued

Using Arrays

Read all the REMARK statements of Figure 8-4, which describe the purpose of the program.

Statement 110 reads the data from statement 120 to assign 12 values to the 12 variables listed in this READ statement. Statement 130 adds the 12 values. This sum is necessary for finding the percentages computed in statements 140 through 250. Statement 140 computes the percentage that month number 1 constitutes of the yearly budget; this is done by rounding the month amount divided by the total amount for all months. Notice that all statements following statement 140 are the same, except for the month number and the variable representing the month.

Using an array, the program shown in Figure 8-5 produces the same results that the program in Figure 8-4 produced. This is shorter and easier to write than the previous program. Statement 110 establishes a 12-position array with one position to hold each of the 12 months. Statement 130 is a FOR statement that causes the FOR-NEXT loop to be repeated 12 times. Statement 140 reads one data item, from the DATA statement below it, into the array named by the subscripted variable B(X). The first time through the loop, X has a value of 1; therefore, the first data item is placed in the first position of the B array. The second time through the loop, X has a value of 2; therefore, the second data item is placed in the second position of the B array. This process continues until all 12 positions have been filled. Statement 160 adds each element of the array to the accumulator T, during the loop.

Statement 180, the FOR statement, starts another loop to be repeated 12 times. Although we have again used the FOR variable X, just as we did in the first FOR statement (statement 130), it's not necessary to do this. We could use any numeric variable except T. We cannot use T because it contains values that we want to use within the loop. In statement 190, after the words "MONTH NUMBER" and a semicolon, an X occurs to represent the changing value of the FOR variable—1 to 12. In the same statement, after the word "IS", followed by a semicolon, we have the formula to compute the percentage of the total budget. Within the formula the subscript variable B(X) refers to each budget month. The FOR variable X increases by 1 each time through the loop, so it will compute the percentage for month 1 the first time through, month 2 the second time through, and so forth.

Whenever a programming application requires that all data be read before any individual data items are manipulated, it is usually best to establish an array for the data items and manipulate the data items within a FOR-NEXT loop.

```
10 REM A PROGRAM TO FIND WHAT PERCENTAGE EACH MONTHLY BUDGET IS OF THE
20 REM TOTAL YEARLY BUDGET (USING ARRAYS).
30 REM
40 REM
50 REM ******************* LEGEND **************
60 REM   T    TOTAL OF MONTHLY BUDGETS
70 REM   X    INDEX VARIABLE
80 REM   B    ARRAY NAME FOR THE 12 MONTHS
90 REM
100 REM************** PROGRAM STARTS HERE ***********
110 DIM B[12]  ←————————— Establish arrays
120 LET T=0  ←————————— Initialize T to 0
130 FOR X=1 TO 12
140 READ B[X]  ←——————————————————————————————— Read DATA
150 DATA 850,900,930,1100,875,960,890,950,925,850,975,1225  ← into arrays
160 LET T=T+B[X]  ←——————— Accumulate array values
170 NEXT X
180 FOR X=1 TO 12                          Computation
190 PRINT "MONTH NUMBER ";X;"IS ";INT(B[X]/T*100+.5);"% OF THE TOTAL BUDGET"
200 NEXT X
999 END
```

Program

```
MONTH NUMBER  1   IS   7    % OF THE TOTAL BUDGET
MONTH NUMBER  2   IS   8    % OF THE TOTAL BUDGET
MONTH NUMBER  3   IS   8    % OF THE TOTAL BUDGET
MONTH NUMBER  4   IS   10   % OF THE TOTAL BUDGET
MONTH NUMBER  5   IS   8    % OF THE TOTAL BUDGET
MONTH NUMBER  6   IS   8    % OF THE TOTAL BUDGET
MONTH NUMBER  7   IS   8    % OF THE TOTAL BUDGET
MONTH NUMBER  8   IS   8    % OF THE TOTAL BUDGET
MONTH NUMBER  9   IS   8    % OF THE TOTAL BUDGET
MONTH NUMBER  10  IS   7    % OF THE TOTAL BUDGET
MONTH NUMBER  11  IS   9    % OF THE TOTAL BUDGET
MONTH NUMBER  12  IS   11   % OF THE TOTAL BUDGET
```

Results

Figure 8-5   A budget program with an array

A Program with Two Numeric Arrays

Read the program remarks in Figure 8-6.

The program asks for keyboard input of a limit amount that limits the budget amounts to be adjusted. Budget amounts for 12 months are then input. The last item to be input is the amount of the budget reduction to be apportioned among those months exceeding the limit amount.

When the budget amounts are input, they are placed into the B array. As you will see later, a second array called N is developed by deducting an amount from selected values in the first array. Finally, both arrays are printed side by side.

Look at the program that makes all this happen. Statement 110 in the program reserves storage for both arrays in the DIM statement. In this case, the number of storage positions reserved for the B array is the exact number required for the values to be input. The N array also has 12 storage positions reserved in the same DIM statement. An array may be dimensioned for a greater number of elements than needed, but it is incorrect to have less than the number required. If an array A had a dimension of 10 and you attempted to input a value into A(11), an error would occur.

Look at symbol 120–140 in the flowchart. This represents the keyboard input for R, a limit amount that determines which budget months must be adjusted. The BASIC statements 120 and 130 accomplish this in the program. Symbol 150 in the flowchart and statement 150 in the program clear the counter C to 0.

Flowchart symbol 160 illustrates the establishment of a FOR-NEXT loop in which the FOR variable is initialized to 1 and the upper limit is set to 12. The coded statement is statement 160 in the program. Symbol 170–180 in the flowchart represents the keyboard input for each monthly budget amount. Look at statement 170 in the program. Near the end of this PRINT statement you can see the variable X, which represents the month number. Look again at statement 160. The FOR variable X will have 1 added to its value each time the loop is executed. Since statement 170 is in the loop, variable X will also step from 1 through 12 and print as shown in the results. Look at the keyboard input in the results and compare it with statement 170. Statement 180 places each input item into positions 1 through 12 of the array B—again making use of the changing value of X. Symbol 190 tests each budget amount after it has been input, to determine whether it exceeds R, the monthly limit. If the input item does not exceed this value, control passes to the NEXT symbol, 210, to continue the loop. If it exceeds R, C is incremented by 1 in symbol 200. C is used to count the number of input items greater than R. Symbol 210 ends the loop. Examine statements 190, 200, and 210 in the BASIC program to see how this part of the loop is written.

Flowchart symbol 220–250 represents statements 220 through 250 in the program. These provide for keyboard input for the variable A, which represents the total amount by which the 12-month budget is to be reduced. Symbol 260–270 and statements 260 and 270 provide column headings for the output in the results.

Statement 280 starts the loop to manipulate the arrays and print the results. Statement 290 compares each of the 12 months with the limit. If the limit is not exceeded, statement 300 places the array element just tested into array N, unchanged. As you can see, in this statement, the subscript for N will always be the same as the subscript for B. This means that the array element will be located in the same position in both arrays. Control is then passed to statement 330 to print the contents of both arrays. Look at the first two lines of output on page 171. The amounts 850 and 900 are printed from both the original budget array B and the new budget array N.

Now look again at statement 290. If the array element is greater than the limit, control passes to statement 320. This statement computes the amount by which an element is to be reduced, by subtracting from the element the amount of the total reduction divided by the number of months to be reduced. This computation places the adjusted amount into the corresponding position of the N array. Arrays B and N are then printed in statement 330. As you can see in the results on page 171, seven of the original budget amounts exceeded 900; therefore, these were reduced by 100. The adjustment was computed by dividing the total reduction amount (700) by 7.

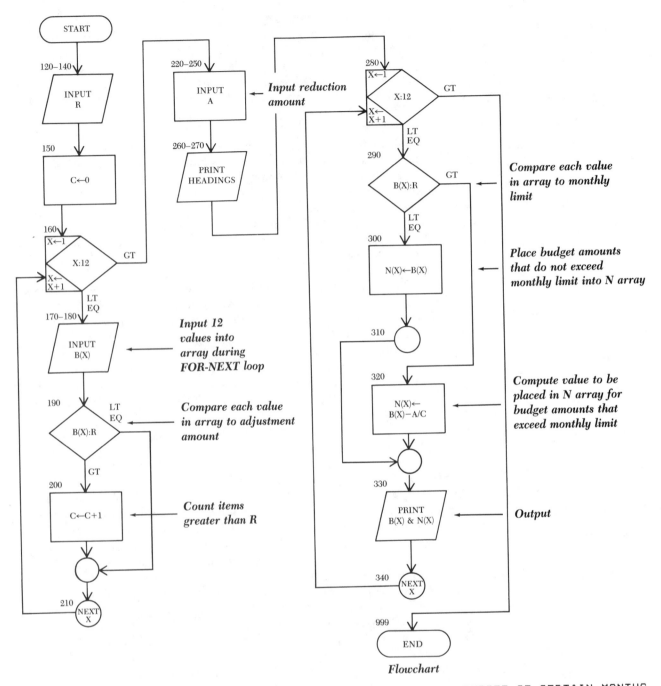

Flowchart

```
10 REM WRITE A PROGRAM THAT WILL REDUCE THE BUDGET OF CERTAIN MONTHS
20 REM BY A VARIABLE AMOUNT, PRINT THE ORIGINAL BUDGET AND THE
30 REM ADJUSTED BUDGET SIDE BY SIDE,
40 REM
50 REM***************** LEGEND ******************
60 REM    B    ORIGINAL BUDGET ARRAY
70 REM    N    ADJUSTED BUDGET ARRAY
80 REM    C    COUNT OF MONTHS OVER LIMIT       R    MONTHLY LIMIT
90 REM    A    AMOUNT BUDGET IS TO BE REDUCED   X    INDEX VARIABLE
100 REM************** PROGRAM STARTS HERE ***********
```

Program

Figure 8-6   Flowchart and program with two arrays

```
110 DIM B[12],N[12]                                            ──────── Establish
120 PRINT "MONTHS TO BE ADJUSTED SHOULD EXCEED WHAT AMOUNT ";           arrays
130 INPUT R  ──────────────────────────────────  Input
140 PRINT                                         monthly
150 LET C=0                                       limit
160 FOR X=1 TO 12
170 PRINT "WHAT IS THE BUDGET AMOUNT FOR MONTH NUMBER ";X;      Loop for input
180 INPUT B[X]                                                  comparison with
190 IF B[X] <= R THEN 210                                       R and incrementing count
200 LET C=C+1
210 NEXT X
220 PRINT
230 PRINT "WHAT IS THE TOTAL REDUCTION AMOUNT ";
240 INPUT A  ──────────────────────────────  Input
250 PRINT                                     reduction
260 PRINT                                     amount
270 PRINT "ORIGINAL BUDGET    NEW BUDGET"  ──── Headings
275 PRINT
280 FOR X=1 TO 12
290 IF B[X]>R THEN 320
300 LET N[X]=B[X]                          ── Loop for
310 GO TO 330                                 output
320 LET N[X]=B[X]-A/C
330 PRINT TAB(8);B[X];TAB(20);N[X]
340 NEXT X
999 END
```

Program (continued)

```
MONTHS TO BE ADJUSTED SHOULD EXCEED WHAT AMOUNT ?900←(VARIABLE R)

WHAT IS THE BUDGET AMOUNT FOR MONTH NUMBER 1    ?850
WHAT IS THE BUDGET AMOUNT FOR MONTH NUMBER 2    ?900
WHAT IS THE BUDGET AMOUNT FOR MONTH NUMBER 3    ?930
WHAT IS THE BUDGET AMOUNT FOR MONTH NUMBER 4    ?1100
WHAT IS THE BUDGET AMOUNT FOR MONTH NUMBER 5    ?875
WHAT IS THE BUDGET AMOUNT FOR MONTH NUMBER 6    ?960
WHAT IS THE BUDGET AMOUNT FOR MONTH NUMBER 7    ?890
WHAT IS THE BUDGET AMOUNT FOR MONTH NUMBER 8    ?950
WHAT IS THE BUDGET AMOUNT FOR MONTH NUMBER 9    ?925
WHAT IS THE BUDGET AMOUNT FOR MONTH NUMBER 10   ?850
WHAT IS THE BUDGET AMOUNT FOR MONTH NUMBER 11   ?975
WHAT IS THE BUDGET AMOUNT FOR MONTH NUMBER 12   ?1225

WHAT IS THE TOTAL REDUCTION AMOUNT ?700←(VARIABLE A)

ORIGINAL BUDGET    NEW BUDGET

        850        850
        900        900
        930        830
        1100       1000
        875        875
        960        860
        890        890
        950        850
        925        825
        850        850
        975        875
        1225       1125
```

Requests for keyboard input for array B (label pointing to the list above)

Keyboard input (label for the right column of inputs)

Results

Figure 8-6 Continued

A Program with a Numeric Array and a String Array

Look at the results shown in Figure 8-7. The purpose of this program is to input months and amounts for a varying number of months; print the number of months, the total amount and the monthly average; and then print a report that shows, by month, how much each amount is above or below the monthly average. Notice the flowchart in the illustration. One of your assignments at the end of this unit is to complete the coding to the right of the flowchart, using the flowchart as a guide.

Symbol 10–20 represents the remarks section. Symbol 110–130 represents the establishments of two arrays (B for amounts and M$ for months) and initializes the variables T and N, the subscript, to zero. These arrays should be large enough to hold at least 12 values. Symbol 140–150 represents the instructions for keyboard input. Symbol 160–170 and symbol 180–190 request keyboard input for each month and each amount. Decision symbol 175 tests for the end of input, that is, determine if "DONE" has been input into the month (M$) array. The total of all amounts is accumulated in T, as shown in process symbol 210. Symbol 220 increments the subscript variable N. Flowline 230 directs control back to the input symbol 160–170 to request another input item.

The calculation of the average amount is shown in symbol 240–250. Symbol 260–280 represents the printing of the number of months, the total amount, and the average amount. A heading is represented by symbol 290–310.

Symbol 320 initiates the FOR-NEXT loop. Note that the test value is $N-1$. M$(N) contains the word "DONE"; since we don't want this to print, N is reduced by 1. Decision symbol 330 compares each array element with the monthly average. If an element is below the average, the below-average amount is computed in the PRINT statement and printed along with the month and the total. If an element is above the average, it is printed in the appropriate column as illustrated in the output. If an element is equal to zero, a zero will be displayed under BELOW AVERAGE.

Note that the FOR statement represented by symbol 320 is initialized to 0. This is necessary, because the first elements of each array were placed in the 0 position of the array.

At the conclusion of this unit, return to this example and complete the program from the flowchart. Check your results with the solution given in the Answers to Application Exercises.

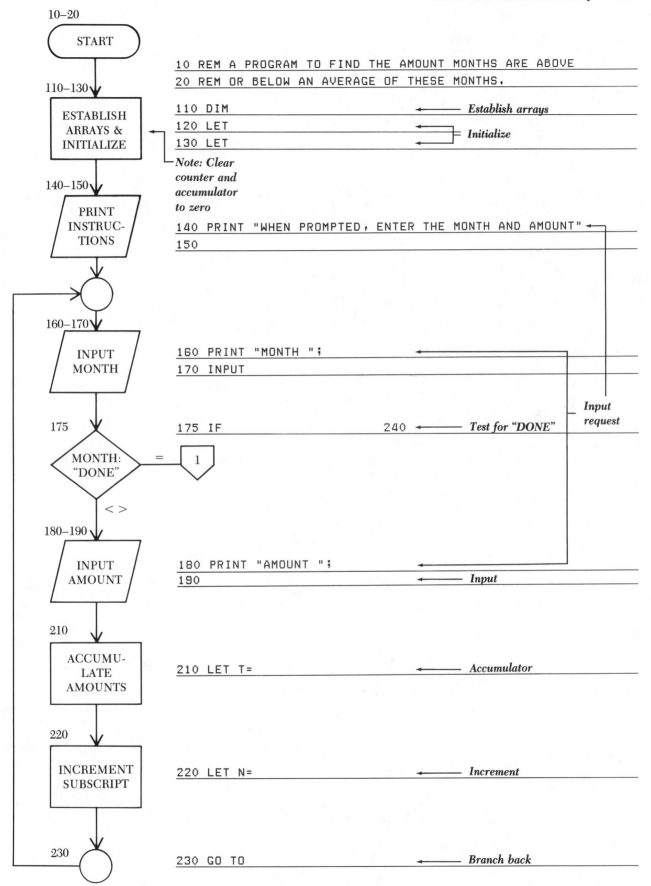

Figure 8-7   A partially completed program with a numeric and a string array

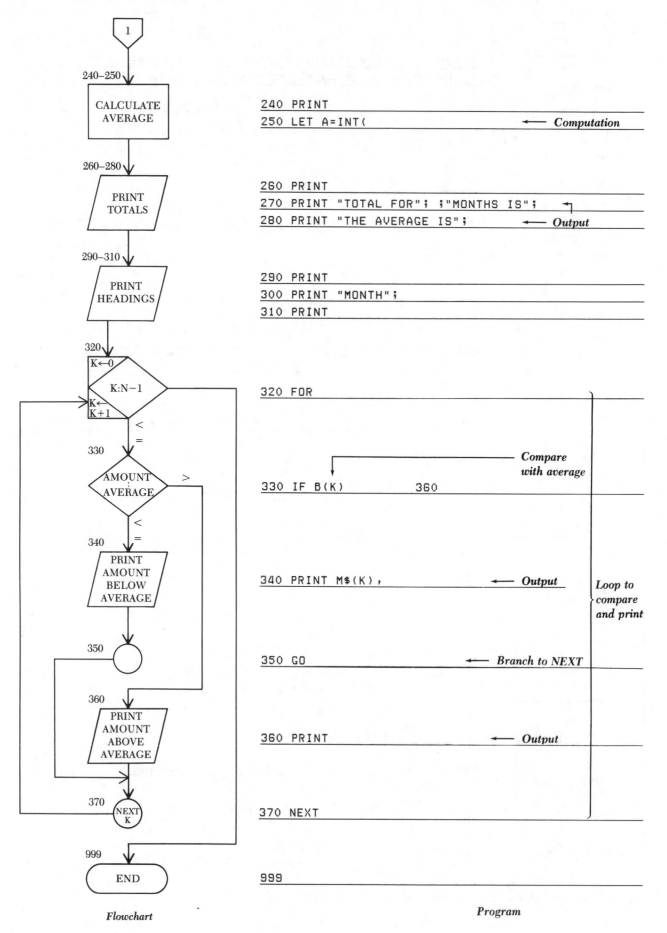

```
        1

240-250
    CALCULATE          240 PRINT
    AVERAGE            250 LET A=INT(                          ←── Computation

260-280
    PRINT             260 PRINT
    TOTALS            270 PRINT "TOTAL FOR"; ;"MONTHS IS";    ⌐
                      280 PRINT "THE AVERAGE IS";             ←── Output

290-310
    PRINT             290 PRINT
    HEADINGS          300 PRINT "MONTH";
                      310 PRINT

320
    K←0
    K:N-1             320 FOR
    K←
    K+1
        <
        =
330                                                          ←── Compare
    AMOUNT    >                                                  with average
    :                 330 IF B(K)        360
    AVERAGE
        <
        =
340
    PRINT
    AMOUNT            340 PRINT M$(K),                       ←── Output
    BELOW
    AVERAGE
                                                                Loop to
350                                                             compare
    ◯                350 GO                   ←── Branch to NEXT   and print

360
    PRINT
    AMOUNT           360 PRINT                               ←── Output
    ABOVE
    AVERAGE

370
    NEXT             370 NEXT
    K

999
    END              999
```

Flowchart   *Program*

Figure 8-7   Continued

```
WHEN PROMPTED, ENTER THE MONTH AND AMOUNT
WHEN THERE ARE NO MORE ENTRIES, ENTER 'DONE'
MONTH ? JAN
AMOUNT ? 850
MONTH ? FEB
AMOUNT ? 900
MONTH ? MAR
AMOUNT ? 930
MONTH ? APR
AMOUNT ? 1100
MONTH ? MAY
AMOUNT ? 1550
MONTH ? JUN
AMOUNT ? 1200
MONTH ? JUL
AMOUNT ? 800
MONTH ? DONE
```

Keyboard input

```
TOTAL FOR 7 MONTHS IS 7330
THE AVERAGE IS 1047
```

MONTH	AMOUNT	ABOVE AVER	BELOW AVER
JAN	850		197
FEB	900		147
MAR	930		117
APR	1100	53	
MAY	1550	503	
JUN	1200	153	
JUL	800		247

Headings

Results

Figure 8-7   Continued

Counting with Arrays

The program in Figure 8-8 counts the votes of three candidates for chairperson without using arrays. A vote for candidate 1, candidate 2, or candidate 3 is indicated by the number 1, 2, or 3 in the DATA statement. Variables P1, P2, and P3 are used to accumulate the vote totals for each candidate.

The more efficient program in Figure 8-9 uses the three-element array P to hold the vote count for each candidate. Statement 60 reads the vote (V) from the DATA statement for candidate 1, 2, or 3. In statement 80, V is used as a subscript variable, indicating which element of the array should be incremented by 1. A vote for candidate 1 would cause the contents of P(1) to be incremented by 1; a vote for candidate 2 would cause the contents of P(2) to be incremented by 1; and a vote for candidate 3 would cause the contents of P(3) to be incremented by 1. Notice that the second program is considerably shorter than the first one.

```
10 DATA 1,3,2,2,2,3,3,2,2,1,1,3,2,1,2,3,3,3,2,2,1
20 DATA 2,1,3,3,3,2,2,2,2,1,1,2,3,3,2,1,1,2,2,3,3,-1
30 LET P1=0
40 LET P2=0
50 LET P3=0
60 READ V
70 IF V=-1 THEN 160
80 IF V=1 THEN 140
90 IF V=2 THEN 120
100 LET P3=P3+1
110 GO TO 60
120 LET P2=P2+1
130 GO TO 60
140 LET P1=P1+1
150 GO TO 60
160 PRINT P1,P2,P3
999 END
```

Figure 8-8   Counting without using an array

```
5 DIM P[3]
10 DATA 1,3,2,2,2,3,3,2,2,1,1,3,2,1,2,3,3,3,2,2,1
20 DATA 2,1,3,3,3,2,2,2,2,1,1,2,3,3,2,1,1,2,2,3,3,-1
30 FOR Z=1 TO 3
40 LET P[Z]=0         Clearing the array to zero since each array
50 NEXT Z             location is a counter
60 READ V
70 IF V=-1 THEN 100
80 LET P[V]=P[V]+1
90 GO TO 60
100 PRINT P[1],P[2],P[3]
999 END
```

Figure 8-9   Counting using an array

PROGRAMMING TECHNIQUES

1. Using the FOR variable as the array element number and subscript:

```
10 DIM X(50)
20 FOR I=1 TO 50
30 PRINT "ITEM NO."; I
40 INPUT X(I)
50 NEXT I
```

2. Clearing an array to zero:

```
10 DIM A(5)
20 FOR I=1 TO 5
30 LET A(I)=0
40 NEXT I
```

3. Counting in an array (continuation of above program):

```
50 PRINT "ENTER CHOICE 1,2,3,4,5, OR -1 TO STOP"
60 INPUT C
65 IF C=-1 THEN 99
70 LET A(C)=A(C)+1
80 GO TO 50
99 END
```

4. Accumulating and averaging the values in an array:

```
120 LET T=0
130 FOR C=1 TO 5
140 LET T=T+M(C)
150 NEXT C
160 PRINT "AVERAGE IS"; T/(C-1)
```

Note: An alternate method is to establish a counter and use the counter as the divisor in statement 160.

5. Copying one array into another array:

```
120 FOR C=1 TO 10
130 LET B(C)=A(C)      (Array B takes on the values of array A)
140 NEXT C
```

DEBUGGING AIDS

ERROR	CAUSE	CORRECTION
10 DIM X(3) 20 FOR I=1 TO 4 30 READ X(I) 40 NEXT I	Subscript exceeds DIM maximum	(Increase size of array) 10 DIM X(10) 20 FOR I=1 TO 4 30 READ X(I) 40 NEXT I
10 DIM X(5) 20 FOR I=1 TO 5 30 INPUT X(1) 40 NEXT I	Incorrect subscript variable used	(Use FOR variable as a subscript) 10 DIM X(5) 20 FOR I=1 TO 5 30 INPUT X(I) 40 NEXT I
10 DIM X(5) 20 FOR I=1 TO 5 30 READ X 40 NEXT I	Failure to use subscript for an array	(All array elements must be subscripted) 10 DIM X(5) 20 FOR I=1 TO 5 30 READ X(I) 40 NEXT I
10 FOR I=1 TO 1000 20 INPUT X(I) 30 NEXT I	Failure to describe array in a DIM statement	(DIMension all arrays) 10 DIM X(1000) 20 FOR I=1 TO 1000 30 INPUT X(I) 40 NEXT I

REFERENCE

DIM STATEMENT SUMMARY

DIM STATEMENT	GENERAL FORM
Specifies the name of one or more arrays and their maximum sizes; precedes first executable statement	10 DIM array name (array size) . . . *Example:* 10 DIM A(50),B$(25)

SUBSCRIPT SUMMARY

DESCRIPTION	VALID FORM	EXAMPLE
A subscript must be:	Constant	S(3)
1. Zero or greater	Variable	A$(I)
2. Equal to or less than the size specified in the DIM statement for the array in which it is used	Variable plus constant	M(X+1)
	Variable minus constant	X(J-1)

APPLICATION EXERCISES

1. Complete the coding of the program in Figure 8-7.
2. Write a single BASIC statement to reserve computer storage for the following arrays:

   C with 20 items, I with 200 items, D$ with 50 items

3. Given the following program and the T array, circle the letter that identifies both the successive values of S and the final value of V when the program is run.

Program	T Array
5 LET S=0	T(1)=2
10 FOR I=2 TO 4 STEP 2	T(2)=3
20 LET S=S+T(I)	T(3)=7
30 NEXT I	T(4)=2
40 LET V=S/5	

	Successive S Values	Final Value of V
a.	0, 3, 1	0.2
b.	0, 3, 1	1
c.	0, 2, 5	1
d.	0, 2, 5	0.2
e.	0, 3, 5	1

4. Complete the following program to input 10 values into the S and T arrays. Accumulate the values in each array. If the total of the values in the S array is less than or equal to the total of the values in the T array, stop the program; if not, print the contents of the S array.

```
10 DIM S(10),T(10)
20 FOR                          ENTER 10 INPUT VALUES
30                              INTO EACH ARRAY
40 NEXT
50 LET A=0                      ACCUMULATOR FOR S ARRAY
60 LET B=0                      ACCUMULATOR FOR T ARRAY
70 FOR
80                              ACCUMULATE TOTALS OF
90                              EACH ARRAY
100 NEXT
110 IF A<=B THEN 999
120 FOR
130                             PRINT THE S ARRAY
140 NEXT
999 END
```

5.   Write a program to place the names of the seven days of the week, beginning with Sunday, into an array from a READ and a DATA statement.

Answers to Application Exercises

1.   (from Figure 8-7)

```
110 DIM B(12),M$(12)
120 LET T=0
130 LET N=0
140 PRINT "WHEN PROMPTED, ENTER THE MONTH AND AMOUNT"
150 PRINT "WHEN THERE ARE NO MORE ENTRIES, ENTER 'DONE'"
160 PRINT "MONTH ";
170 INPUT M$(N)
175 IF M$(N)="DONE" THEN 240
180 PRINT "AMOUNT ";
190 INPUT B(N)
210 LET T=T+B(N)
220 LET N=N+1
230 GO TO 160
240 PRINT
250 LET A=INT(T/N)
260 PRINT
270 PRINT "TOTAL FOR";N;"MONTHS IS";T
280 PRINT "THE AVERAGE IS";A
290 PRINT
300 PRINT "MONTH","AMOUNT","ABOVE AVER","BELOW AVER"
310 PRINT
320 FOR K=0 TO N-1
330 IF B(K)>A THEN 360
340 PRINT M$(K),B(K)"                ",A-B(K)
350 GO TO 370
360 PRINT M$(K),B(K),B(K)-A
370 NEXT K
999 END
```

Figure 8-10   A completed program with a numeric and a string array

2.
```
10 DIM C(20),I(200),D$(50)
```

3.   e

4.
```
10 DIM S(10),T(10)
20 FOR I=1 TO 10
30 INPUT S(I),T(I)
40 NEXT I
50 LET A=0
60 LET B=0
70 FOR I=1 TO 10
80 LET A=A+S(I)
90 LET B=B+T(I)
100 NEXT I
110 IF A<=B THEN 999
120 FOR I=1 TO 10
130 PRINT S(I)
140 NEXT I
999 END
```

5.
```
10 DIM D$(7)
20 DATA "SUNDAY","MONDAY","TUESDAY","WEDNESDAY"
30 DATA "THURSDAY","FRIDAY","SATURDAY"
40 FOR K=1 TO 7
50 READ D$(K)
60 NEXT K
99 END
```

PROGRAMMING PROBLEMS

8-1. Calories Program

Given the number of calories per day for one week and an ideal average calories count, write a program to adjust the calories count of each day so the average calories of the adjusted calories per day will equal the ideal calories count. If the average calories is less than or equal to the ideal average, no adjustment is necessary.

Programming tips:

1. Use the general flowchart in Figure 8-11 as a guide for preparing a detailed flowchart.
2. Truncate calories to a whole number when placing the calories count in the adjusted array.
3. Initialize total to zeros before entering FOR-NEXT loops.
4. The difference between the original calories count and the adjusted calories count can be computed within the PRINT statement.
5. The formula to find the adjustment rate is:
   (average calories − ideal calories)/ideal calories.
6. Each item in the original array multiplied by the adjustment rate equals the difference. The original value minus the difference equals the adjusted value.

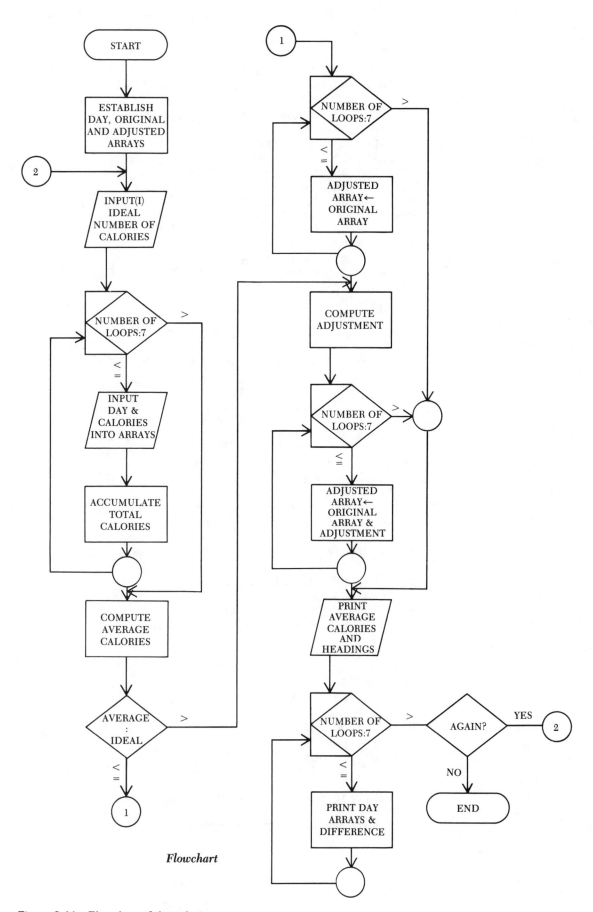

Flowchart

Figure 8-11   Flowchart of the calories program

Results:

```
ENTER THE IDEAL NUMBER OF CALORIES
? 1400
ENTER DAY OF WEEK AND NUMBER OF CALORIES

WHAT DAY OF THE WEEK? MONDAY
HOW MANY CALORIES? 1350
WHAT DAY OF THE WEEK? TUESDAY
HOW MANY CALORIES? 1400
WHAT DAY OF THE WEEK? WEDNESDAY
HOW MANY CALORIES? 1500
WHAT DAY OF THE WEEK? THURSDAY
HOW MANY CALORIES? 1325
WHAT DAY OF THE WEEK? FRIDAY
HOW MANY CALORIES? 1375
WHAT DAY OF THE WEEK? SATURDAY
HOW MANY CALORIES? 1000
WHAT DAY OF THE WEEK? SUNDAY
HOW MANY CALORIES? 1550

AVERAGE CALORIES FOR THE WEEK 1357

DAY           ORIGINAL   ADJUSTED   DIFFERENCE

MONDAY         1350       1350        0
TUESDAY        1400       1400        0
WEDNESDAY      1500       1500        0
THURSDAY       1325       1325        0
FRIDAY         1375       1375        0
SATURDAY       1000       1000        0
SUNDAY         1550       1550        0
TO TRY AGAIN TYPE YES? YES

ENTER THE IDEAL NUMBER OF CALORIES
? 1300
ENTER DAY OF WEEK AND NUMBER OF CALORIES

WHAT DAY OF THE WEEK? SAT
HOW MANY CALORIES? 1050
WHAT DAY OF THE WEEK? SUN
HOW MANY CALORIES? 1600
WHAT DAY OF THE WEEK? MON
HOW MANY CALORIES? 1375
WHAT DAY OF THE WEEK? TUES
HOW MANY CALORIES? 1400
WHAT DAY OF THE WEEK? WED
HOW MANY CALORIES? 1550
WHAT DAY OF THE WEEK? THUR
HOW MANY CALORIES? 1300
WHAT DAY OF THE WEEK? FRI
HOW MANY CALORIES? 1400

AVERAGE CALORIES FOR THE WEEK 1382
```

Figure 8-12   Results of the calories program

```
DAY          ORIGINAL   ADJUSTED   DIFFERENCE

SAT          1050       983        67
SUN          1600       1498       102
MON          1375       1288       87
TUES         1400       1311       89
WED          1550       1452       98
THUR         1300       1217       83
FRI          1400       1311       89
TO TRY AGAIN TYPE YES? NO
```

Note: Due to computer differences, your results may not match exactly.

Figure 8-12   Continued

8-2. Golf-Handicap Program

Given a varying number of golfers and their golf score handicaps, write a program to schedule a golf tournament. Golfers with similar handicaps should be grouped together in a foursome. Follow these guidelines:

1. Include the following DATA statements in your program:

    ```
    DATA 5,4,3,1,8,35,4,10,1,40,7,30,6,20,2,20
    DATA 15,10,16,15,9,30,10,25,13,25,12,5,11,10,14,30
    ```

2. Each pair of numbers in the DATA statements represents the golfer's number and handicap (golfer 5 has a handicap of 4, golfer 3 has a handicap of 1, etc.). The values should be placed in the handicap array, X, in golfer number order.
3. Golfer numbers should be placed in a second array, the foursome array, Z, according to their handicaps.
4. Allow for as many as 72 participants.
5. Golfers with below-average handicaps should tee off first.

    Programming tips:

1. Draw a flowchart of the solution.
2. Data should be read into a handicap array by a FOR-NEXT loop with two READ statements. The first READ indicates the position of the array (READ K), and the second READ indicates the handicap value that is to go into the array (READ X(K)).
3. While reading the data into the handicap array, accumulate a total to be used to find the average handicap.
4. Before the FOR-NEXT loop is entered to place the golfer numbers into the foursome array according to their handicaps, two counters should be initialized. One counter will place golfer numbers with below-average handicaps into the low-order position of the foursome array (LET L=1), and the other will place the remaining golfer numbers into the high-order positions of the foursome array (LET H=number of golfers). The counters must be incremented and decremented as values are placed into the low-order or high-order positions of the foursome array from within the loop.
5. When displaying the foursome array, use subscript arithmetic to display four values per line (Z(I), Z(I+1), Z(I+2), Z(I+3)).

Results:

```
HOW MANY GOLFERS? 16

GOLFER #   HANDICAP

     1            40
     2            20
     3            1
     4            10
     5            4
     6            20
     7            30
     8            35
     9            30
    10            25
    11            10
    12            5
    13            25
    14            30
    15            10
    16            15

TEE OFF #       FOURSOME

     1          3     4     5    11
     2         12    15    16    14
     3         13    10     9     8
     4          7     6     2     1
```

Figure 8-13   Results of the golf-handicap program

9 Two-Dimensional Arrays

OBJECTIVES

When you complete this unit, you will be able to:

1. Write a dimension statement, given a description of one or more one- or two-dimensional arrays
2. Given a problem with or without a flowchart:
   a. Write a program to read data into a two-dimensional array, manipulate its contents, and write out the array and/or results of the manipulation
   b. Write a program using nested FOR and NEXT statements to process a two-dimensional array
3. Code and execute a BASIC solution to a problem that requires placing values into a two-dimensional array, manipulating the array, and outputting results

INTRODUCTION

What Are Two-Dimensional Arrays?

In a previous unit we discussed arrays of one dimension. Sometimes it is necessary to store numeric or string values in a matrix where the values must be accessed by their row and column locations. Processing two-dimensional arrays is usually accomplished within nested FOR-NEXT loops.

Nested FOR-NEXT Loops

Programmers often use one FOR-NEXT loop within another FOR-NEXT loop; this is called a *nested* FOR-NEXT loop. A nested FOR-NEXT loop is one whose range is contained entirely within the range of another FOR-NEXT loop. Figure 9-1 shows a FOR-NEXT loop (statements 40 through 60) nested within another (statements 20 through 70). When the outer FOR statement is first encountered in the program, A is replaced by 1. Statements following the FOR statement, if any, are executed until the next inner FOR statement is encountered. At this point, B is replaced by 1. The inner FOR-NEXT loop advances faster than the outer loop and is executed 10 times as B advances from 1 to 10. The eleventh time, when B is incremented to 11, control drops to the statement following statement 60, because the test value was exceeded. The outer FOR-NEXT loop then continues. The next time that the outer FOR statement is executed, A becomes 2. Statements following the outer FOR statement are then executed. When the inner FOR statement is encountered, B is again initialized to 1 and the inner FOR-NEXT loop is executed 10 times. This process continues until the FOR variable in the outer FOR statement exceeds its test value.

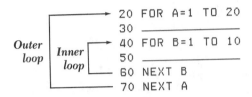

Figure 9-1   Nested FOR-NEXT loops

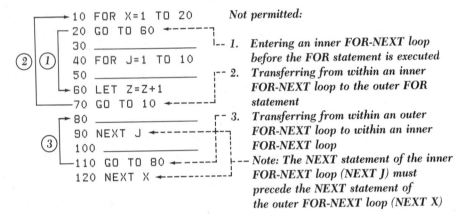

Figure 9-2   Nested FOR-NEXT loop rules

There are several transfers within nested FOR-NEXT loops that usually result in an incorrect program. In Figure 9-2, encircled arrow 1 shows a transfer from the outer FOR-NEXT loop to the inner FOR-NEXT loop without initializing the inner FOR statement at line 40. This transfer is incorrect. Encircled arrow 2 shows another improper transfer, from the middle of the inner FOR-NEXT loop to the outer FOR statement; this reinitializes X to 1 instead of incrementing it by 1. The transfer should occur to NEXT statement 120, to continue the outer FOR-NEXT loop. Encircled arrow 3 shows an incorrect transfer into the middle of the inner FOR-NEXT loop from the outer loop.

Another requirement for nested FOR-NEXT loops is that the last statement in an inner FOR-NEXT loop should never be beyond the last statement of the outer FOR-NEXT loop in which it is contained.

Figure 9-3 illustrates a nest of three FOR-NEXT loops. Statement 50 will be executed one million times, because the outer loop executes 100 times; the next inner loop, 100 multiplied by 100, or 10,000 times; and the innermost loop, 10,000 multiplied by 100, or a million times. This occurs because each time the innermost loop is executed, control goes to the next outer loop, which is incremented by 1, and the inner loop is then executed the times indicated. This short program does take quite a bit of computer time, so we suggest that you do *not* run this program on your computer.

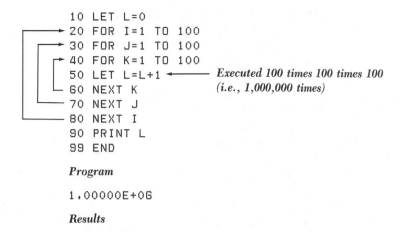

```
10 LET L=0
20 FOR I=1 TO 100
30 FOR J=1 TO 100
40 FOR K=1 TO 100
50 LET L=L+1   ←——— Executed 100 times 100 times 100
60 NEXT K              (i.e., 1,000,000 times)
70 NEXT J
80 NEXT I
90 PRINT L
99 END
```

Program

1.00000E+06

Results

Figure 9-3   Two nested FOR-NEXT loops

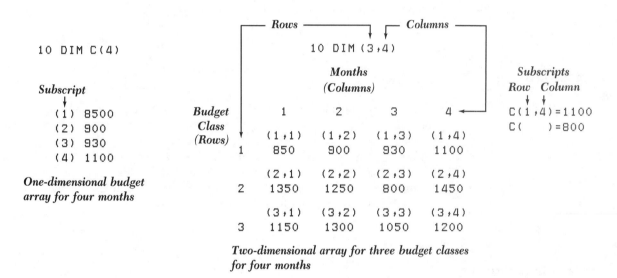

Two-dimensional array for three budget classes for four months

Figure 9-4   A two-dimensional array

Two-Dimensional Arrays

In the left portion of Figure 9-4, you can see the one-dimensional C array representing four months; this is similar to an array we discussed in an earlier unit. When discussing the one-dimensional array, we said that it was simply a list or table of related data items of defined length stored in reserved areas of computer storage. In the C array in Figure 9-4, the DIM statement in line 10 defines the length as four. A two-dimensional array has both a defined length (called *rows*) and a defined width (called *columns*). You can see that the two-dimensional C array on the right in Figure 9-4 consists of three rows for different budget classes, and four columns for different months. The rows are horizontal; the columns are vertical. If you have trouble remembering this, it might be helpful to think of columns as the vertical columns or pillars at the front of a building and rows as the horizontal rows in a theater.

In the unit on one-dimensional arrays, we mentioned that (for our purposes) the main difference between one- and two-dimensional arrays is the number of subscripts required to refer to them. Only one subscript is needed to refer to a particular element of a one-dimensional array. For instance, C(4) refers to the fourth element of the array, which has a value of 1100. In the two-dimensional array on the right in Figure 9-4, two subscripts are required to describe the element or location containing 1100, because this is a two-dimensional array. Since 1100 is located in row 1, column 4, we can describe its location as C(1,4), as we have shown to the right of the array. Now to be sure that you understand this, enter the proper subscripts within the empty parentheses, to identify the location in the C array containing the value of 800. Don't forget that the row is always entered as the first subscript, and the column is entered second.

Following the array name C, you should have entered 2,3 inside the parentheses, to represent the second row and the third column, where the value 800 is stored. Like the one-dimensional array, on most systems the two-dimensional array can contain string values as well as numeric values. The maximum length of a string value within an array varies among different BASIC systems.

At the conclusion of this unit, you might want to try describing other locations for practice. We have entered the subscripts within parentheses above the values in each array location, so you can check them yourself.

Subscripts

The requirements for subscripting two-dimensional arrays are the same as those for one-dimensional arrays. Subscripts must be positive integers and can be either a variable, a constant, or both. Two-dimensional arrays have the same capabilities for dealing with array elements as do one-dimensional arrays. Each element can be read, written, manipulated, and controlled within FOR-NEXT loops. The only additional requirement is that you specify two subscripts. Later in the unit we will present several illustrations using two-dimensional arrays.

The DIM Statement

A DIM statement is required to reserve storage for two-dimensional arrays, just as for one-dimensional arrays. The only difference is that more entries are required within the parentheses following the name of a two-dimensional array. You will see examples of two acceptable DIM statements in Figure 9-5. The same provisions that apply to DIM statements for one-dimensional arrays, regarding maximum size and placement in the program, also apply to two-dimensional arrays. It is also important to remember the proper order for entering subscripts: rows are first, followed by columns. One-dimensional and two-dimensional numeric and string arrays can be described in a single DIM statement, as illustrated in statement 50 of Figure 9-5.

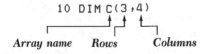

```
10 DIM C(3,4)
```
Array name   Rows   Columns

```
50 DIM C(3,4),R(50),X$(10,10)
```

Figure 9-5   DIM statements for one- and two-dimensional arrays

Programs with Two-Dimensional Arrays

In Figure 9-6, the program at the top of the figure sums each *column* of the X array, and the second program below sums each *row* of the X array. To make these programs easier to follow, a graphic representation of the X array appears on the right in the middle of the figure.

Look at the program at the top of the figure. Statement 20 establishes X as an array containing two rows and three columns. Statements 30 through 80 assign values to each array element. (These assignments could also be made with a READ or an INPUT statement.) Statement 90 is the FOR statement for the outer loop. The outer loop of nested FOR-NEXT loops executes slowest because the FOR variable is incremented only after the inner FOR-NEXT loop has been completed, whereas the inner FOR-NEXT loop, beginning at statement 110, executes fastest because it is completed each time the outer FOR variable is incremented. To determine which FOR-NEXT loop is to go fastest and which is to go slowest, you must decide how you want to manipulate the array. When referring to an array element, the row subscript must be first and the column subscript second. It is strongly recommended that you use R to represent the row and C to represent the column.

If you want to manipulate each element within a column, the column is represented by the FOR variable of the outer or slowest loop. Statement 90 of the first program assigns the value 1 to C, representing column 1. Statement 110 assigns the value 1 to R, representing row 1. Statement 120 adds the element at $X(1,1)$, a value of 10, to a total represented by T. Statement 130 passes control back to the inner FOR statement, because the inner loop executes repeatedly until the test value is exceeded. When statement 110 is executed the second time, C will still have a value of 1 and R will have a value of 2. Now when statement 120 is executed, the element at $X(2,1)$, a value of 30, will be added to T. T now has a value of 40. Statement 130 sends control back to statement 110 for one more increment. Since the inner loop has been executed the correct number of times, because R has exceeded the test value of 2, control passes to statements 140 and 150, which print the total of the column. The first line of ouput prints the correct total of column 1, which is 40, as shown.

Statement 160 is the next statement to be executed. It passes control back to statement 90, which adds 1 to C. C now has a value of 2. Statement 100 initializes T to 0, since we have totaled column 1 and we now want to add the elements in the second column. Statement 110 assigns 1 to R again. When statement 120 is executed this time, the element at $X(1,2)$—row 1, column 2—will be added to T. On the second pass through this inner loop, $X(2,2)$ will be added to T to give the total of the elements in the second column. Statement 90 will increment C by 1 again and start the two loops again for the third and last time. C will have a value of 3, and the inner loop then adds $X(1,3)$ and $X(2,3)$ to get the total of the last column.

The second program in Figure 9-6 adds rows. To add the elements in each row, we start with a FOR statement that increments the FOR variable R, which is the slowest, as shown in statement 90. In the inner loop, the FOR variable C will execute the fastest, as shown in statement 110. On the first pass through the inner loop, $X(1,1)$ is added to T, then $X(1,2)$ is added, and finally $X(1,3)$. T now contains the total of the elements in the first row (70). When the outer loop is executed for the second and final time, $X(2,1)$, $X(2,2)$, and $X(2,3)$ are added to form the sum of the elements in the second row.

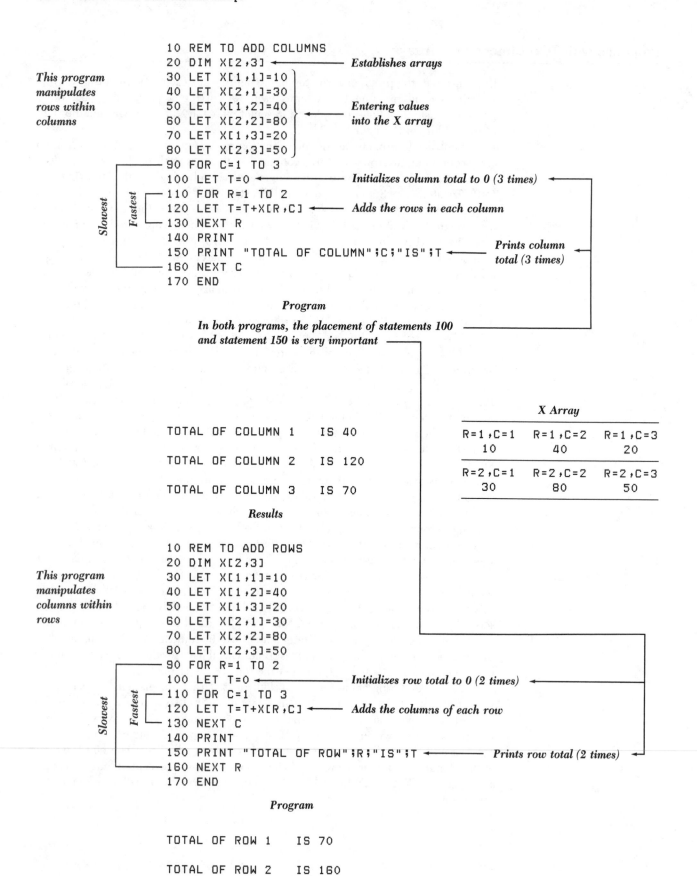

This program manipulates rows within columns

```
10 REM TO ADD COLUMNS
20 DIM X[2,3]          ← Establishes arrays
30 LET X[1,1]=10
40 LET X[2,1]=30
50 LET X[1,2]=40       ← Entering values
60 LET X[2,2]=80          into the X array
70 LET X[1,3]=20
80 LET X[2,3]=50
90 FOR C=1 TO 3
100 LET T=0            ← Initializes column total to 0 (3 times)
110 FOR R=1 TO 2
120 LET T=T+X[R,C]     ← Adds the rows in each column
130 NEXT R
140 PRINT
150 PRINT "TOTAL OF COLUMN";C;"IS";T   ← Prints column
160 NEXT C                                total (3 times)
170 END
```

Program

In both programs, the placement of statements 100 and statement 150 is very important

```
TOTAL OF COLUMN 1    IS 40

TOTAL OF COLUMN 2    IS 120

TOTAL OF COLUMN 3    IS 70
```

Results

X Array		
R=1,C=1	R=1,C=2	R=1,C=3
10	40	20
R=2,C=1	R=2,C=2	R=2,C=3
30	80	50

This program manipulates columns within rows

```
10 REM TO ADD ROWS
20 DIM X[2,3]
30 LET X[1,1]=10
40 LET X[1,2]=40
50 LET X[1,3]=20
60 LET X[2,1]=30
70 LET X[2,2]=80
80 LET X[2,3]=50
90 FOR R=1 TO 2
100 LET T=0            ← Initializes row total to 0 (2 times)
110 FOR C=1 TO 3
120 LET T=T+X[R,C]     ← Adds the columns of each row
130 NEXT C
140 PRINT
150 PRINT "TOTAL OF ROW";R;"IS";T   ← Prints row total (2 times)
160 NEXT R
170 END
```

Program

```
TOTAL OF ROW 1    IS 70

TOTAL OF ROW 2    IS 160
```

Figure 9-6 Adding rows and columns   *Results*

The Budget Array

The array in Figure 9-7 will be used in the next two programs of this unit. The columns of the array represent the 12 months of the year; the rows represent 10 budget categories, which are described on the left. To find the clothing budget for the month of September, look for the value in row 5 and column 9, where you find 0. How much will be spent for education during the month of December? The correct answer is 44, which appears in row 9, column 12.

Figure 9-7 also shows the results of a program that accepts a code from a keyboard and then takes the action specified by the code. If code 1 is entered, the program requests a specific budget-category number and a month number and then prints the contents of this location. If code 2 is entered, the totals of the monthly budgets are printed. Code 3 ends the program.

The flowchart and the program that produced the results are shown in Figure 9-8. The start symbol in the flowchart represents the program remarks and statement 110, which establishes the 10-by-12 budget array. Symbol 120 establishes the outer FOR-NEXT loop that will increment the column subscript, C, the slowest. Symbol 130 establishes the inner loop that will increment the row subscript, R, the fastest. Symbol 140–260 represents the reading of the data items into the array B.

Can you see why C is in the outer loop and R in the inner loop? Look at the 12 DATA statements in the program, each representing one month. Each DATA statement contains 10 entries—one for each budget category in a month. Since DATA statements assign values sequentially from left to right, the data items will be placed into every row of a column. When 10 items have been assigned to a column, the next DATA statement causes values to be assigned to the next column, and so on, until all columns have been filled.

Suppose there were ten DATA statements, each representing a budget category, containing entries for each of the 12 months. How would they change this portion of the program? Remember, if the elements of the row are to be manipulated—in this case, read—the row subscript is incremented slowest in the outer loop. Therefore, if this were the case, the two FOR statements would be interchanged, as would the two NEXT statements.

In the flowchart, symbol 290–300 requests keyboard input to determine which code is to be entered. The BASIC coding is in statements 290 and 300. Statement 310 prints the requested code. Decision symbols 320, 330, and 340 test the code to determine what action to take next. Statement 320 passes control to statement 360 if the code is 1; statement 330 passes control to statement 420 if the code is 2; statement 340 passes control to statement 510 if the code is 3. If the code is not 1, 2, or 3, the program branches to statement 530, where an error message is printed. Statement 540 transfers control back to statement 290 to get corrected input. Look again at symbol 320. If the code is 1, the exit to the right is taken to off-page connector 1. The off-page connector symbol is used to show the connection of flowchart symbols on different pages. Connector 1 points to symbol 360–370, which asks for keyboard input: the expense category number, R, and the month number, C. We are asking the program to look for the value stored in a specific row and column of the array. Whatever is input for R and C can then be used to print the element stored at B(R,C). Look at the output produced in Figure 9-7 as a result of statements 360 through 400 in Figure 9-8.

In the flowchart off-page connector 5 and statement 410 on page 194 transfer control back to statement 290 on page 193 where another code is requested. Symbol 330 illustrates that the exit to the right is taken, if the code assigned by input from the keyboard is 2. Statement 330 provides for a transfer to statement 420 as a result of this condition.

Code 2 means that the requester wants the total for each budget month printed. Since we want to total each of the 12 columns, C will be the FOR variable in

Expense Category	No.	Jan 1	Feb 2	Mar 3	Apr 4	May 5	Jun 6	Jul 7	Aug 8	Sep 9	Oct 10	Nov 11	Dec 12
Food	1	187	190	196	232	189	203	189	202	195	187	205	254
Housing	2	150	150	150	150	150	150	150	150	150	150	150	150
Util.	3	128	135	140	165	131	137	127	136	139	128	139	187
Trans.	4	102	108	112	132	105	109	101	108	111	102	111	154
Cloth.	5	85	90	93	110	88	91	84	90	0	85	93	132
Med. care	6	68	72	74	88	70	72	67	71	73	68	74	110
Recrea.	7	58	13	65	77	60	62	57	61	64	58	64	99
Savings	8	42	45	46	55	44	45	41	44	45	52	47	77
Educ.	9	17	68	19	22	18	18	16	17	108	17	20	44
Misc.	10	8	29	5	69	20	73	7	71	38	8	75	18

Data

```
WHAT IS THE CODE ? 1
CODE = 1  ←—— Code 1 selects the budget amount, given the budget category and month

WHAT IS THE EXPENSE NUMBER AND MONTH NUMBER ? 5,8
THE AMOUNT OF THE BUDGET
FOR CATEGORY NUMBER 5                                        Output from
AND FOR MONTH NUMBER 8                                       statements 360–400
IS 90


WHAT IS THE CODE ? 2
CODE = 2  ←—— Code 2 totals the budget for each month

TOTAL BUDGET FOR MONTH 1 IS 845

TOTAL BUDGET FOR MONTH 2 IS 900

TOTAL BUDGET FOR MONTH 3 IS 900

TOTAL BUDGET FOR MONTH 4 IS 1100

TOTAL BUDGET FOR MONTH 5 IS 875

TOTAL BUDGET FOR MONTH 6 IS 960
                                                             Output from
TOTAL BUDGET FOR MONTH 7 IS 839                              statements 470–480

TOTAL BUDGET FOR MONTH 8 IS 950

TOTAL BUDGET FOR MONTH 9 IS 923

TOTAL BUDGET FOR MONTH 10 IS 855

TOTAL BUDGET FOR MONTH 11 IS 978

TOTAL BUDGET FOR MONTH 12 IS 1225

WHAT IS THE CODE ? 3
CODE = 3  ←—— Code 3 ends the report

                        Output from
END OF REPORT  ←——      statement 510
```

Results

Figure 9-7   Data and results of a program with a two-dimensional array

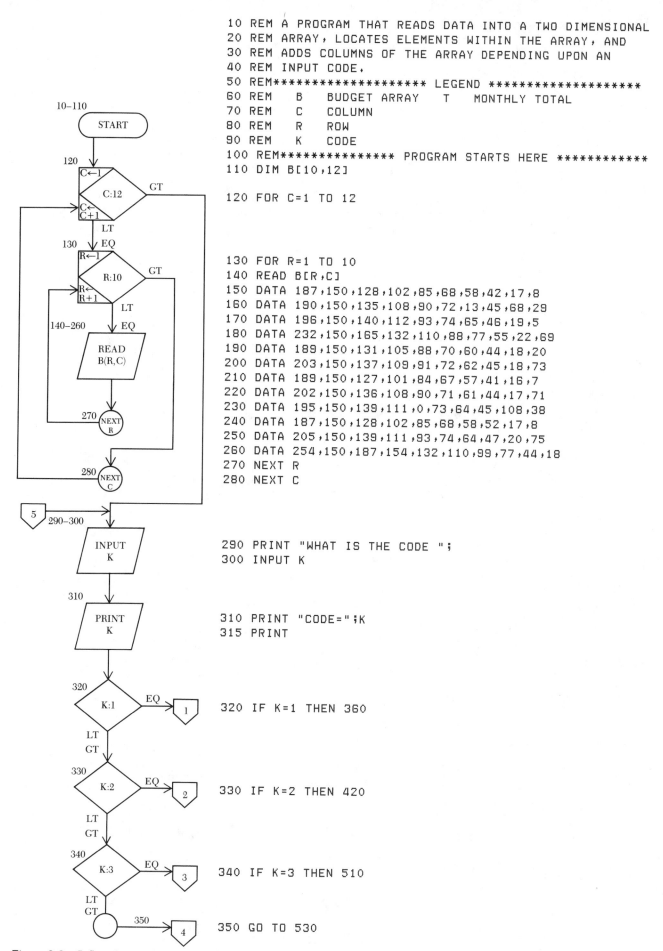

```
10 REM A PROGRAM THAT READS DATA INTO A TWO DIMENSIONAL
20 REM ARRAY, LOCATES ELEMENTS WITHIN THE ARRAY, AND
30 REM ADDS COLUMNS OF THE ARRAY DEPENDING UPON AN
40 REM INPUT CODE.
50 REM******************** LEGEND ********************
60 REM    B    BUDGET ARRAY    T    MONTHLY TOTAL
70 REM    C    COLUMN
80 REM    R    ROW
90 REM    K    CODE
100 REM************** PROGRAM STARTS HERE ************
110 DIM B[10,12]

120 FOR C=1 TO 12



130 FOR R=1 TO 10
140 READ B[R,C]
150 DATA 187,150,128,102,85,68,58,42,17,8
160 DATA 190,150,135,108,90,72,13,45,68,29
170 DATA 196,150,140,112,93,74,65,46,19,5
180 DATA 232,150,165,132,110,88,77,55,22,69
190 DATA 189,150,131,105,88,70,60,44,18,20
200 DATA 203,150,137,109,91,72,62,45,18,73
210 DATA 189,150,127,101,84,67,57,41,16,7
220 DATA 202,150,136,108,90,71,61,44,17,71
230 DATA 195,150,139,111,0,73,64,45,108,38
240 DATA 187,150,128,102,85,68,58,52,17,8
250 DATA 205,150,139,111,93,74,64,47,20,75
260 DATA 254,150,187,154,132,110,99,77,44,18
270 NEXT R
280 NEXT C




290 PRINT "WHAT IS THE CODE ";
300 INPUT K



310 PRINT "CODE=";K
315 PRINT




320 IF K=1 THEN 360




330 IF K=2 THEN 420




340 IF K=3 THEN 510




350 GO TO 530
```

Figure 9-8 A flowchart and a program with a two-dimensional array

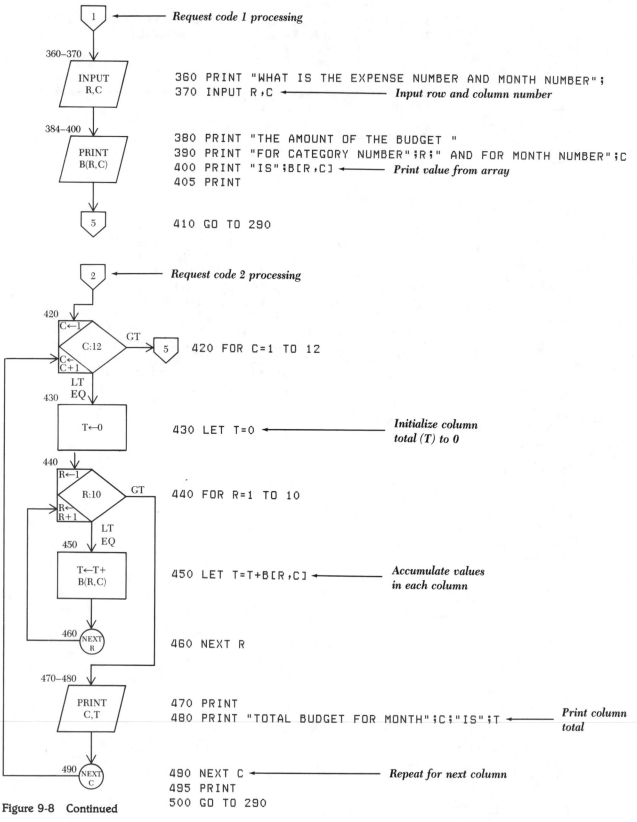

```
360-370     360 PRINT "WHAT IS THE EXPENSE NUMBER AND MONTH NUMBER";
            370 INPUT R,C ◄──────────── Input row and column number

384-400     380 PRINT "THE AMOUNT OF THE BUDGET "
            390 PRINT "FOR CATEGORY NUMBER";R;" AND FOR MONTH NUMBER";C
            400 PRINT "IS";B[R,C] ◄──── Print value from array
            405 PRINT

            410 GO TO 290
```

Request code 1 processing

Request code 2 processing

```
420         420 FOR C=1 TO 12

430         430 LET T=0 ◄──────────── Initialize column
                                        total (T) to 0

440         440 FOR R=1 TO 10

450         450 LET T=T+B[R,C] ◄──── Accumulate values
                                        in each column

460         460 NEXT R

470-480     470 PRINT
            480 PRINT "TOTAL BUDGET FOR MONTH";C;"IS";T ◄── Print column
                                                              total

490         490 NEXT C ◄──────────── Repeat for next column
            495 PRINT
            500 GO TO 290
```

Figure 9-8   Continued

Request code 3 processing

510 PRINT "END OF REPORT"

520 GO TO 550

530 PRINT "VALID CODES ARE 1,2 AND 3. TRY AGAIN." ← *Error recovery*

540 GO TO 290

550 END

Flowchart

Figure 9-8   Continued

the outer loop, as shown in statement 420. Symbol 430 and statement 430 clear T to 0, because the sum of each column will be accumulated here. On page 194 statement 440 increments the row subscript R, with a limit of 10, because there are 10 expense categories—each represented by a row number. Statement 450 adds each expense category to a total that is printed by statements 470 and 480 each time the inner loop is completed. After the total of each of the 12 months has been printed, statement 500 transfers control back to statement 290 to request another code.

Flowchart symbol 340 illustrates that the exit to the right is taken, if the input code is 3. Statement 340 transfers control to statement 510 to print an end message and stop the program.

Partially Completed Budget Program

Read the REMARK statements explaining the program in Figure 9-10 which produces the results in Figure 9-9.

At the conclusion of this unit, we will ask you to study this problem and partial solution, and then complete the program with the aid of the flowchart.

You should note several points before completing this program: Statements 110 through 280 are identical to statements 110 through 280 of the previous program, Figure 9-8, since we are using the same array. Statement 310, the FOR statement, begins a loop to print the entire array. It is not necessary to use nested FOR-NEXT loops in this section of the program, because the column number in statements 320 and 330 is represented by a subscript that is a constant rather than a variable. A nested FOR-NEXT loop could be used instead of the constant as the column subscript; the printed results would be identical.

Symbols 380 through 440 of the flowchart are used to step through each expense category, that is, row. This is why the outer FOR statement is used to increment the row—FOR variable R. On the other hand, symbols 490 through 570 illustrate the steps necessary to search columns; therefore, the FOR variable C is in the outer loop. At the conclusion of this unit, study this problem, complete the program from the flowchart, and check your results with the solutions given in the Answers to Application Exercises.

Counting with a Two-Dimensional Array

Do you recall how a single array was used to keep counts? This technique was used to count votes for three candidates. The program in Figure 9-11 on page 201 uses a two-dimensional array to keep count of the ratings given to these candidates. Each candidate is rated on a scale from 1 for excellent to 5 for poor. The ratings for each of the three candidates are shown in DATA statements 20, 30, and 40. Statements 50 through 90 clear the T array to 0. We must do this because each position of the array will act as an individual counter—a count of the number of individual ratings for each candidate. Take a moment to fill the T array with zeros.

The nested FOR-NEXT loops in statements 100 through 150 control reading of data into the X array at statement 120 and counting the ratings at statement 130. We will now enter values into these arrays as directed by the program. When statement 100 is executed, R will be equal to 1. In the space provided on the right, put a 1 under R, which represents the row. Statement 110 initializes C to 1, so write 1 under C, which represents the column. Statement 120 now reads the first data item, 1, and puts it into row 1 and column 1 of the X array. Put 1 in the X array.

Statement 130 counts the ratings. This means add a 1 into row 1, column 1 of the T array. R is used as the first subscript of T, and it has value of 1. Look at the

Output from the budget array, statements 290–340

BUDGET

187	190	196	232	189	203	189	202	195	187	205	254
150	150	150	150	150	150	150	150	150	150	150	150
128	135	140	165	131	137	127	136	139	128	139	187
102	108	112	132	105	109	101	108	111	102	111	154
85	90	93	110	88	91	84	90	0	85	93	132
68	72	74	88	70	72	67	71	73	68	74	110
58	13	65	77	60	62	57	61	64	58	64	99
42	45	46	55	44	45	41	44	45	52	47	77
17	68	19	22	18	18	16	17	108	17	20	44
8	29	5	69	20	73	7	71	38	8	75	18

BUDGET CATEGORIES CONTAINING ITEMS OVER $100

```
              1
              2
              3
              4      Output from statements 370–440    (2)
              5
              6
              9
```

MONTH	BUDGET CATEGORY	LOWEST AMOUNT
1	10	8
2	7	13
3	10	5
4	9	22
5	9	18
6	9	18
7	10	7
8	9	17
9	5	0
10	10	8
11	9	20
12	10	18

Output from statements 450–570   (3)

Figure 9-9   Results of a partially completed program with a two-dimensional array

second subscript used to designate the column for the T array. This subscript is represented by X(R,C). To get the second subscript, BASIC goes to the X array for the contents of X(1,1). There is a 1 in this position; therefore, the effect of this instruction is to add a 1 to T(1,1). Since T(1,1) contained 0 initially, the result will be 1. Put 1 in T(1,1).

Statement 140 transfers control back to statement 110, which increments C by 1. Change the column variable C to 2. Statement 120 now reads the second data element from statement 20, a 1, into row 1 and column 2 of the X array. Write 1 there. Statement 130 now adds 1 to T(1,1), because R is still equal to 1, and to column 1, because the column representation is X(R,C)—R has a value of 1 and C has a value of 2. Look at the contents of X(1,2)—it contains 1, and that is why a 1 will be added to T(1,1). Carry out this addition in the T array. T(1,1) will now contain 2—C then becomes 3. Statement 120 reads the third data item (3) into row 1, column 3. Enter this value into the X array.

When statement 130 is executed, 1 will be added to row 1 and column 3 of the T array. The column is 3 because that column is contained in X(1,3). The program

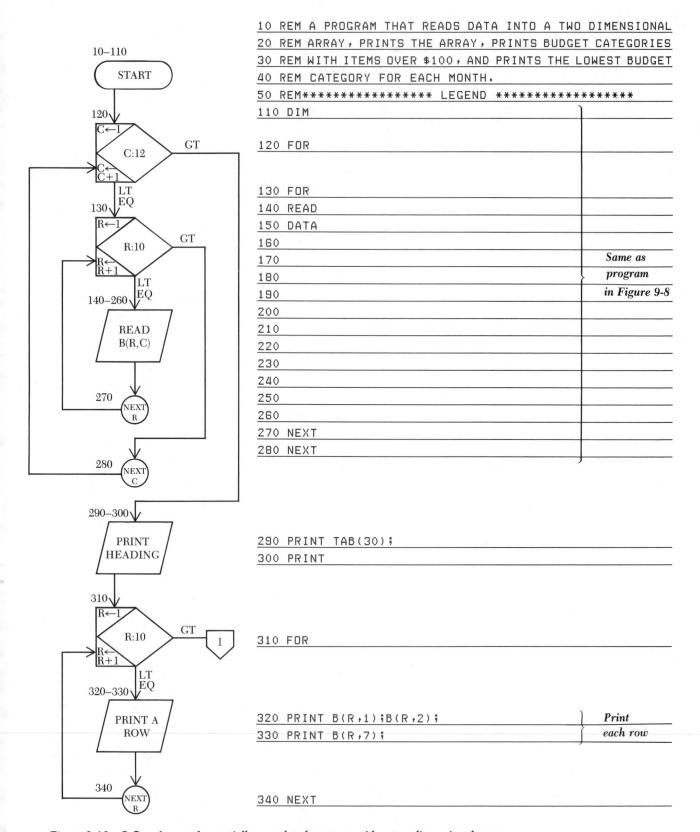

```
10 REM A PROGRAM THAT READS DATA INTO A TWO DIMENSIONAL
20 REM ARRAY, PRINTS THE ARRAY, PRINTS BUDGET CATEGORIES
30 REM WITH ITEMS OVER $100, AND PRINTS THE LOWEST BUDGET
40 REM CATEGORY FOR EACH MONTH.
50 REM***************** LEGEND *****************
110 DIM
120 FOR
130 FOR
140 READ
150 DATA
160
170
180
190
200
210
220
230
240
250
260
270 NEXT
280 NEXT
290 PRINT TAB(30);
300 PRINT
310 FOR
320 PRINT B(R,1);B(R,2);
330 PRINT B(R,7);
340 NEXT
```

Same as program in Figure 9-8

Print each row

Figure 9-10   A flowchart and a partially completed program with a two-dimensional array

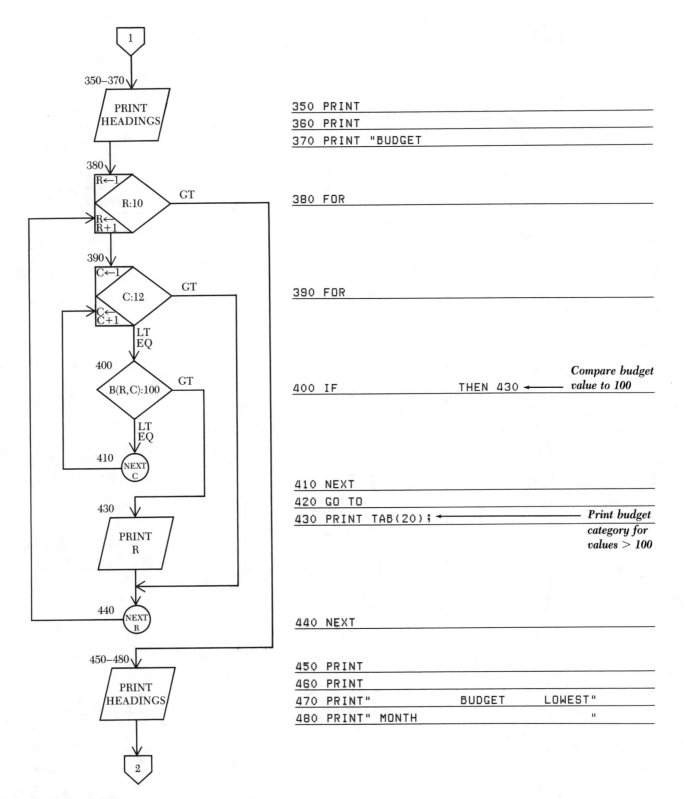

350 PRINT _____

360 PRINT _____

370 PRINT "BUDGET _____

380 FOR _____

390 FOR _____

400 IF _____ THEN 430 ⟵——— *Compare budget value to 100*

410 NEXT _____

420 GO TO _____

430 PRINT TAB(20); ⟵——— *Print budget category for values > 100*

440 NEXT _____

450 PRINT _____

460 PRINT _____

470 PRINT"   BUDGET   LOWEST"

480 PRINT" MONTH   "

Figure 9-10   Continued

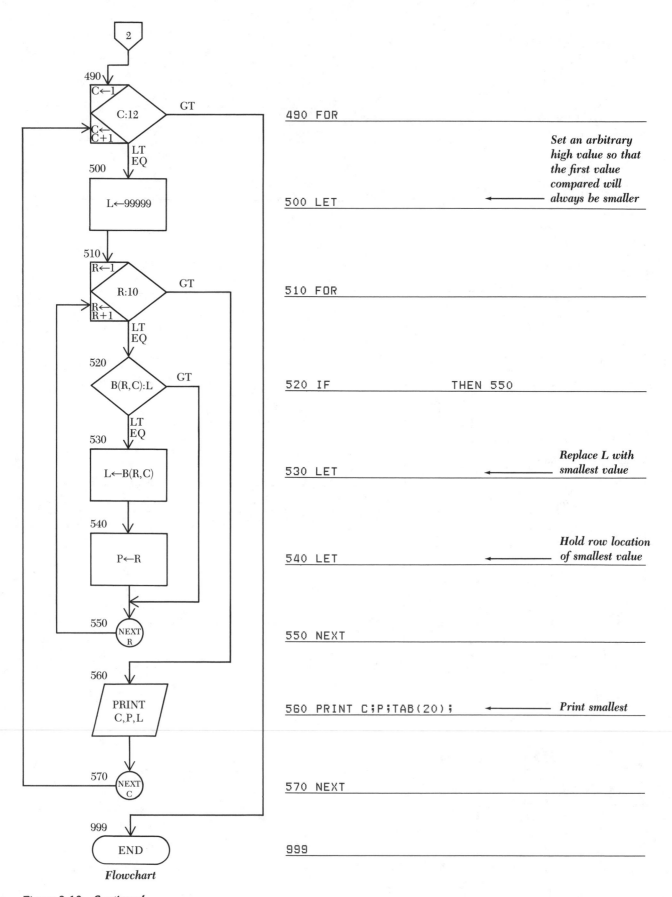

490 FOR _____

Set an arbitrary high value so that the first value compared will always be smaller

500 LET _____

510 FOR _____

520 IF _____ THEN 550 _____

Replace L with smallest value

530 LET _____

Hold row location of smallest value

540 LET _____

550 NEXT _____

560 PRINT C;P;TAB(20); ←——— *Print smallest*

570 NEXT _____

999 _____

Flowchart

Figure 9-10 Continued

continues using the contents of the X array as a subscript for the T array, until the nested FOR-NEXT loops are completed.

At the conclusion of this unit, continue inserting values into both arrays until they are complete. Check your work with the results shown in Figure 9-11.

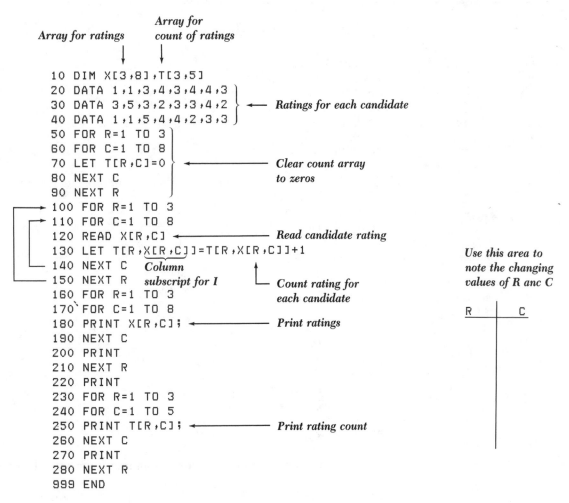

```
                   Array for
Array for ratings  count of ratings

10 DIM X[3,8],T[3,5]
20 DATA 1,1,3,4,3,4,4,3
30 DATA 3,5,3,2,3,3,4,2   ← Ratings for each candidate
40 DATA 1,1,5,4,4,2,3,3
50 FOR R=1 TO 3
60 FOR C=1 TO 8
70 LET T[R,C]=0   ← Clear count array
80 NEXT C            to zeros
90 NEXT R
100 FOR R=1 TO 3
110 FOR C=1 TO 8
120 READ X[R,C]   ← Read candidate rating
130 LET T[R,X[R,C]]=T[R,X[R,C]]+1
140 NEXT C    Column
150 NEXT R    subscript for I
160 FOR R=1 TO 3              ← Count rating for
170 FOR C=1 TO 8                each candidate
180 PRINT X[R,C];   ← Print ratings
190 NEXT C
200 PRINT
210 NEXT R
220 PRINT
230 FOR R=1 TO 3
240 FOR C=1 TO 5
250 PRINT T[R,C];   ← Print rating count
260 NEXT C
270 PRINT
280 NEXT R
999 END
```

Use this area to note the changing values of R anc C

R	C

Figure 9-11   Counting with a two-dimensional array

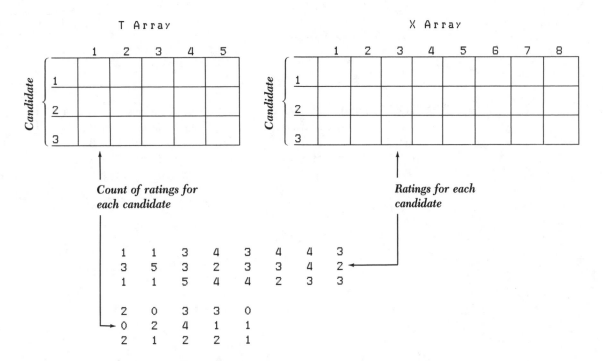

PROGRAMMING TECHNIQUES

1. Processing rows within a column:

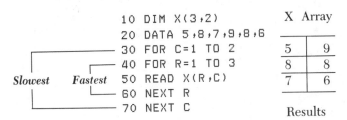

```
10 DIM X(3,2)
20 DATA 5,8,7,9,8,6
30 FOR C=1 TO 2
40 FOR R=1 TO 3
50 READ X(R,C)
60 NEXT R
70 NEXT C
```

X Array

5	9
8	8
7	6

Results

2. Processing columns within a row (continuation of program above):

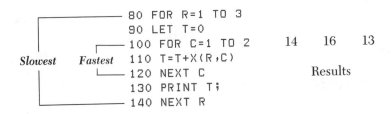

```
80 FOR R=1 TO 3
90 LET T=0
100 FOR C=1 TO 2
110 T=T+X(R,C)
120 NEXT C
130 PRINT T;
140 NEXT R
```

14   16   13

Results

3. Initializing an array to zero:

```
10 DIM A(2,2)
20 FOR R=1 TO 2
30 FOR C=1 TO 2
40 LET A(R,C)=0
50 NEXT C
60 NEXT R
```

A Array

0	0
0	0

Results

4. Counting in an array (using the A array from programming technique 3):

```
10 DIM A(2,2),B(2,3)
20 DATA 1,2,2,1,1,1
30 FOR R=1 TO 2
40 FOR C=1 TO 3
50 READ B(R,C)
60 LET A(R,B(R,C))=A(R,B(R,C))+1
70 NEXT C
80 NEXT R
```

B Array

1	2	2
1	1	1

Results

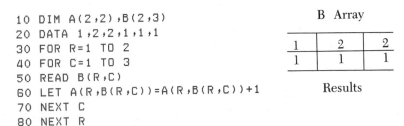

Row 1, column 1 of A array = count of the 1s in row 1 of B array
Row 1, column 2 of A array = count of the 2s in row 1 of B array
Row 2, column 1 of A array = count of the 1s in row 2 of B array
Row 2, column 2 of A array = count of the 2s in row 2 of B array

A Array

1	2
3	0

Results

5. Copying array C$ into array M$ (values have already been placed in the C$ array):

```
100 DIM C$(3,4),M$(3,4)
200 FOR R=1 TO 3
300 FOR C=1 TO 4
400 LET M$(R,C)=C$(R,C)
500 NEXT C
600 NEXT R
```

C$ Array

A	Z	X	B
M	B	T	C
Q	Z	A	G

M$ Array

A	Z	X	B
M	B	T	C
Q	Z	A	G

6. Printing an array:

```
10 DIM X(10,8)
    :
    :
100 FOR R=1 TO 10
110 FOR C=1 TO 8
120 PRINT X(R,C);
130 NEXT C
140 PRINT ←————————
150 NEXT R
```

Results:

Note: Statement 140 is required to display each row on one line.

DEBUGGING AIDS

ERROR	CAUSE	CORRECTION
10 DIM A(5,6) 20 FOR R=1 TO 5 30 FOR C=1 TO 6 40 READ A(R,C) 50 NEXT R 60 NEXT C	Unmatching FOR-NEXT statements	(Interchange NEXT statements) 10 DIM A(5,6) 20 FOR R=1 TO 5 30 FOR C=1 TO 6 40 READ A(R,C) 50 NEXT C 60 NEXT R
170 FOR R=1 TO 10 180 FOR C=1 TO 5 190 INPUT X(C,R) 200 NEXT C 210 NEXT R	Array subscripts reversed	(Interchange subscripts) 170 FOR R=1 TO 10 180 FOR C=1 TO 5 190 INPUT X(R,C) 200 NEXT C 210 NEXT R
10 DIM Z(7,5) 20 FOR R=1 TO 10 30 FOR C=1 TO 5 40 LET Z(R,C)=0 50 NEXT C 60 NEXT R	Array size exceeded	(Increase array size) 10 DIM Z(10,5) 20 FOR R=1 TO 10 30 FOR C=1 TO 5 40 LET Z(R,C)=0 50 NEXT C 60 NEXT R

REFERENCE

Processing Two-Dimensional Arrays

Use R to represent row subscript

$$X(R,C)$$

Use C to represent column subscript

Two-dimensional arrays can be processed:

Down (rows within columns)

Across (columns within rows)

Row subscript advances fastest

Column subscript advances fastest

FOR-NEXT Loop Rules

Permitted:

1. Transferring from within the FOR-NEXT loop to outside the loop
2. Transferring from outside the FOR-NEXT loop to the FOR statement, after the loop has been completed

Not permitted:

1. Entering a FOR-NEXT loop before the FOR statement is executed
2. Transferring from within a FOR-NEXT loop to the FOR statement, before the loop is completed
3. Entering an inner FOR-NEXT loop before its FOR statement is executed (nested FOR-NEXT loops only)
4. Transferring from within an inner FOR-NEXT loop to the outer loop's FOR statement (nested FOR-NEXT loops only)
5. Transferring from within an outer FOR-NEXT loop to within an inner FOR-NEXT loop (nested FOR-NEXT loops only)
6. Using the same FOR variable for the FOR statements of nested FOR-NEXT loops

APPLICATION EXERCISES

1. Complete the coding of the program in Figure 9-10.
2. Write a single BASIC statement to reserve computer storage for the following arrays:

   A with 20 by 10 items (20 rows by 10 columns), H with 100 items, S$ with 5 by 6 items

3. The three daily meals served by 10 restaurants are rated as superb, good, fair, or awful. Assume that READ and DATA statements have placed the ratings in a 10 by 3 array. Write a program to read a restaurant's rating for each of the three daily meals and place them in an array. If the rating is not superb or good, replace the rating in the array with "unacceptable".
4. Given the following partially completed program:

   ```
   10 DIM M(3,6)
   15 A=0
   20 FOR R=1 TO 3
   30 FOR C=1 TO 6
   40 INPUT M(R,C)
   45 A=A+M(R,C)
   50 NEXT C
   60 NEXT R
   ```

   Complete the program to:
   a. Add the columns and print the total of each column if A > 1000; otherwise, add the rows and print the total of each row
   b. Print a total of all the values in the array

5. Assume that data has been placed into the Z array as follows:

	1	2	3	4
1	3	9	5	4
2	6	8	4	3
3	9	7	3	2
4	10	6	2	1

What will the following program print as output?

```
10 DIM Z(4,4)
20 LET X=5
30 FOR R=1 TO 4 STEP 3
40 FOR C=2 TO 3
50 LET X=X+Z(R,C)
60 NEXT C
70 NEXT R
80 PRINT X
99 END
```

Answers to Application Exercises

1. (From Figure 9-10)

```
10 REM A PROGRAM THAT READS DATA INTO A TWO DIMENSIONAL
20 REM ARRAY, PRINTS THE ARRAY, PRINTS BUDGET CATEGORIES
30 REM WITH ITEMS OVER $100, AND PRINTS THE LOWEST BUDGET
40 REM CATEGORY FOR EACH MONTH.
50 REM**************** LEGEND *****************
60 REM    B    BUDGET ARRAY    C    COLUMNS
70 REM    R    ROWS
80 REM    L    LOWEST BUDGET CATEGORY
90 REM    P    LOCATION OF LOWEST BUDGET CATEGORY
100 REM**************** PROGRAM STARTS HERE ************
110 DIM B[10,12]
120 FOR C=1 TO 12
130 FOR R=1 TO 10
140 READ B[R,C]
150 DATA 187,150,128,102,85,68,58,42,17,8
160 DATA 190,150,135,108,90,72,13,45,68,29
170 DATA 196,150,140,112,93,74,65,46,19,5
180 DATA 232,150,165,132,110,88,77,55,22,69
190 DATA 189,150,131,105,88,70,60,44,18,20
200 DATA 203,150,137,109,91,72,62,45,18,73
210 DATA 189,150,127,101,84,67,57,41,16,7
220 DATA 202,150,136,108,90,71,61,44,17,71
230 DATA 195,150,139,111,0,73,64,45,108,38
240 DATA 187,150,128,102,85,68,58,52,17,8
250 DATA 205,150,139,111,93,74,64,47,20,75
260 DATA 254,150,187,154,132,110,99,77,44,18
270 NEXT R
280 NEXT C
290 PRINT TAB(30);"BUDGET"
300 PRINT
310 FOR R=1 TO 10
```

Figure 9-12 A completed program with a two-dimensional array

```
320 PRINT B[R,1];B[R,2];B[R,3];B[R,4];B[R,5];B[R,6];
330 PRINT B[R,7];B[R,8];B[R,9];B[R,10];B[R,11];B[R,12]
340 NEXT R
350 PRINT
360 PRINT
370 PRINT "BUDGET CATEGORIES CONTAINING ITEMS OVER $100"
380 FOR R=1 TO 10
390 FOR C=1 TO 12
400 IF B[R,C]>100 THEN 430
410 NEXT C
420 GO TO 440
430 PRINT TAB(20);R
440 NEXT R
450 PRINT
460 PRINT
470 PRINT "    BUDGET       LOWEST"
480 PRINT "MONTH CATEGORY   AMOUNT"
490 FOR C=1 TO 12
500 LET L=99999
510 FOR R=1 TO 10
520 IF B[R,C]>L THEN 550
530 LET L=B[R,C]
540 LET P=R
550 NEXT R
560 PRINT C;P;TAB(20);L
570 NEXT C
999 END
```

Figure 9-12 continued

2. DIM A(20,10),H(100),S$(5,6)

3.
```
10 DIM R$(10,3)
20 FOR R=1 TO 10
30 FOR C=1 TO 3
40 READ R$(R,C)
50 IF R$(R,C)>"FAIR" THEN 70
60 LET R$(R,C)="UNACCEPTABLE"
70 NEXT C
80 NEXT R
99 END
```

4. a.
```
200 IF A <= 1000 THEN 310
210 FOR C=1 TO 6
220 LET T=0
230 FOR R=1 TO 3
240 LET T=T+M(R,C)
250 NEXT R
260 PRINT T
270 NEXT C
280 GO TO 380
310 FOR R=1 TO 3
320 LET T=0
330 FOR C=1 TO 6
340 LET T=T+M(R,C)
350 NEXT C
360 PRINT T
370 NEXT R
```
   b.
```
380 PRINT A
999 END
```

5. 27

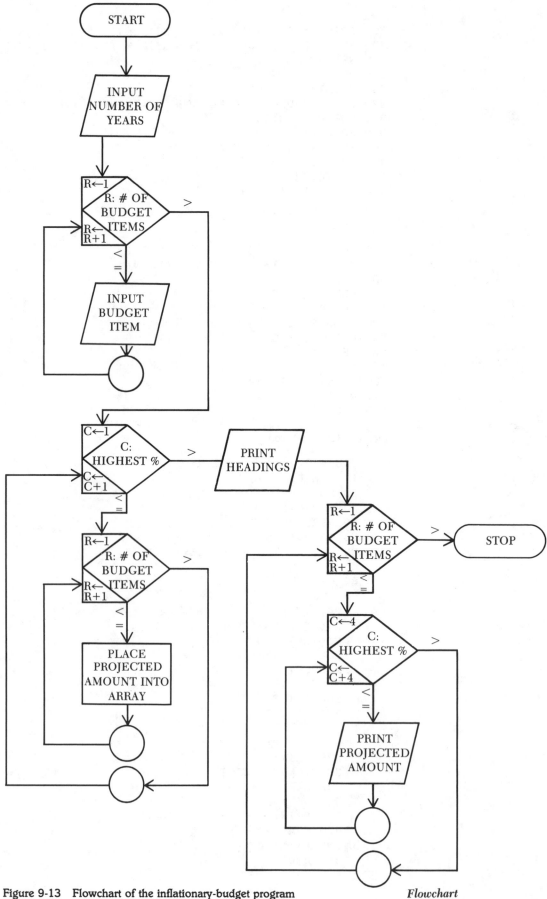

Figure 9-13 Flowchart of the inflationary-budget program   *Flowchart*

PROGRAMMING PROBLEMS

9-1. Inflationary Budget Program

Given yearly budget totals for ten budget items, write a program to print the projected amounts of these budget items for a varying number of years with various rates of inflation.

The projected inflation amount can be calculated by multiplying the budget amount by 1 plus the inflation rate raised to the power of the number of years to be projected.

Programming tips:

1. Use the general flowchart in Figure 9-13 as a guide to prepare a more detailed flowchart.
2. When printing projected amounts, truncate the values to whole numbers.
3. Within two FOR-NEXT loops, compute the inflation amount for ten budget items from 1 to 20 percent.
4. The formula for computing the inflation amount is:

   INFLATION AMT=BUDGET AMT*(1+C/100) ^NO. OF YRS (exponent)

   (C should be represented as a FOR variable)
5. Budget items should be placed into a one-dimensional array, and the computed adjusted amounts should be placed into a two-dimensional array.

```
HOW MANY YEARS WOULD YOU LIKE TO LOOK AHEAD ? 5

ENTER PRESENT AMOUNT OF BUDGET ITEM # 1 ? 2429
ENTER PRESENT AMOUNT OF BUDGET ITEM # 2 ? 1800
ENTER PRESENT AMOUNT OF BUDGET ITEM # 3 ? 1692
ENTER PRESENT AMOUNT OF BUDGET ITEM # 4 ? 1355
ENTER PRESENT AMOUNT OF BUDGET ITEM # 5 ? 1041
ENTER PRESENT AMOUNT OF BUDGET ITEM # 6 ? 907
ENTER PRESENT AMOUNT OF BUDGET ITEM # 7 ? 738
ENTER PRESENT AMOUNT OF BUDGET ITEM # 8 ? 583
ENTER PRESENT AMOUNT OF BUDGET ITEM # 9 ? 384
ENTER PRESENT AMOUNT OF BUDGET ITEM # 10 ? 421


IN 5 YEARS YOUR BUDGET COULD LOOK LIKE THIS
WITH INFLATION RATES OF:

   4%        8%        12%       16%       20%

  2955      3568      4280      5101      6044
  2189      2644      3172      3780      4478
  2058      2486      2981      3553      4210
  1648      1990      2387      2845      3371
  1266      1529      1834      2186      2590
  1103      1332      1598      1905      2256
   897      1084      1300      1550      1836
   709       856      1027      1224      1450
   467       564       676       806       955
   512       618       741       884      1047
```

Results

Figure 9-14   Results of the inflationary-budget program

9-2. Checkbook-Reconciliation Program

Given a beginning bank balance, checks issued and checks outstanding during a certain period, and deposits not yet credited by the bank, write a program that lists outstanding checks and computes the adjusted bank balance.

The adjusted bank balance is equal to the bank balance plus deposits not yet credited by the bank minus outstanding checks.

Programming tips:

1. Prepare a detailed flowchart of the solution.
2. Establish a 20 × 3 two-dimensional array capable of holding 20 issued checks with three fields—check number, date issued, and amount. Establish a second array of the same size for outstanding checks.
3. Keep count of the number of checks issued. This count will be used in the loop to determine the outstanding checks.
4. Keep count of the number of outstanding checks. The total count will be used to prepare the outstanding check record. As you develop this count, it will be used as the row subscript to place values into the outstanding check array.

Results:

```
ENTER CHECK #, DATE(MODAYR-082582), AMOUNT (XX,XX)
FOR ALL CHECKS OUTSTANDING FROM LAST BANK STATEMENT
AND ISSUED SINCE LAST BANK STATEMENT
WHEN ALL CHECKS HAVE BEEN ENTERED, TYPE -1,-1,-1

? 1927,071585,6.50
? 1929,072885,3.50
? 1935,080385,50
? 1936,080885,15.45
? 1937,080885,3.63
? 1938,081085,30
? 1939,081285,22.75
? 1940,081585,33.62
? 1941,082085,40
? -1,-1,-1

ENTER BALANCE FROM YOUR BANK STATEMENT? 640.41
ENTER DEPOSITS NOT CREDITED BY BANK
ENTER -2 WHEN THERE ARE NO MORE DEPOSITS
? 200
? 55
? -2

ENTER 'Y' IF CHECK WAS RETURNED BY BANK OTHERWISE ENTER 'N'

CHECK # 1927 FOR $ 6.5 ? Y
CHECK # 1929 FOR $ 3.5 ? Y
CHECK # 1935 FOR $ 50 ? N
CHECK # 1936 FOR $ 15.45 ? Y
CHECK # 1937 FOR $ 3.63 ? Y
CHECK # 1938 FOR $ 30 ? N
CHECK # 1939 FOR $ 22.75 ? Y
CHECK # 1940 FOR $ 33.62 ? Y
CHECK # 1941 FOR $ 40 ? N
```

Figure 9-15   Results of the bank-reconciliation program

```
OUTSTANDING CHECK RECORD

CHK #           DATE            AMT
1935            80382           50
1938            81082           30
1941            82082           40

TOTAL OUTSTANDING CHECKS----- 120

ADJUSTED BANK BALANCE IS----- 775.41

THIS SHOULD AGREE WITH YOUR CHECKBOOK BALANCE
```

Figure 9-15   Continued

10 User-Defined Functions and Subroutines

OBJECTIVES

When you complete this unit, you will be able to:

1. Write a user-defined function and a statement that requires the use of that function for a given problem
2. Write a subroutine and a main program that references the subroutine for a given problem
3. Code and execute a BASIC solution to a problem that requires a user-defined function and a subroutine

INTRODUCTION

What Is a User-Defined Function?

A user-defined function is a single statement describing an arithmetic expression; this function can be referenced one or more times from the program within which it is defined. Values represented by variables within the user-defined function can be changed for each reference.

What Is a Subroutine?

A subroutine is a group of statements contained within a program; it can be referenced one or more times from different locations within the program.

Using User-Defined Functions and Subroutines

You learned in a previous unit that frequently used functions are often provided by computer manufacturers. Programmers occasionally need to use the same arithmetic expression several times within the same program, but with different values. In this situation, the programmer can define the expression in a user-defined function at the beginning of the program and then refer to it when needed, rather than write the entire expression each time.

A programmer might often need to use a particular group of statements more than once and in different places within a program. Under these circumstances, a subroutine is often used.

The User-Defined Function

A subprogram is one or more BASIC statements that are referred to one or more times by the program in which the subprogram is contained. The user-defined function subprogram contains a BASIC arithmetic statement that is referred to one or more times by the program. In Figure 10-1, statement 10 is an illustration of a user-defined function subprogram; it consists of a single statement preceded by the statement name DEF. This is used most often in programs that require the repeated use of a rather complex expression. Statement 10 in Figure 10-1 is a user-defined function subprogram called C. Most systems require that the programmer use a single-letter variable following FN, to identify the function. Some systems also require a space between FN and the variable. Following DEF FNC is a D within parentheses. The variable within parentheses is called a *dummy argument*. The dummy argument must be a numeric variable. Some systems permit more than one dummy argument, but here we will illustrate the single-argument function only. The dummy argument, D, is used in the expression to the right of the equals sign. The expression illustrated is $5/9*(F - 32)$, a formula used to convert Fahrenheit temperatures to Celsius. Functions must be defined before they are used. They are often placed at the beginning of the program before any other executable statements. After the user-defined function has been defined, it can be invoked as illustrated in statement 30. F is given a value in statement 20. Statement 30 invokes the function each time the FOR-NEXT loop is executed, and this results in the output shown below the program. The purpose of this program is simply to show the mechanics of a user-defined function in a program and is not meant to show an efficient use of a user-defined function.

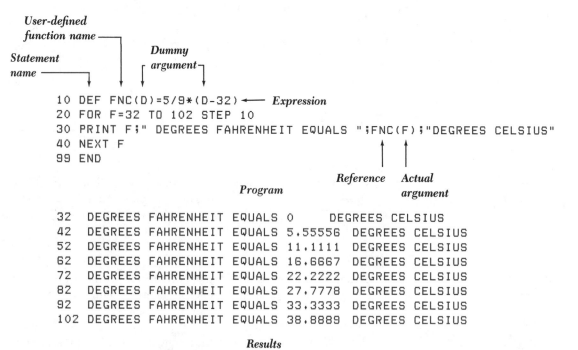

Figure 10-1   User-defined function

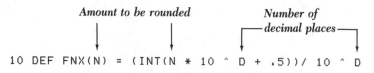

Figure 10-2   Rounding function

The Rounding Function

Figure 10-2 is the definition of a function that can be used to round a value to a specified number of decimal places. Before a programmer can use a user-defined function, all variables within the function definition must be assigned a value. In this figure, the value to be rounded, N, and the number of decimal places, D, must be assigned values before the function FNX is used.

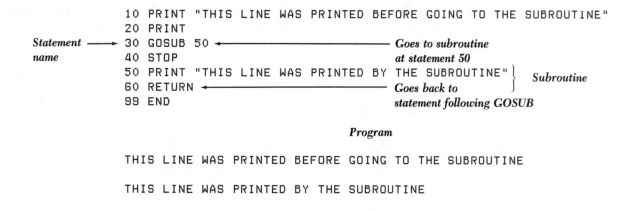

```
10 PRINT "THIS LINE WAS PRINTED BEFORE GOING TO THE SUBROUTINE"
20 PRINT
30 GOSUB 50        ←———————————————— Goes to subroutine
40 STOP                                 at statement 50
50 PRINT "THIS LINE WAS PRINTED BY THE SUBROUTINE"  }  Subroutine
60 RETURN  ←————————————————— Goes back to
99 END                          statement following GOSUB
```

Statement name

Program

```
THIS LINE WAS PRINTED BEFORE GOING TO THE SUBROUTINE

THIS LINE WAS PRINTED BY THE SUBROUTINE
```

Results

Figure 10-3 Subroutine

The Subroutine

Figure 10-3 illustrates another type of subprogram, the subroutine. Like the user-defined function, it is written by the programmer and can be invoked one or more times from within a program. The difference between these two subprograms is that the subroutine usually has more than one statement, and it requires the use of two statements that we have not discussed before. Look at statement 30, which says GOSUB 50. This statement passes control to a subroutine beginning at statement 50. After statement 50 is executed, the RETURN statement sends control back to the statement following the one that invoked the subroutine. In this case, control passes to statement 40.

Subroutines are usually placed at the end of the program before the END statement. The statement preceding the subroutine should be either a STOP statement, as in statement 40, or a GO TO statement passing control to the END statement. If this is not done, the subroutine will be executed unintentionally.

Subroutines have several advantages. If a set of statements will be used more than once in a program, they can be included only once in a subroutine and then used from any place in the program. Another advantage is that the programmer can use subroutines to break up a large program into more manageable segments. These segments can then be written and tested independently and consolidated later into one program. Programs written this way are often easier to write and have fewer errors.

Using User-Defined Functions

Figure 10-4 shows a partially completed list of user-defined functions used to convert selected weights and measures to the metric system. The first example converts miles to kilometers by multiplying the number of miles by the constant 1.60934. M is used as the dummy argument in the definition of this user-defined function named A. We have given examples 2 through 8 different names since this would be necessary if all were defined in the same program. We have also given each dummy argument a different variable name, but this would not be necessary even if all these functions were used in the same program as long as the argument is assigned its intended value before being used. In example 9, name the function I and complete it.

A correct definition of the function is DEF FNI(R)=R*1.09361. When this function is used, R should be expressed in meters. The function then computes meters expressed in yards. At the conclusion of this unit, you will be asked to complete this metric-conversion table as part of the Application Exercises.

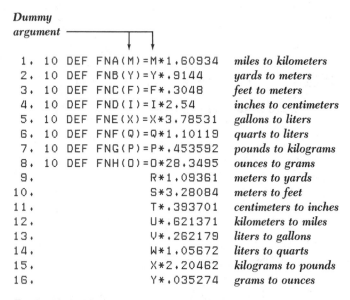

Figure 10-4   Metric-conversion functions

The Punch Program

Figure 10-5 shows the results of a program that converts certain measurements in a punch recipe to the metric system. The program requests the name of each ingredient and its unit of measure and amount and then prints the equivalent metric measurement. The flowchart and the partially completed program that produced these results are shown in Figure 10-6. We will complete this program together.

The START symbol in the flowchart covers statements 10 through 100 for REMARKS (which are not shown) and statements 110 and 120 to define metric-conversion functions. The function in statement 110 defines the conversion of gallons to liters, rounded to two places. When used, G, representing a value in gallons, will be multiplied by the constant 3.7853 and then rounded to give the equivalent measure in liters. Now complete statement 120, used to convert pounds to kilograms.

The correct statement is

```
120 DEF FNB(P)=(INT((P*.453592)*10^2+.5))/10^2.
```

Flowchart symbol 140–150 requests input. Write statement 150.

```
ENTER INGREDIENT, WHEN FINISHED TYPE DONE
?JELLO
ENTER UNIT OF MEASURE-GALLONS
QUARTS,POUNDS OR OUNCES AND AMOUNT?OUNCES,9
 .5625    POUNDS OF JELLO IS EQUIVALENT TO
 .26      KILOGRAMS OR   260   GRAMS
```
— *Output from statements 140–190*
— *Output from statements 320–350*

```
ENTER INGREDIENT, WHEN FINISHED TYPE DONE
?BOILING WATER
ENTER UNIT OF MEASURE-GALLONS
QUARTS,POUNDS OR OUNCES AND AMOUNT?QUARTS,1
 .25      GALLONS OF BOILING WATER IS EQUIVALENT TO
 .95      LITERS
```
Output from statements 290–300

```
ENTER INGREDIENT, WHEN FINISHED TYPE DONE
?COLD WATER
ENTER UNIT OF MEASURE-GALLONS
QUARTS,POUNDS OR OUNCES AND AMOUNT?QUARTS,2
 .5       GALLONS OF COLD WATER IS EQUIVALENT TO
 1.89     LITERS
```

```
ENTER INGREDIENT, WHEN FINISHED TYPE DONE
?SUGAR
ENTER UNIT OF MEASURE-GALLONS
QUARTS,POUNDS OR OUNCES AND AMOUNT?POUNDS,2
 2        POUNDS OF SUGAR IS EQUIVALENT TO
 .91      KILOGRAMS OR 910 GRAMS
```
— *Output from statements 340–350*

```
ENTER INGREDIENT, WHEN FINISHED TYPE DONE
?LEMON JUICE
ENTER UNIT OF MEASURE-GALLONS
QUARTS,POUNDS OR OUNCES AND AMOUNT?QUARTS,1
 .25      GALLONS OF LEMON JUICE IS EQUIVALENT TO
 .95      LITERS
```
Output from statements 270–300

```
ENTER INGREDIENT, WHEN FINISHED TYPE DONE
?PINEAPPLE JUICE
ENTER UNIT OF MEASURE-GALLONS
QUARTS,POUNDS OR OUNCES AND AMOUNT?GALLONS,1
 1        GALLONS OF PINEAPPLE JUICE IS EQUIVALENT TO
 3.79          LITERS
```

```
ENTER INGREDIENT, WHEN FINISHED TYPE DONE
?CRUSHED APPLE
ENTER UNIT OF MEASURE-GALLONS
QUARTS,POUNDS OR OUNCES AND AMOUNT?OUNCES,8
 .5       POUNDS OF CRUSHED APPLE IS EQUIVALENT TO
 .23      KILOGRAMS OR   230 GRAMS
```

```
ENTER INGREDIENT, WHEN FINISHED TYPE DONE
?CRUSHED BANANAS
ENTER UNIT OF MEASURE-GALLONS
QUARTS,POUNDS OR OUNCES AND AMOUNT?POUNDS,1
 1     POUNDS OF CRUSHED BANANAS IS EQUIVALENT TO
 .45      KILOGRAMS OR 450   GRAMS
```

```
ENTER INGREDIENT, WHEN FINISHED TYPE DONE
?DONE
```

Figure 10-5   Results of a program to convert a punch recipe to the metric system

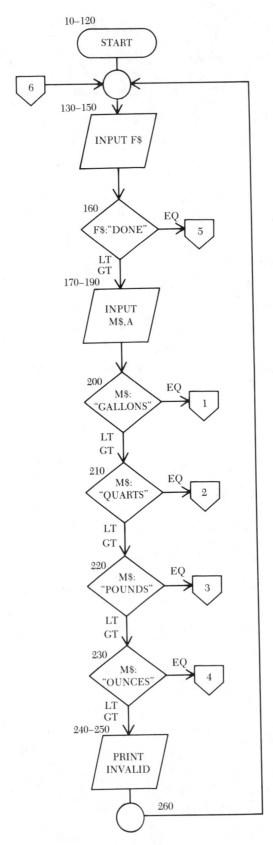

Figure 10-6 A flowchart and a partially completed program that converts a punch recipe to the metric system

Function to convert gallons to liters

Function to convert pounds to kilograms →

```
110 DEF FNA(G)=(INT(G*3.7853)*10^2+.5)/10^2
120 DEF FNB(P)=(     (  .453592)
```

```
130 PRINT
140 PRINT "ENTER INGREDIENT, WHEN FINISHED TYPE DONE"
150
```

```
160 IF            THEN 999
```
Tests for end

```
170 PRINT"ENTER UNIT OF MEASURE-GALLONS"
180 PRINT"QUARTS,POUNDS OR OUNCES AND AMOUNT"
190
```

```
200 IF M$                    THEN 290
```

```
210 IF M$                    THEN 270
```
Tests for unit of measure

```
220 IF M$                    THEN 340
```

```
230 IF M$                    THEN 320
```

```
240 PRINT"INVALID INPUT, CHECK SPELLING"
```
Validity check
```
250 PRINT"OF UNIT OF MEASURE AND TRY AGAIN"
```

```
260 GO TO 130
```

Figure 10-6   Continued

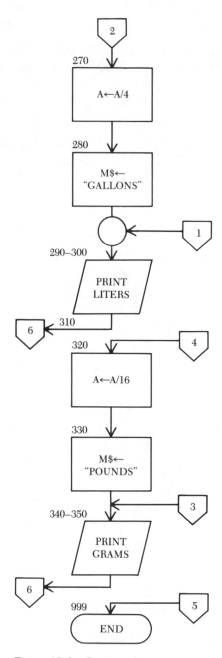

Figure 10-6   Continued

You should have written 150 INPUT F$. Decision symbol 160 tests to see whether there is any more input. If the word "DONE" is entered at the keyboard, the program should stop. Complete statement 160 to do this.

The statement is 160 IF F$="DONE" THEN 999. Statements 170 and 180 ask for input from the keyboard for the unit of measure and the amount. Write statement 190, using the input symbol as a guide.

```
270 LET _____        ←———— Convert quarts to
                                                        gallons




280 LET _____




290 PRINT A;M$;" OF  ";F$;" IS EQUIVALENT TO"  _____

300 PRINT FNA(A);" LITERS" _____

310 GO TO 130 _____



320 LET _____        ←———— Convert ounces
                                                        to pounds




330 LET _____




340 PRINT "A";M$;" OF  ";F$;" IS EQUIVALENT TO" _____

350 PRINT FNB(A);" KILOGRAMS OR ";FNB(A)*1000;" GRAMS" ____

360 GO TO 130 _____

999 END _____
```

Figure 10-6 Continued

 The correct statement is 190 INPUT M$,A. Decision symbol 200 tests to see whether the unit of measure is gallons; if it is, control passes to statement 290. Write statement 200 to accomplish this.

 The correct statement is 200 IF M$="GALLONS" THEN 290. Statements 210, 220, and 230 test for other units of measure. Complete these statements.

The statements should read as follows:

```
210 IF M$="QUARTS" THEN 270
220 IF M$="POUNDS" THEN 340
230 IF M$="OUNCES" THEN 320
```

If a unit of measure does not match any of these tests, the input is declared invalid and control passes back to statement 140 to request corrected input. This is accomplished in statements 240 through 260.

Examine symbol 200 again. If the unit of measure is equal to gallons, the exit to connector symbol 1 is taken. Another off-page connector symbol 1 is located on the next page where it connects to symbol 290–300, if the unit of measure is gallons. Statements 290 and 300 print the conversion of gallons to liters.

Look again at symbol 210. If the unit of measure is quarts, the exit to the right is taken to off-page connector symbol 2 on the next page. Off-page connector symbol 2 leads into symbol 270, which converts quarts to gallons by dividing by 4 before converting the amount to liters. The programmer could write a function to convert quarts to liters directly, rather than dividing by 4 before using the gallons-to-liters function. If that is done, statement 270, which changes the unit of measure from quarts to gallons, could be eliminated. Complete statements 270 and 280.

Statement 270 should be LET A=A/4, and statement 280 should be LET M$="GALLONS".

Look at decision symbols 220 and 230. These test for the unit of measure of pounds or ounces. If the unit of measure is pounds, function B is used to convert the pounds to kilograms and grams. If the unit of measure is ounces, the value as well as the name must be converted to pounds before the function is used. Go to the next page and complete statements 320 and 330 to do this.

Statement 320 is LET A=A/16, and statement 330 is M$="POUNDS".

Output from statements 130–230 —→

```
ENTER NUMBER OF PLAYERS?10
ENTER PLAYER # 1     AT BATS AND HITS ?9,1
ENTER PLAYER # 2     AT BATS AND HITS ?5,0
ENTER PLAYER # 3     AT BATS AND HITS ?7,3
ENTER PLAYER # 4     AT BATS AND HITS ?11,2
ENTER PLAYER # 5     AT BATS AND HITS ?12,4
ENTER PLAYER # 6     AT BATS AND HITS ?8,5
ENTER PLAYER # 7     AT BATS AND HITS ?3,0
ENTER PLAYER # 8     AT BATS AND HITS ?2,0
ENTER PLAYER # 9     AT BATS AND HITS ?9,5
ENTER PLAYER # 10    AT BATS AND HITS ?13,2
```

```
PLAYER #   BATTING AVERAGE
```

Results from first subroutine call —→

```
    6           .625
    9           .556
    3           .429
    5           .333
    4           .182
   10           .154
    1           .111
    2           0
    7           0
    8           0
```

Figure 10-7   Results of a program to compute and sort baseball averages

```
             ┌ ENTER  PLAYER  #  1     FIELDING  CHANCES  AND  ERRORS?11,1
             │ ENTER  PLAYER  #  2     FIELDING  CHANCES  AND  ERRORS?13,3
             │ ENTER  PLAYER  #  3     FIELDING  CHANCES  AND  ERRORS?6,1
             │ ENTER  PLAYER  #  4     FIELDING  CHANCES  AND  ERRORS?8,1
Output from  │ ENTER  PLAYER  #  5     FIELDING  CHANCES  AND  ERRORS?3,1
statements 300-380 ┤ ENTER PLAYER # 6   FIELDING  CHANCES  AND  ERRORS?9,3
             │ ENTER  PLAYER  #  7     FIELDING  CHANCES  AND  ERRORS?7,1
             │ ENTER  PLAYER  #  8     FIELDING  CHANCES  AND  ERRORS?6,1
             │ ENTER  PLAYER  #  9     FIELDING  CHANCES  AND  ERRORS?7,1
             └ ENTER  PLAYER  # 10     FIELDING  CHANCES  AND  ERRORS?15,2

                    PLAYER  #   FIELDING  AVERAGE

             ┌        1              .909
             │        4              .875
             │       10              .867
             │        7              .857
Results from │        9              .857
second subroutine ┤    3             .833
call         │        8              .833
             │        2              .769
             │        5              .667
             └        6              .667

             ┌ ENTER  PLAYER  #  1     INNINGS  PITCHED  AND  EARNED  RUNS  ALLOWED?3,5
             │ ENTER  PLAYER  #  2     INNINGS  PITCHED  AND  EARNED  RUNS  ALLOWED?15,2
             │ ENTER  PLAYER  #  3     INNINGS  PITCHED  AND  EARNED  RUNS  ALLOWED?8,1
             │ ENTER  PLAYER  #  4     INNINGS  PITCHED  AND  EARNED  RUNS  ALLOWED?6,2
Output from  │ ENTER  PLAYER  #  5     INNINGS  PITCHED  AND  EARNED  RUNS  ALLOWED?3,1
statements 460-550 ┤ ENTER PLAYER # 6   INNINGS  PITCHED  AND  EARNED  RUNS  ALLOWED?8,3
             │ ENTER  PLAYER  #  7     INNINGS  PITCHED  AND  EARNED  RUNS  ALLOWED?9,2
             │ ENTER  PLAYER  #  8     INNINGS  PITCHED  AND  EARNED  RUNS  ALLOWED?5,1
             │ ENTER  PLAYER  #  9     INNINGS  PITCHED  AND  EARNED  RUNS  ALLOWED?20,3
             └ ENTER  PLAYER  # 10     INNINGS  PITCHED  AND  EARNED  RUNS  ALLOWED?14,1

                    PLAYER  #   EARNED  RUN  AVERAGE

             ┌       10              .5
             │        3              .88
             │        2              .93
             │        9             1.05
Results from │        8             1.4
third subroutine ┤     7            1.56
call         │        5             2.33
             │        4             2.33
             │        6             2.63
             └        1            11.67
```

Figure 10-7   Continued

The Baseball-Averages Program

The results in Figure 10-7 show the output of a program that requests batting, fielding, and pitching facts about each member of a Little League baseball team. The program computes the batting average, fielding average, and earned-run average for each player, and then uses a subroutine that sorts the averages in sequence. The program prints the batting and fielding averages in descending order and the earned-run average in ascending order. We will write parts of this program together.

Look at the START symbol in the flowchart in Figure 10-8. It represents REMARK statements 10 through 100, which are omitted from this illustration;

statement 110, a function to round a value to a varying number of decimal places; and statement 120 to establish the array A, which will contain the averages of 1 to 50 players. Symbol 130–140 requests keyboard input. Given statement 130, write statement 140.

Statement 140 should be INPUT N.

Look at flowchart symbol 150. It establishes the beginning of a FOR-NEXT loop to accept from a keyboard the times at bat (B) and the number of hits (H) of N players. Complete statements 150 and 170 to do this.

Statement 150 should be FOR X=1 TO N, and statement 170 should be INPUT B,H. Decision symbol 180 tests B for zero, because B is a divisor in the formula for computing the batting average, and we must never divide by zero. If B equals zero, we place a zero in that player's position of the array after skipping the computation of the batting average. Now write statements 180 and 220.

Statement 180 is IF B=0 THEN 220. Statement 220 is LET A(X)=0.

Look back at statement 110. The expression uses the variable D to indicate the number of decimal places that should remain after this rounding function is invoked. Look at symbol 190. The number 3, indicating three decimal places, is assigned to D. Write statement 190.

LET D=3 is correct.

Symbol 200 computes the rounded batting average of a player and stores it in the A array. Notice that the argument for function I is a numeric expression rather than a single variable. When this form is used, the expression is first converted to a single value. This value replaces the dummy argument, and then the expression in the user-defined function is calculated. Flowline 210 and statement 210 transfer control to the NEXT statement to continue the loop. Complete statement 230.

Statement 230 should be NEXT X.

Look at off-page connector symbol 1 and flowchart symbol 240. This symbol is used to show transfer to a subroutine. Off-page connector 1 indicates that control is being passed to the subroutine, flowchart symbol (630–770) in Figure 10-9. Statement 240 accomplishes this. In the program, it is GOSUB 770. The terminal symbol at the top of the flowchart in Figure 10-9 represents REMARK statements 630 through 760, which are not shown in the program, and statement 770, which defines two arrays to be used in the subroutine. Recall that subroutines can be entered at any point; therefore, statement 240 would still be correct if it read GOSUB 630 rather than GOSUB 770. The subroutine will sort elements from an array named A into descending sequence and then place them in an array named Z. Array C will contain the locations of each element before it was sorted.

Many different sorting methods exist; some are more efficient than others. In this subroutine we attempted to program a sort similar to a manual sort that you might use if a computer were not available. This sort probably uses more computer time than some others, but it is easier to follow and it gets the job done.

Using symbol 780 as a guide, write the FOR statement for the outer loop.

It is FOR K1=1 TO N. N represents the number of elements in the array.

Look at symbol 790. B1 will be used to hold the largest value, as the program steps through the array. It was initialized with a −1 so that every value in the array will be greater than this initial value. Now complete statement 790.

The correct statement is LET B1=−1.

Next write the FOR statement for the inner loop, using symbol 800 as a guide.

You should have written FOR N1=1 TO N.

Look at symbol 810. Here an element in the array is compared with B1. If the element is equal to or less than B1, the exit to the right is taken, to the NEXT symbol, continuing the loop. If the array element is greater than B1, the downward exit is taken. Complete statements 810 and 840.

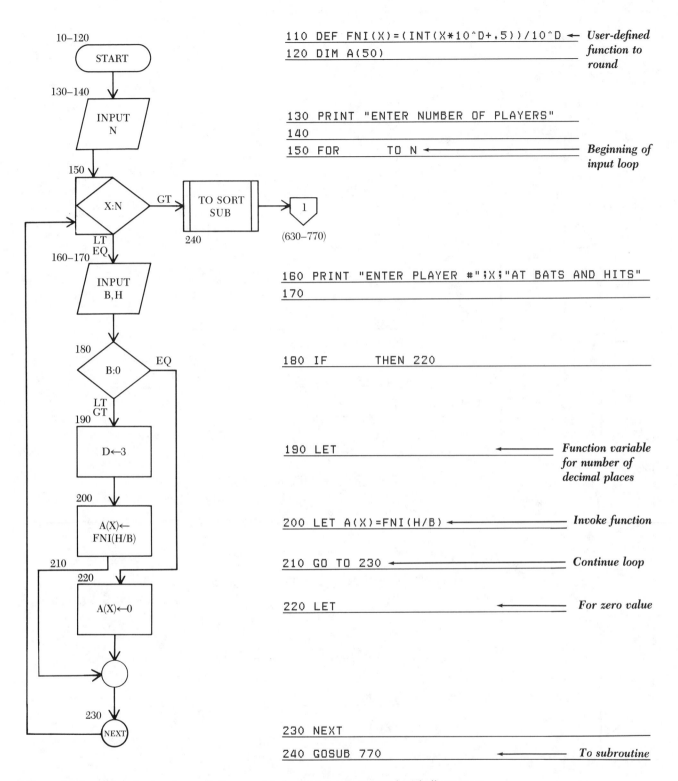

Figure 10-8 A flowchart and a partially completed program to compute baseball averages

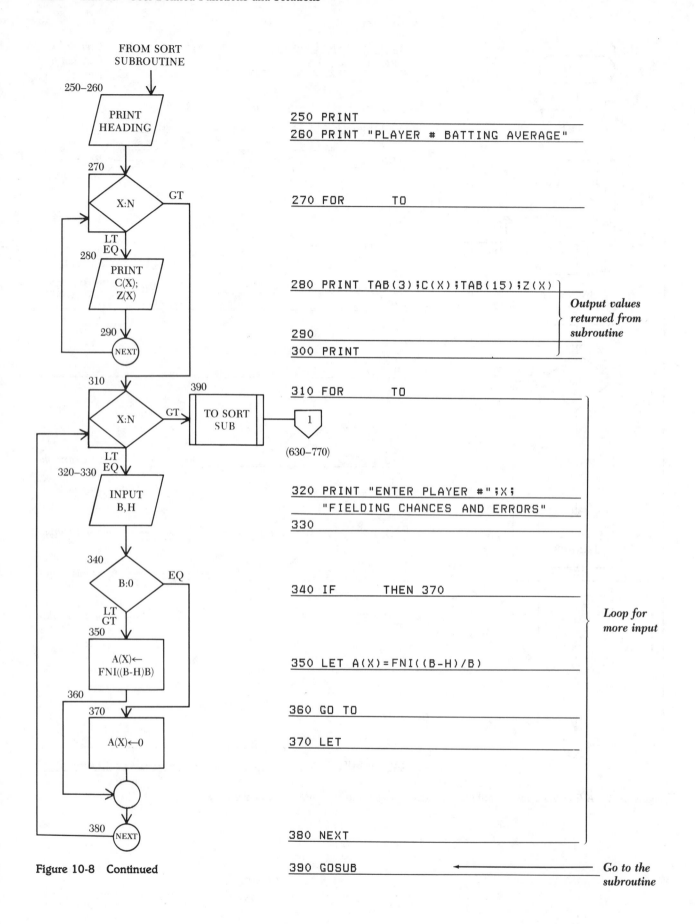

FROM SORT
SUBROUTINE

250–260
PRINT
HEADING

270
X:N   GT

LT
EQ
280
PRINT
C(X);
Z(X)

290
NEXT

310
X:N   GT   390   TO SORT SUB   1

LT
EQ
320–330
INPUT
B,H

340
B:0   EQ

LT
GT
350
A(X)←
FNI((B-H)B)

360

370
A(X)←0

380
NEXT

```
250 PRINT
260 PRINT "PLAYER # BATTING AVERAGE"


270 FOR       TO


280 PRINT TAB(3);C(X);TAB(15);Z(X)          Output values
                                            returned from
                                            subroutine
290
300 PRINT


310 FOR       TO


(630–770)


320 PRINT "ENTER PLAYER #";X;
        "FIELDING CHANCES AND ERRORS"
330


340 IF        THEN 370


350 LET A(X)=FNI((B-H)/B)


360 GO TO

370 LET


380 NEXT

390 GOSUB                          Go to the
                                   subroutine
```

Output values returned from subroutine

Loop for more input

Figure 10-8   Continued

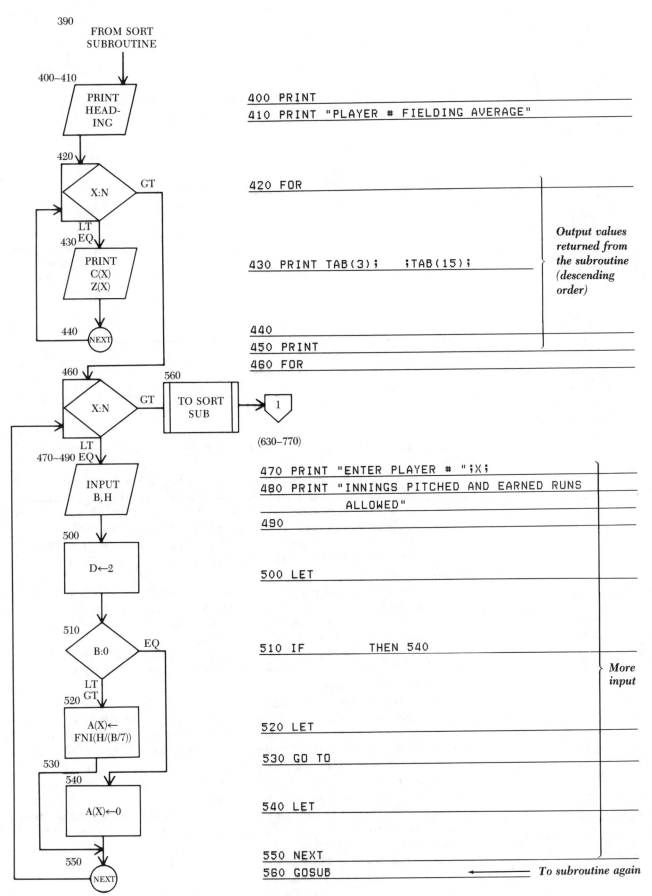

390
FROM SORT
SUBROUTINE

400–410
PRINT
HEAD-
ING

```
400 PRINT
410 PRINT "PLAYER # FIELDING AVERAGE"
```

420
X:N   GT

```
420 FOR
```

LT
EQ
430

PRINT
C(X)
Z(X)

```
430 PRINT TAB(3);    ;TAB(15);
```

*Output values
returned from
the subroutine
(descending
order)*

440
NEXT

```
440
450 PRINT
460 FOR
```

460
X:N   GT

560
TO SORT
SUB

1

(630–770)

LT
EQ
470–490

INPUT
B,H

```
470 PRINT "ENTER PLAYER # ";X;
480 PRINT "INNINGS PITCHED AND EARNED RUNS
            ALLOWED"
490
```

500
D←2

```
500 LET
```

510
B:0   EQ

```
510 IF        THEN 540
```

*More
input*

LT
GT
520

A(X)←
FNI(H/(B/7))

```
520 LET
```

530

```
530 GO TO
```

540
A(X)←0

```
540 LET
```

550
NEXT

```
550 NEXT
560 GOSUB
```
To subroutine again

Figure 10-8   Continued

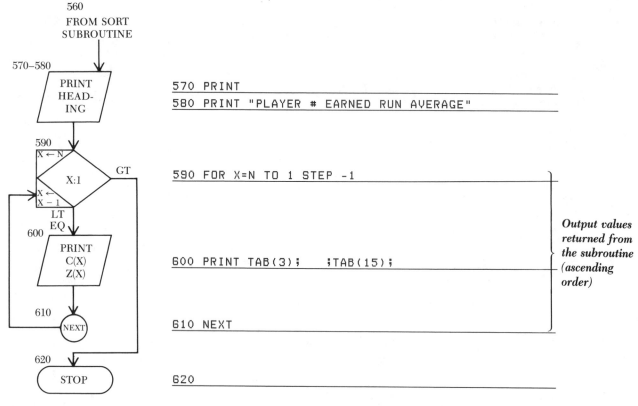

Figure 10-8 Continued

Statement 810 should be IF A(N1)<B1 THEN 840, and statement 840 should be NEXT N1.

Symbol 820 specifies that B1 should be replaced by A(N1), because this exit is taken only when the array element is larger than the value in B1. The next symbol, 830, keeps track of the location of this larger element by placing the value of the FOR variable (the element number) in H1. Complete statements 820 and 830.

They are LET B1=A(N1) and LET H1=N1. This inner loop will be executed N times; when it is finished, B1 will contain the largest value in the array A, and H1 will contain its location.

Symbols 850 and 860 place the largest value and its location into the first positions of the Z and C arrays, respectively. Symbol 870 replaces the previous largest value with −1, because we do not want to consider the contents of this array location again. Write these three LET statements.

Statement 850 is LET Z(K1)=B1, statement 860 is LET C(K1)=H1, and statement 870 is LET A(H1)=−1. Statement 880 ends the outer loop. Complete it.

The statement is NEXT K1.

Up to this point the outer loop has executed once and the inner loop N times, to find the largest value in the array. Since we replaced the largest value with −1, the largest of the remaining values can now be found. The outer loop now executes for the second time. All elements of the array are searched again in the inner loop, and the next largest value will find its way to B1—its location will be in H1.

These values will be stored in the second positions of arrays Z and C, respectively. The process continues until N positions have been sorted in descending order. The last statement of a subroutine returns control to the statement following the GOSUB statement. (Subroutines are usually placed at the end of the program.) Complete statements 890 and 999.

Statement 890 is RETURN and statement 999 is END.

Note: REMARK statements 630–760 are not shown

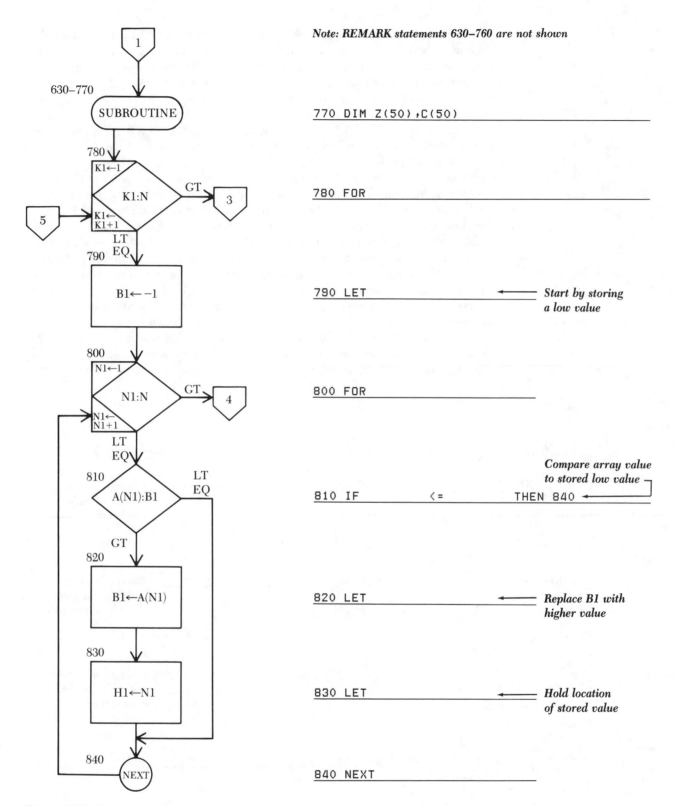

770 DIM Z(50),C(50)

780 FOR

790 LET ⟵ *Start by storing*
a low value

800 FOR

Compare array value
to stored low value ⌐
810 IF   <=   THEN 840 ⟵

820 LET ⟵ *Replace B1 with*
higher value

830 LET ⟵ *Hold location*
of stored value

840 NEXT

Figure 10-9   A sort subroutine

The RETURN statement causes control to pass back to symbol 250 after the subroutine has been completed because this is the statement that follows the statement that called the subroutine. Statements 250 and 260 print page headings for the first report—a list of players and their batting averages. Symbol 270 begins the FOR-NEXT loop to print the contents of the sorted array. Symbol 290 ends the loop. Complete statements 270 and 290.

Statement 270 is FOR X=1 TO N and statement 290 is NEXT X. Statement 280 prints the player's number and the batting average from arrays C and Z.

Symbols 310 through 380 repeat the same steps as symbols 150 through 230, with one exception. Symbol 350 uses a formula to find a player's fielding average that is different from the one used to compute the player's batting average. Look at symbol 390. Control passes to the subroutine again just as it did at symbol 240, but this time it will sort other values that have been placed in the A array. You will be asked to complete statements 310 through 440 as part of the Application Exercises.

Symbols 460 through 550 repeat the steps of symbols 150 through 230 and symbols 310 through 380, except for the computation of the earned-run average. The formula for this computation appears in symbol 520. The subroutine is invoked at symbol 560 to sort the new contents of the A array. You will be asked to complete statements 470 through 580 as part of the Application Exercises.

Symbols 590 through 610 are used to print the contents of arrays C and Z, showing the earned-run average of each player. These averages should be listed in ascending rather than descending sequence, because a lower average indicates a

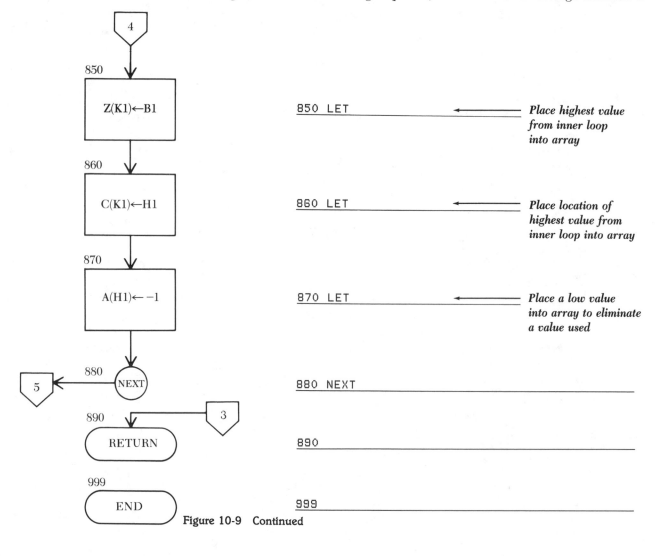

Figure 10-9 Continued

better pitching performance by the player. These averages occur in descending order after the sort, so they are written from the arrays in reverse order. This is accomplished by using the −1 decrement in the FOR statement, number 590. This retrieves array items from the last position of the array first. Complete statements 600 and 610 to finish the FOR-NEXT loop.

Statement 600 should be PRINT TAB(3);C(X);TAB(15);Z(X). Statement 610 should be NEXT X.

Symbol 620 represents the statement to be placed in front of the subroutine. Write statement 620.

Statement 620 can be either STOP or GO TO 999 to prevent entering the subroutine without executing a GOSUB statement.

PROGRAMMING TECHNIQUES

1. Transferring a value to a subroutine:

```
10 PRINT "VALUE TO BE SENT TO SUBROUTINE"
20 INPUT V
30 LET D=V
40 GOSUB 100
         .
         .
         .
```

Subroutine
```
100 IF D<=0 THEN 120
110 PRINT SQR(D)
120 RETURN
```

2. Transferring an array to a subroutine:

```
10 DIM X(10),D(10)
20 FOR I=1 TO 10
30 READ X(I)
40 LET D(I)=X(I)
50 NEXT I
60 GOSUB 100
         .
         .
         .
```

Subroutine
```
100 FOR J=1 TO 10
110 PRINT D(J)
120 NEXT J
130 RETURN
```

3. Writing a function for a frequently used equation:

```
10 DEF FNA(B)=(B*H)/2
20 READ B,H
30 PRINT FNA(B)
40 INPUT X,H
50 LET T=B+FNA(X)
60 LET C=10
70 LET H=15
80 PRINT FNA(C)
90 PRINT FNA(C/3)
```

DEBUGGING AIDS

ERROR	CAUSE	CORRECTION
10 FNA(A)=SQR(A)*1.5	Did not use DEF	10 DEF FNA(A)=SQR(A)*1.5
10 DEF FNT(X)=X+Y*7 20 INPUT X 30 PRINT FNT(X)	All variables not given values	10 DEF FNT(X)=X+Y*7 20 INPUT X,Y 30 PRINT FNT(X)
10 DEF FNZ(V)=V^2+.5 20 INPUT V 30 LET FNZ(V)=V*2	Using function on left side of equals sign	10 DEF FNZ(V)=V^2+.5 20 INPUT V 30 LET X=FNZ(V)*2
10 READ X 20 GOSUB 100 30 GO TO 10 . . . 100 LET X=X+5 110 PRINT X 120 END	Failure to include RETURN statement	10 READ X 20 GOSUB 100 30 GO TO 10 . . . 100 LET X=X+5 110 PRINT X 120 RETURN 130 END
10 INPUT Z 20 LET X=Z*Z 30 GOSUB 50 40 PRINT X 50 LET T=15 60 LET X=X*T 70 RETURN 80 END	Failure to place STOP statement before subroutine	10 INPUT Z 20 LET X=Z*Z 30 GOSUB 50 40 PRINT X 45 STOP 50 LET T=15 60 LET X=X*T 70 RETURN 80 END

REFERENCE

Summary of the User-Defined Function

1. Description:
   a. A single-statement function defined in the program in which it is used
   b. Usually defines a rather complex arithmetic expression that is referred to more than once in a program
   c. Results in one computed value
2. Definition: DEF FN name (dummy argument) = arithmetic expression
3. Example:

   ```
   10 DEF FNR(V)=INT(V*100+.5)/100
   ```

4. Use:

   ```
   10 LET V=152.6389
   20 PRINT FNR(V)
   ```

5. Placement: Before first executable statement
6. Name: One letter A through Z (preceded by a space on some systems)
7. Dummy argument:
   a. Can be repeated in definition
   b. Can be a variable, an expression, or a constant

Summary of the Subroutine

1. Description: A group of one or more statements within a program that are referenced one or more times from different points in the program

2. Definition:

   (program)
   GOSUB statement number of subroutine
      (subroutine)
   RETURN

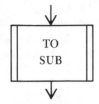

*Flowchart
symbol*

3. Example:

```
50 GOSUB 100
    .
    .
    .
100 .
110 .
120 RETURN
```

4. Placement: Usually near the end of the program before the END statement

5. Dummy argument: Values are usually sent to the subroutine through dummy variables and dummy arrays

---

APPLICATION EXERCISES

1. Complete the metric-conversion table in Figure 10-4.
2. Complete the coding of the program in Figure 10-8.
3. Write user-defined functions for the following:
   a. $m = mx + b$
   b. $y = y^2 - 2$
   c. $v = v/r$
   d. $y = (y - k)^2/4(x - h)$
4. Given the quadratic-equation function $fx = ax^2 + bx + c$, complete the program shown in Figure 10-10.

```
10 DEF FNA(Y)=          ◄———— User-defined function: quadratic equation
20 DEF FNB(N)=          ◄———— User-defined function:
30 READ A,B,C,X                round to three decimal places
40 DATA 1.2345,2.9876,6.4321,4
50 LET Z=               ◄———— Invoke quadratic function
60 PRINT A;B;C;X;       ◄———— Print rounded value (use rounding function)
70 READ A,B,C,D
80 DATA 2.5656,3.2323,4.5564,8
90 PRINT A;B;C;D;       ◄———— Print rounded value of quadratic function
100 END
```

Figure 10-10   A partially completed program with two user-defined functions

5. Show the output that would result from the program in Figure 10-11.

```
10 REM THE ARRAYS ARE AS FOLLOWS:
20 REM N$=NAME        U=NO. OF UNITS        G=GPA
30 REM N1=NO. OF STUDENTS TO BE ANALYZED  U1=STANDARD NO. OF UNITS
40 REM D=DUMMY ARRAY FOR VALUES TO BE COMPARED TO STANDARD
50 REM G1=STANDARD GPA
60 REM V1=DUMMY ARGUMENT FOR STANDARD
70 DIM N$(10),U(10),G(10),D(10)
80 PRINT "ENTER THE NUMBER OF STUDENTS TO BE ANALYZED ";
90 INPUT N1
100 PRINT
110 FOR I=1 TO N1
120 READ N$(I),U(I),G(I)
130 NEXT I
140 PRINT "ENTER THE STANDARD NO. OF UNITS CARRIED ";
150 INPUT U1
160 PRINT
170 PRINT "ENTER THE STANDARD GPA ";
180 INPUT G1
190 PRINT
195 REM WRITE THE STATEMENTS THAT WILL COPY THE VALUES REQUIRED BY THE
197 REM SUBROUTINE
200 FOR I=1 TO N1
210 LET D(I)=U(I)
220 NEXT I
225 LET V1=U1
230 PRINT "THE FOLLOWING PEOPLE EXCEED ";U1;"UNITS:"
240 PRINT
250 PRINT "NAME ";TAB(15);"UNITS"
260 PRINT
280 GOSUB 510
290 PRINT
295 REM WRITE THE STATEMENTS THAT WILL COPY THE VALUES REQUIRED BY THE
297 REM SUBROUTINE
300 FOR I=1 TO N1
310 LET D(I)=G(I)
320 NEXT I
325 LET V1=G1
330 PRINT "THE FOLLOWING PEOPLE EXCEED ";G1;"GPA"
340 PRINT
350 PRINT "NAME";TAB(15);"GPA"
360 PRINT
380 GOSUB 510
390 PRINT
400 PRINT "THE FOLLOWING RECORDS WERE ANALYZED:"
405 PRINT
410 PRINT "NAME";TAB(15);"UNITS";TAB(30);"GPA"
415 PRINT
420 FOR I=1 TO N1
430 PRINT N$(I);TAB(15);U(I);TAB(30);G(I)
440 NEXT I
450 DATA "ABBOT",34,2.9
460 DATA "BRENNEN",28,3.2
470 DATA "DOBY",20,3.7
480 DATA "MANTEL",40,2.5
490 DATA "TROOPE",32,2.8
500 STOP
```

Figure 10-11   A program that uses a subroutine to find the largest value

```
505 REM WRITE THE SUBROUTINE
510 FOR I=1 TO N1
520 IF D(I)<=V1 THEN 540
530 PRINT N$(I);TAB(15);D(I)
540 NEXT I
550 RETURN
560 END


ENTER THE NUMBER OF STUDENTS TO BE ANALYZED   ? 5

ENTER THE STANDARD NO. OF UNITS CARRIED   ? 36

ENTER THE STANDARD GPA   ? 3.1
```

Figure 10-11   Continued

6. Write a program to accomplish the following:
   a. Establish a 20 by 10 array called A$ and another dummy array called E$ with the same dimensions
   b. Input two values to indicate the number of rows and columns to be used each time the program is run
   c. Input string values into the A$ array
   d. Transfer the A$ array to a subroutine via the dummy array E$
   e. Transfer the number of rows and columns to the subroutine via the dummy variables W1 and M1
   f. In the subroutine, print each string equal to the value "NONE"
   g. Print "END OF PROGRAM" in the main body of the program

Answers to Application Exercises

1. Solution for Figure 10-4

(Continued from Figure 10-4)

```
 9. 10 DEF FNI(R)=R*1.09361      meters to yards
10. 10 DEF FNJ(S)=S*3.28084      meters to feet
11. 10 DEF FNK(T)=T*.393701      centimeters to inches
12. 10 DEF FNL(U)=U*.621371      kilometers to miles
13. 10 DEF FNM(V)=V*.262179      liters to gallons
14. 10 DEF FNN(W)=W*1.05672      liters to quarts
15. 10 DEF FNO(X)=X*2.20462      kilograms to pounds
16. 10 DEF FNP(Y)=Y*.035274      grams to ounces
```

Figure 10-12   Additional metric-conversion functions

2. Solution for Figure 10-8

```
10 REM A PROGRAM THAT COMPUTES AVERAGES AND
20 REM CALLS A SUBROUTINE TO SORT THE AVERAGES.
30 REM
40 REM
50 REM ******************** LEGEND ****************
60 REM    N        NUMBER OF PLAYERS    X       FOR VARIABLE
70 REM    B,H      INPUT VARIABLES
80 REM    D        # OF DECIMAL PLACES FOR FNI ROUNDING FUNCTION
90 REM    A        ARRAY FOR INPUT
100 REM ************ PROGRAM STARTS HERE ************
110 DEF FNI(M)=(INT(M*10 ^ D+.5))/10 ^ D
120 DIM A[50]
130 PRINT "ENTER NUMBER OF PLAYERS";
140 INPUT N
150 FOR X=1 TO N
160 PRINT "ENTER PLAYER # ";X;" AT BATS AND HITS ";
170 INPUT B,H
180 IF B=0 THEN 220
190 LET D=3
200 LET A[X]=FNI(H/B)
210 GO TO 230
220 LET A[X]=0
230 NEXT X
240 GOSUB 770
250 PRINT
260 PRINT " PLAYER #  BATTING AVERAGE"
265 PRINT
270 FOR X=1 TO N
280 PRINT TAB(3);C[X];TAB(15);Z[X]
290 NEXT X
300 PRINT
310 FOR X=1 TO N
320 PRINT "ENTER PLAYER # ";X;" FIELDING CHANCES AND ERRORS";
330 INPUT B,H
340 IF B=0 THEN 370
350 LET A[X]=FNI((B-H)/B)
360 GO TO 380
370 LET A[X]=0
380 NEXT X
390 GOSUB 770
400 PRINT
405 PRINT
410 PRINT " PLAYER #  FIELDING AVERAGE"
415 PRINT
420 FOR X=1 TO N
430 PRINT TAB(3);C[X];TAB(15);Z[X]
440 NEXT X
450 PRINT
460 FOR X=1 TO N
470 PRINT " ENTER PLAYER # ";X;
480 PRINT " INNINGS PITCHED AND EARNED RUNS ALLOWED";
490 INPUT B,H
500 LET D=2
510 IF B=0 THEN 540
```

Figure 10-13 A completed program to compute and sort baseball averages

```
520 LET A[X]=FNI(H/(B/7))
530 GO TO 550
540 LET A[X]=0
550 NEXT X
560 GOSUB 770
570 PRINT
580 PRINT " PLAYER #  EARNED RUN AVERAGE"
585 PRINT
590 FOR X=N TO 1 STEP -1
600 PRINT TAB(3);C[X];TAB(15);Z[X]
610 NEXT X
620 STOP
630 REM ************ SORT SUBROUTINE ************
640 REM NUMBER OF ITEMS TO BE SORTED (MAXIMUM 50)
650 REM MUST BE PLACED IN N. ITEMS TO BE SORTED
660 REM MUST BE PLACED IN ARRAY A(50). RESULTS OF
670 REM THE SORT WILL BE RETURNED IN THE Z ARRAY.
680 REM THE FOLLOWING VARIABLE NAMES ARE USED IN
690 REM THE SUBROUTINE AND SHOULD NOT BE USED IN
700 REM THE CALLING PROGRAM.
710 REM***************** LEGEND *****************
720 REM   K1    OUTER LOOP INDEX VARIABLE
730 REM   N1    INNER LOOP INDEX VARIABLE
740 REM   B1    LARGEST VALUE   H1   LARGEST VALUE LOCATION
750 REM   Z(50) SORT ARRAY      C(50) PLAYER ARRAY
760 REM *********** PROGRAM STARTS HERE ***********
770 DIM Z[50],C[50]
780 FOR K1=1 TO N
790 LET B1=-1
800 FOR N1=1 TO N
810 IF A[N1] <= B1 THEN 840
820 LET B1=A[N1]
830 LET H1=N1
840 NEXT N1
850 LET Z[K1]=B1
860 LET C[K1]=H1
870 LET A[H1]=-1
880 NEXT K1
890 RETURN
999 END
```

Figure 10-13   Continued

3. a. DEF FNA(M)=M*X+B
   b. DEF FNB(Y)=Y^2-2
   c. DEF FNC(V)=V/R
   d. DEF FND(Y)=(Y-K)^2/(4*(X-H))

4. Solution for Figure 10-10

```
10 DEF FNA(Y)=A*Y ^ 2+B*Y+C
20 DEF FNB(N)=INT(N*1000+.5)/1000
30 READ A,B,C,X
40 DATA 1.2345,2.9876,6.4321,4
50 LET Z=FNA(X)
60 PRINT A;B;C;X;FNB(Z)
70 READ A,B,C,D
80 DATA 2.5656,3.2323,4.5564,8
90 PRINT A;B;C;D;FNB(FNA(D))
100 END
```

```
1.2345    2.9876    6.4321    4    38.135
2.5656    3.2323    4.5564    9    194.613
```

Figure 10-14 A completed program and results of a program with two user-defined functions

5. Solution for Figure 10-11

```
ENTER THE NUMBER OF STUDENTS TO BE ANALYZED    ? 5

ENTER THE STANDARD NO. OF UNITS CARRIED    ? 36

ENTER THE STANDARD GPA    ? 3.1

THE FOLLOWING PEOPLE EXCEED 36 UNITS:

NAME            UNITS

MANTEL          40

THE FOLLOWING PEOPLE EXCEED    3.1 GPA

NAME            GPA

BRENNEN         3.2
DOBY            3.7

THE FOLLOWING RECORDS WERE ANALYZED:
NAME            UNITS        GPA

ABBOT           34           2.9
BRENNEN         28           3.2
DOBY            20           3.7
MANTEL          40           2.5
TROOPE          32           2.8
```

Figure 10-15 Results of a program that uses a subroutine to find the largest value in an array

6.

```
10 DIM A$(20,10),E$(20,10)
20 INPUT W,M
30 FOR R=1 TO W
40 FOR C=1 TO M
50 INPUT A$(R,C)
60 LET E$(R,C)=A$(R,C)
70 NEXT C
80 NEXT R
90 LET W1=W
100 LET M1=M
110 GOSUB 1000
120 PRINT "END OF PROGRAM"
130 STOP
1000 FOR R=1 TO W1
1010 FOR C=1 TO M1
1020 IF E$(R,C)<>"NONE" THEN 1040
1030 PRINT "ROW";R;"COLUMN";C;"IS ";E$(R,C)
1040 NEXT C
1050 NEXT R
1060 RETURN
9999 END
```

Figure 10-16 A program that searches a two-dimensional array in a subroutine

PROGRAMMING PROBLEMS

10-1. Prediction Program

Given a list of heights and weights for a group of children, predict the weight of a child, given his or her height.
Data:

Heights: 49 51 50 47 49 48
Weights: 74 80 78 72 70 72

Formulas:

S1 = Sum of the first list (heights)
S2 = Sum of the second list (weights)
S3 = Sum of the products of the first list and the second list: $(49 * 74) + (51 * 80)$, etc.
S4 = Sum of the first list squared: $(49^2 + 51^2)$, etc.
N = Number of values in each list
Slope = $(N*S3-(S1*S2))/(N*S4-S1**2)$
Regression line = $(S2/N)-((Slope*S1)/N)$
Prediction = Regression line + slope*input value for prediction

Establish a user-defined function to round. Use a subroutine to accumulate and print the contents of a dummy array.

Programming tips:

1. Use the flowchart in Figure 10-17 as a guide.

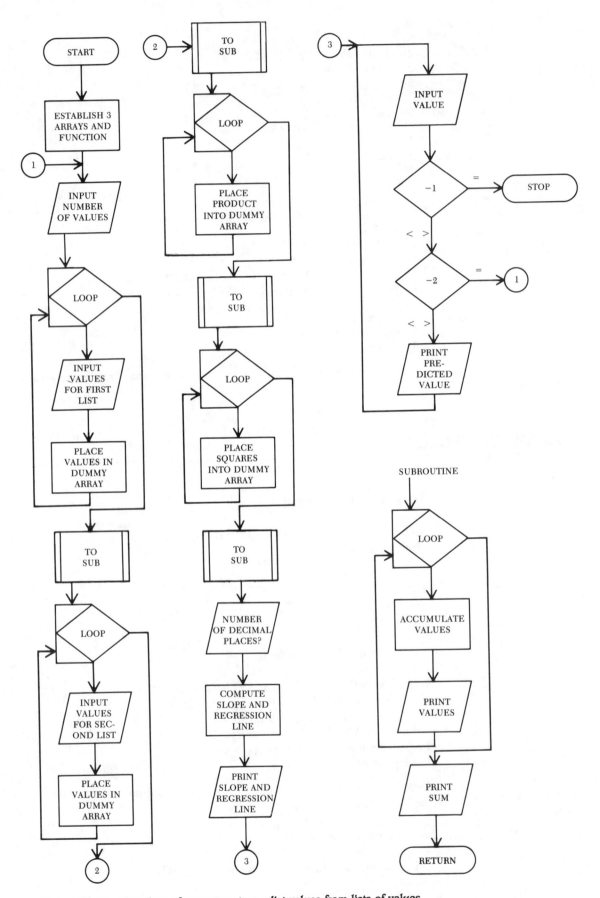

Figure 10-17 Flowchart of a program to predict values from lists of values

2. Use FOR-NEXT loops to place values to be accumulated into a dummy array before branching to the subroutine.
3. After returning from the subroutine, place the accumulated total into different variables (S1,S2,S3,S4) so that they can be used in later calculations.
4. Values sent to the subroutine and the total of these values should be printed in the subroutine.
5. Round all results to the number of decimal places indicated but do not use the rounded values of the slope and regression line when computing the predicted value.

Results:

```
ENTER NUMBER OF VALUES IN LIST ?6
ENTER VALUES FOR FIRST LIST
?49
?51
?50
?47
?49
?48
VALUES:
 49     51     50     47     49    48  SUM IS 294
ENTER VALUES FOR SECOND LIST
?74
?80
?78
?72
?70
?72
VALUES:
 74    80    78    72    70    72    SUM IS 446
VALUES:
 3626    4080    3900    3384    3430    3456    SUM IS 21876
VALUES:
 2401    2601    2500    2209    2401    2304    SUM IS 14416
ENTER NUMBER OF DECIMAL PLACES?0

SLOPE IS 2

REGRESSION LINE IS-33

ENTER INPUT VALUE, -1 TO STOP, -2 FOR NEW LISTS ?50
PREDICTED VALUE IS 77
ENTER INPUT VALUE, -1 TO STOP, -2 FOR NEW LISTS ?46
PREDICTED VALUE IS 68
ENTER INPUT VALUE, -1 TO STOP, -2 FOR NEW LISTS ?55
PREDICTED VALUE IS 88
ENTER INPUT VALUE, -1 TO STOP, -2 FOR NEW LISTS ?-2
ENTER NUMBER OF VALUES IN LIST ?3
ENTER VALUES FOR FIRST LIST
?50
?46
?55
VALUES:
 50    46    55   SUM IS 151
ENTER VALUES FOR SECOND LIST
?77
?68
?88
```

Figure 10-18   Results of a program to predict values from lists of values

```
VALUES:
 77   68   88   SUM IS 233
VALUES:
 3850  3128  4840   SUM IS 11818
VALUES:
 2500  2116  3025   SUM IS 7641
ENTER NUMBER OF DECIMAL PLACES?2

SLOPE IS 2.22

REGRESSION LINE IS-34.14

ENTER INPUT VALUE, -1 TO STOP, -2 FOR NEW LISTS ?51
PREDICTED VALUE IS 79.15
ENTER INPUT VALUE, -1 TO STOP, -2 FOR NEW LISTS ?44
PREDICTED VALUE IS 63.6
ENTER INPUT VALUE, -1 TO STOP, -2 FOR NEW LISTS ?58
PREDICTED VALUE IS 94.7
ENTER INPUT VALUE, -1 TO STOP, -2 FOR NEW LISTS ?-1
```

Figure 10-18 Continued

10-2. Questionnaire Program

Given the results of a psychological questionnaire used to predict the character of six athletes, write a program to print the results of the questionnaire, a summary of the responses, and the average score of each athlete.
Questionnaire responses:

			Score on trait				
Athlete	1	2	3	4	5	6	7
1	7	2	7	6	3	2	2
2	6	3	8	5	2	1	7
3	8	4	7	6	4	3	9
4	5	3	8	5	4	2	7
5	7	5	6	4	5	2	8
6	8	4	9	6	4	3	8

Use a subroutine to print different size arrays, the 6 by 7 questionnaire results, array (P), and the 9 by 7 questionnaire summary, array (D).

Use array A as a 9 by 7 dummy array for passing values to the subroutine. Use dummy variables to pass the number of rows and columns for the array to be printed in the subroutine.

Programming tips:

1. Draw a flowchart of the solution using the following tips in the order shown.
2. Write a user-defined function to average and round each athlete's traits to one decimal place. The formula is:

INT(total/no. of values*10+.5)/10

3. Prepare a DATA statement showing each athlete's scores:

   ```
   DATA 7,2,7,6,3,2,2
   DATA 6,3,8,5,2,1,7, etc.
   ```

4. Use nested FOR-NEXT loops in the main body of the program to read data into the P array, and at the same time place the P array into the dummy array A for printing.
5. Input row and column limits for the first array to be printed. Send these limits via dummy variables to the subroutine and then print the dummy array A in the subroutine.
6. Clear the D array to 0 before computing the questionnaire summary.
7. Use nested FOR-NEXT loops in the main body of the program to add responses from the questionnaire summary. Since the rating for each trait is to be examined, the inner FOR-NEXT loop should control the 6 rows, the outer loop should control the 7 columns, and the resulting count should be placed in the D array. The following statement can be used to accumulate the trait ratings:

   ```
   D(P(R,C),C)=D(P(R,C),C)+1
   ```

8. Use another set of nested FOR-NEXT loops to place the D array into the dummy array A for printing.

Results:

```
AN EXPLANATION OF THE TRAITS IS AS FOLLOWS:
1-AMBITION, 2-COACHABILITY, 3-EMOTIONAL CONTROL,
4-DESIRE, 5-CONFIDENCE, 6-LEADERSHIP, 7-AGGRESSIVENESS,
RATINGS--9 HIGH TO 1 LOW

ENTER NUMBER OF ROWS AND COLUMNS?6,7

          QUESTIONNAIRE RESULTS
PLAY,             TRAITS
  #    1    2    3    4    5    6    7

  1    7    2    7    6    3    2    2
  2    6    3    8    5    2    1    7
  3    8    4    7    6    4    3    9
  4    5    3    8    5    4    2    7
  5    7    5    6    4    5    2    8
  6    8    4    9    6    4    3    8

ENTER NUMBER OF ROWS AND COLUMNS?9,7

          QUESTIONNAIRE SUMMARY
RAT,            TRAITS
       1    2    3    4    5    6    7

  1    0    0    0    0    0    1    0
  2    0    1    0    0    1    3    1
  3    0    2    0    0    1    2    0
  4    0    2    0    1    3    0    0
  5    1    1    0    2    1    0    0
  6    1    0    1    3    0    0    0
  7    2    0    2    0    0    0    2
  8    2    0    2    0    0    0    2
  9    0    0    1    0    0    0    1
```

Figure 10-19   Results of a program to analyze questionnaires

```
AVERAGE SCORE FOR PLAYERS
PLAY.#

1    4.1
2    4.6
3    5.9
4    4.9
5    5.3
6    6
```

Figure 10-19 Continued

11 Data Files

OBJECTIVES

When you complete this unit, you will be able to:

1. Write programs for sequential data files on disk to:
   a. Load data records onto a new file from READ and DATA statements or INPUT statements
   b. Retrieve data records from the beginning to the end of an existing file, and then process and display the data on a screen or printer
   c. Maintain the file by allowing transactions to be entered from a keyboard via INPUT statements that will:
      (1) Add a new record to an existing file
      (2) Delete a record from an existing file
      (3) Change (update) a record in an existing file
   d. Enter inquiries about data records in any sequence from a keyboard via INPUT statements, and display the records on a screen or printer
2. Eliminate an entire sequential file from a disk in either the immediate mode or program mode

INTRODUCTION

What Is a Data File?   A data file is a collection of related records treated as a unit. For example, a group of employee-payroll records constitute a payroll data file; a group of student-grade records constitute a student-grade data file.

What Is a Record?   A record is a collection of related fields of data treated as a unit. For example, each employee's payroll record could contain a set of fields—such as employee number, employee name, pay rate, and number of dependents.

What Is a Field?   A field is a specified area within a record, used for a particular category of data. For example, within an employee's payroll record, one field could be used for the

245

employee number, a second field for the employee name, another for the employee's pay rate, and another for the employee's number of dependents.

Using a Data File

Up to this point you have entered data into memory in one of three ways: using an assignment (LET) statement, a combination of READ and DATA statements, or an INPUT statement. The LET and READ/DATA statements are coded as part of the program and are best used when values do not change between runs of the program and the volume of the data is relatively small. The INPUT statement is best used when data changes between runs of the program and the volume of data is relatively small. The data entered under any of these methods is usable by only a single program. Also, up to this point, when a program was run, the only methods of output from memory were onto a screen or a printed page.

In BASIC a data file can be used to store data separately from any particular program, on media such as magnetic disks and magnetic tapes. A data file can be used for long-term storage of large amounts of data that could be changed between runs of a program and can be accessed by more than one program.

There are two types of data files: *sequential* (serial) and *direct* (random). Records in a sequential file are retrieved in the same order as they are stored in the file—that is, one after another. Either magnetic disk or magnetic tape can be used for sequential files. Records in a direct file can be retrieved in any order, irrespective of the order in which they are stored in the file. Magnetic disks can be used for direct files; magnetic tape cannot.

Many considerations are involved in deciding whether to use sequential or direct files. Furthermore, sequential files require a decision regarding use of magnetic disk versus magnetic tape. In this beginning course, for simplicity and brevity, *we will deal only with sequential files on disks.*

Sequential-File Operations

We will examine four basic operations common to all data-file processing, whether computerized or not. The file will be a household budget file. Each record in the file will consist of four fields: (1) budget code (e.g., 2100); (2) description (e.g., HOUSING); (3) monthly expense amount (e.g., 150); and (4) annual budget amount (e.g., 1900). The four operations will be accomplished by four separate and distinct programs using a common sequential disk file. The operations involve: (1) loading data records onto a new file from READ/DATA statements; (2) retrieving the records from the beginning of the file to the end and displaying each record, including the amount of difference between expense and budget; (3) inquiring through keyboard entry about individual records, and then retrieving and displaying them; and (4) maintaining the file by adding new records, deleting records, and changing records. For brevity, the size of the file and the volume of transactions will be small. However, everything you do is applicable to larger files and larger numbers of transactions.

Overview of Processing a Household-Budget File

Before we investigate each of the four programs to process the household-budget file, we will look at some of the file conditions and the displayed results associated with these programs.

Figure 11-1 shows the contents of the budget file after the loading program has been executed.

RECORD	BUDGET CODE	DESCRIPTION	EXPENSE	BUDGET
1	2100	HOUSING	150	1900
2	4500	TAXES	75	1900
3	99999	0	0	0

Figure 11-1   Contents of sequential file following run of loading program

Figure 11-2 shows the results of the program for retrieving and displaying the file. In addition to displaying the four fields from each record, the program calculates and displays the amount of difference between expense and budget. Printed headings have been eliminated, to shorten the program and concentrate attention on file processing. The flag record with the budget code of 99999 is not printed.

Budget code	Description	Expense	Budget	Over(-)/ under
2100	HOUSING	150	1900	1750
4500	TAXES	75	1900	1825

Figure 11-2   Display of entire contents of sequential file following run of retrieve and display program

Budget code	Description	Expense	Budget
4500	TAXES	75	1900
2100	HOUSING	150	1900

Figure 11-3   Display of selected sequential-file records following run of inquiry program

Figure 11-3 shows a display of records after execution of the file-inquiry program. This figure does not show the messages requesting the input of the desired budget code; it shows only the records that are retrieved. Note that the records are retrieved in a sequence different from that in which they are stored. This is possible only when the sequential file is stored on disk; it cannot be done on a tape file.

Figure 11-4 shows the contents of the budget file after the maintenance program has been executed. Compare the contents after maintenance in Figure 11-4 with the contents of the file after loading in Figure 11-1, and note that there are differences. Record 1 now contains a new record with a budget code of 1800, added to the beginning of the file. Record 2 contains the record with a budget code of 2100. This record, originally the first record, has now been changed in the description and expense fields. The third record, having a budget code of 3200, is added to the middle of the file. Record 4, with a budget code of 5000, is added to the end of the file. Notice that the record with a budget code of 4500 is not in the file. It was originally the second record in the file after loading, but was deleted during execution of the maintenance program.

RECORD	BUDGET CODE	DESCRIPTION	EXPENSE	BUDGET	
1	1800	FOOD	230	2500	*Added to beginning of file*
2	2100	HOUSING-OPER	220	1900	*Changed*
3	3200	HOUSING-RENT	200	2400	*Added to middle of file* *4500 deleted*
4	5000	CLOTHING	180	1300	*Added to end of file*
5	99999	0	0	0	*Same*

Figure 11-4   Contents of sequential file following maintenance program

File Loading (Figures 11-5 through 11-10)

Figure 11-5 shows a system flowchart for the program for loading a sequential file. In previous units we have shown only logic in program flowcharts. A system flowchart gives an overall picture of the components involved in the execution of the load program, but not the detailed logic of the program. In this case we can see that input is entered through READ and DATA statements. Output uses a magnetic disk for the budget file named "BDGSEQ" and a screen or printer display for an "END OF FILE LOADING" message.

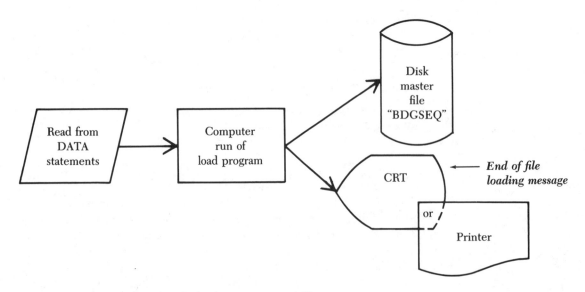

Figure 11-5   System flowchart for loading a sequential file

BUDGET CODE	DESCRIPTION	EXPENSE	BUDGET
2100	"HOUSING"	150	1900
4500	"TAXES"	75	1900
99999	"0"	0	0

Figure 11-6   Data to be read from DATA statements and loaded onto a sequential file

Figure 11-6 illustrates the data to be loaded onto the budget master file. Note that all fields other than the budget description are numeric. Note in particular that, for budget code 99999, the zero in the description field is within quotations, because all entries in this field are strings; whereas the zeros in the expense and budget fields are not. In later illustrations the quotations marks will not be shown.

	BEFORE LOADING				AFTER LOADING			
RECORD	BUDGET CODE	DESCRIPTION	EXPENSE	BUDGET	BUDGET CODE	DESCRIPTION	EXPENSE	BUDGET
1					2100	HOUSING	150	1900
2					4500	TAXES	75	1900
3					99999	0	0	0

Figure 11-7   Contents of sequential file before and after loading (writing) file

Figure 11-7 illustrates the contents of the budget master file before and after loading. Before loading, the file is empty. After loading, the file contains the three records read from the DATA statements.

```
END OF FILE LOADING
```

Figure 11-8   Output displayed by program for loading a sequential file

Figure 11-8 shows the "END OF FILE LOADING" message that is displayed on the screen or printer at the conclusion of the loading program. We could have displayed each record that was loaded onto the file, but we did not, because we wanted to emphasize the file-loading process.

Figure 11-9 lists the legend for the variables. To keep the program as brief as possible, this legend will not be shown in the program.

E1   Expenses
B1   Budget amount
N1$ Description
N1   Budget code

Figure 11-9   Legend for variables used in program for loading a sequential file

The detailed logic for the program for loading a sequential file is illustrated in Figure 11-10.

The BASIC language for data file processing varies widely among different types of computers. For that reason, the BASIC program will be listed only in the

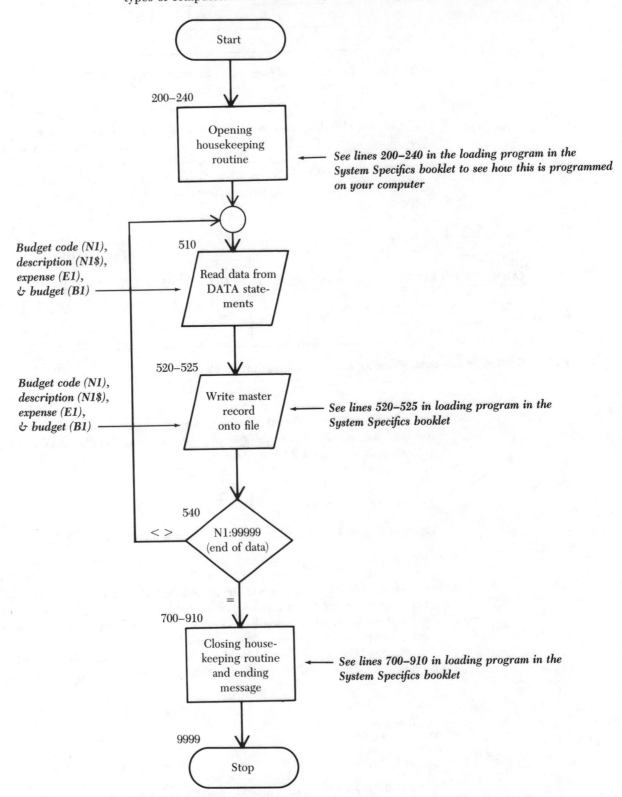

Figure 11-10   Logic flowchart for program for loading a sequential file

System Specifics booklet. In this text we will concentrate on the detailed logic for each program by use of the flowchart.

Symbol 200–240 calls for an opening (housekeeping) routine. In this area the BASIC language varies with different computers. Look at the note to the right of the symbol, which reminds you to look later at program statements 200 through 240 in the System Specifics booklet. Actions in an opening (housekeeping) routine include opening and naming the file and setting the file pointer to the beginning of the file at record number 1.

It would be helpful at this point to compare the data stored in a file with the data stored in DATA statements, since they are quite similar. Recall that a pointer started at the first data item of the lowest-numbered DATA statement and advanced sequentially through the data, as each item was read. Each data file also has a pointer starting at the first data item in the first record of the file and advancing sequentially through each field in the record, as each field is either read from the file or written on the file. In the loading program the data is written on the file. In the remaining three programs the data will be read from the file.

Symbol 510 covers the reading of the four items of data (N1, N1$, E1, and B1) from a DATA statement. These items of data could have been entered via INPUT statements; the net result would be the same: the values for each record would be entered in memory.

In symbol 520–525 the values for each record are written onto the file, rather than displayed on a screen or printer. Here also the BASIC language varies among different computers, so remember to look at lines 520 through 525 in the loading program in the System Specifics booklet.

Symbol 540 tests budget code N1 to see whether the record just loaded onto the file is the end-of-data flag record with a budget code of 99999. If not, the program branches back to symbol 510 to read the data for another record. If this is the end of the data, the program branches to symbol 700–910 to the closing (housekeeping) routine and to display the "END OF FILE LOADING" message. The closing (housekeeping) routine also varies among different computers, so remember to study lines 700–910 of the program in the System Specifics booklet. The program then terminates at symbol 9999.

In the remaining three programs, the opening and closing (housekeeping) routines will be similar to the routines in this program.

File Retrieval and Display (Figures 11-11 through 11-15)

Figure 11-11 is the system flowchart for the program for retrieving and displaying a sequential file. The input for this program is the master file named "BDGSEQ", and the output is displayed on either a screen or a printer.

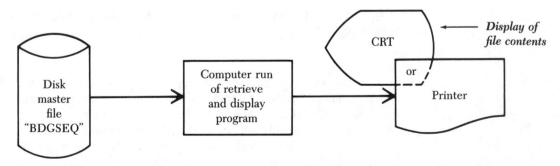

Figure 11-11   System flowchart for retrieving and displaying a sequential file

Figure 11-12 illustrates the contents of the file before and after execution of the program for file retrieval and display. Since the file is used only as input and nothing is written on it, the contents remain unchanged.

RECORD	BUDGET CODE	DESCRIPTION	EXPENSE	BUDGET
1	2100	HOUSING	150	1900
2	4500	TAXES	75	1900
3	99999	0	0	0

Figure 11-12   Contents of sequential file before and after (unchanged) retrieval and display of entire file

Figure 11-13 shows the display of the file retrieval program. As we mentioned earlier, the four fields from each record are displayed, as well as the calculated difference between expense and budget. In addition, an end-of-program message is printed as shown.

Budget code	Description	Expense	Budget	Over(-)/ under
↓	↓	↓	↓	↓
2100	HOUSING	150	1900	1750
4500	TAXES	75	1900	1825

END OF FILE RETRIEVAL

Figure 11-13   Output displayed by program for retrieving and displaying a sequential file

Figure 11-14 is the legend for the program. The variables are the same as those used in the loading program with the addition of D1, which represents the over/under budget amount.

$B1$ Budget amount
$D1$ Over(-)/under budget amount
$E1$ Expenses
$N1$ Budget code
$N1\$$ Description

Figure 11-14   Legend for variables used in program for retrieving and displaying a sequential file

The detailed logic for the file-retrieval program is illustrated by the flowchart in Figure 11-15. Symbol 200–240 covers the opening housekeeping routine, which is similar to the opening routine for the loading program.

Symbol 400–404 calls for reading the four items of data ($N1$, $N1\$$, $E1$, and $B1$) from the master file, rather than from DATA statements, as was done in the loading program. This coding also varies with different computers.

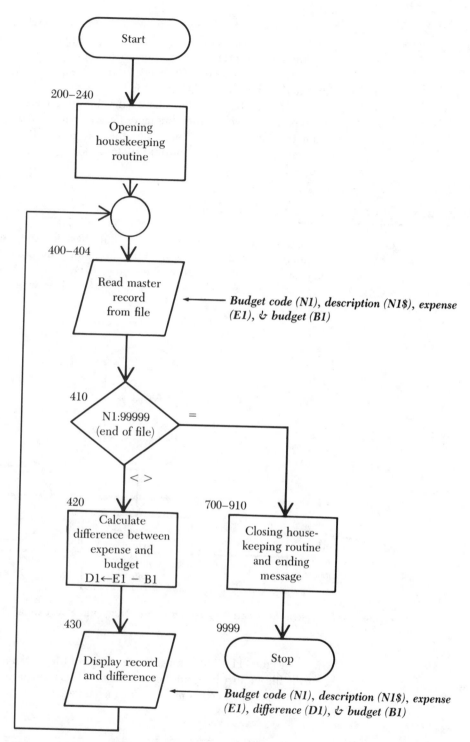

Figure 11-15   Logic flowchart for program for retrieving and dislaying a sequential file

In symbol 410 budget code N1 is tested to see whether the flag record (that is, the end of file) has been read. If N1 does not equal 99999, the end of file has not been reached, so the program continues to symbol 420.

At symbol 420 the difference between expense and budget is calculated and assigned to the variable D1. Next, in symbol 430, the four variables from the file (N1, N1$, E1, and B1) and the calculated value of D1 are displayed on the screen or printer. The flowchart then branches back to symbol 400–404 to read another record from the file. This continues until the flag record 99999 is recognized; then the program branches to symbol 700–910 for a closing housekeeping routine and displays the ending message.

File Inquiry (Figures 11-16 through 11-20)

Figure 11-16 illustrates the system flowchart for the program for sequential-file inquiry. There are two sources of input for this program: an inquiry from the keyboard and the disk master file named "BDGSEQ". The output is a display on the screen or printer, whenever a match is found between the inquiry record and a master record.

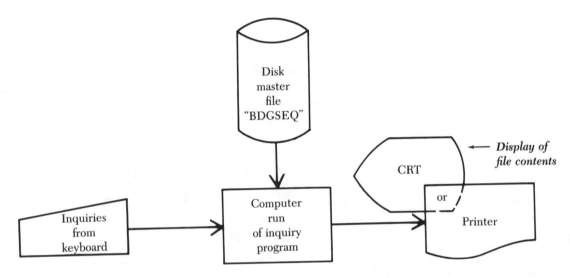

Figure 11-16   System flowchart for program for inquiring with a sequential file

Figure 11-17 illustrates the contents of the disk file before and after execution of the file-inquiry program. Since the disk file is used only as input and since nothing is written on it, the contents remain unchanged.

RECORD	BUDGET CODE	DESCRIPTION	EXPENSE	BUDGET
1	2100	HOUSING	150	1900
2	4500	TAXES	75	1900
3	99999	0	0	0

Figure 11-17   Contents of sequential file Before and After execution of file-inquiry program

Figure 11-18 shows the displayed results of the inquiry program. These displayed results include the inquiry budget code typed by the user. If a matching code is found in the master file, four fields from the master record are displayed. If a match is not found, a message is printed to indicate this. Finally, when there are no more requests, an ending message is printed. Note that the records are not retrieved in the same order as they are stored.

```
ENTER BUDGET CODE FOR RECORD YOU WANT TO SEE
(TO STOP TYPE 99999)    ?4500

4500              TAXES              75              1900

ENTER BUDGET CODE FOR RECORD YOU WANT TO SEE
(TO STOP TYPE 99999)    ?2100

2100              HOUSING            150             1900

ENTER BUDGET CODE FOR RECORD YOU WANT TO SEE
(TO STOP TYPE 99999)    ?1800

BUDGET CODE   1800     NOT FOUND IN FILE.

ENTER BUDGET CODE FOR RECORD YOU WANT TO SEE
(TO STOP TYPE 99999)    ?99999


END OF INQUIRIES
```

Figure 11-18   Output displayed by program for inquiring with a sequential file

Figure 11-19 contains the legend of the symbols used in the program. N is the only different symbol: it stands for the inquiry budget code.

B1   Budget amount
E1   Expenses
N   Inquiry budget code
N1   Budget code
N1$ Description

Figure 11-19   Legend for variables used in program for inquiring with a sequential file

The detailed logic for the file inquiry is illustrated by the flowchart in Figure 11-20. Symbol 200–230 covers the opening housekeeping routine, which is similar to the opening routines for the two previous programs. Symbol 310–320 sets the pointer at the beginning of the file. For the first time in this program, the pointer is set in the opening housekeeping routine. However, since the records are retrieved in a sequence other than that in which they are stored, the pointer must be reset before each new inquiry is made. Therefore, we have put this step just before inquiry budget code N is input. Like opening (housekeeping) and closing routines, this is another procedure that varies with different computers, so remember to examine the BASIC language in the program, beginning at statement 310 in the System Specifics booklet.

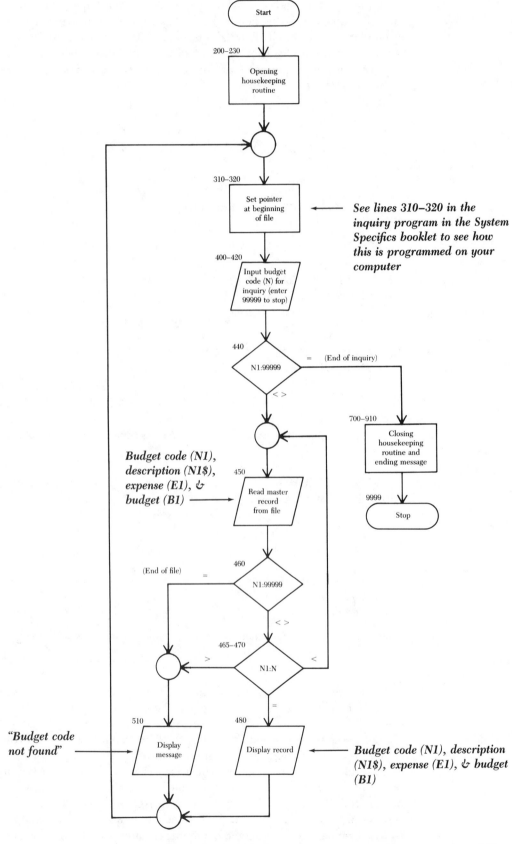

Figure 11-20   Logic flowchart for program for inquiring with a sequential file

Symbol 400–420 calls for the user to input the inquiry budget code (N) corresponding to the budget record from the file that is to be displayed. In symbol 440 inquiry budget code N is tested to see whether the user wants to end the input. If N is equal to 99999, the program branches to symbol 700–910 to the closing housekeeping routine and ending message. If N is not equal to 99999, the flowchart continues to symbol 450.

At symbol 450 four items of data (N1, N1$, E1, B1) are read from the master file. In symbol 460 the master record budget code (N1) is compared to 99999 as an end-of-file check. If N1 is equal to 99999, this means that the entire file has been searched and no match has been found for the inquiry budget code (N), so the program branches to symbol 510. At symbol 510 a message is displayed indicating that the budget code was not found. The flowchart then branches back to symbol 310 to set the pointer at the beginning of the file, before requesting another inquiry. If N1 does not equal 99999 at symbol 460, the flowchart continues to symbol 465–470.

At symbol 465–470 budget code N1 from the master record is compared with inquiry budget code N. If master code N1 is greater than inquiry code N, there is no need to search any further, because the inquiry code cannot be found. This happens because the master file is in ascending budget-code sequence; therefore, when N1 is greater than N, everything else beyond N1 is also greater than N so no match can be found. In this case, the program branches to symbol 510 to print a message indicating that the budget code was not found, and then it branches to symbol 310–320 to reset the pointer at the beginning of the file and make another inquiry.

At symbol 465–470, if master budget code N1 is less than inquiry code N, it is possible that the desired record is still in the file, so the program branches back to symbol 450 to read another master record. On the other hand, if N1 equals N at symbol 470, the flowchart continues to symbol 480. At symbol 480 the four fields of the master record are displayed; then the flowchart branches back to symbol 310–320 to reset the pointer at the beginning of the file and make another inquiry. The inquiry process continues until a value of 99999 is input for N. Then at symbol 440, the program branches to symbol 700–910 to the closing housekeeping routine.

File Maintenance

For clarity, the system flowchart for the file-maintenance program is illustrated in two separate parts of Figure 11-21.

Figure 11-21(a), the system flowchart for the first part of the file-maintenance program, covers updating in the form of add, change, and delete transactions. Transactions are entered through the keyboard, and master records are read from the old master file name "BDGSEQ". The program outputs onto an updated temporary file named "TEMP".

Any error messages are displayed on the screen or printer. When the last transaction and the last record from the old master file have been processed, the temporary file will contain a completely changed (updated) file of budget records.

Figure 11-21(b), the system flowchart for the second part of the maintenance program, covers copying the updated temporary file named "TEMP" onto a new updated master file named "BDGSEQ". The temporary file may then be used for back-up once it has been copied.

(a)

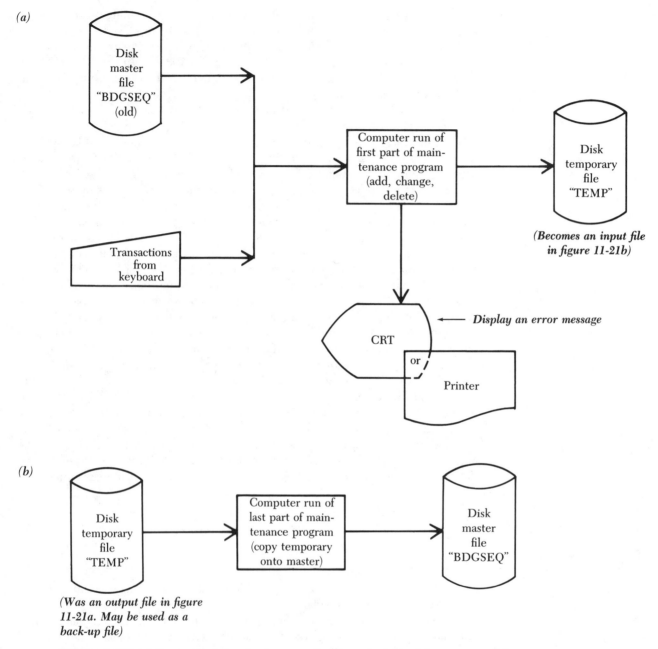

Figure 11-21 (a) System flowchart for first part of program for maintaining a sequential file (adds, changes, and deletes); (b) system flowchart for last part of program (copies temporary file onto master)

Figure 11-23 summarizes the 11 transactions for the maintenance program. The transaction number will help you relate each transaction to the file contents after maintenance in Figure 11-22 and output display in Figure 11-24. The transaction code definitions are summarized in the note at the bottom of Figure 11-23. The maintenance program is the most complicated of all sequential-file programs, so you should study these illustrations carefully and refer to them as you examine the remaining illustrations in this unit.

Figure 11-22 shows the contents of the master file named "BDGSEQ" before and after the maintenance program was executed. To the right of the "after maintenance" section is a one-word description of the type of change that affected each record.

RECORD	BEFORE MAINTENANCE				AFTER MAINTENANCE				
	BUDGET CODE	DESCRIPTION	EXPENSE	BUDGET	BUDGET CODE	DESCRIPTION	EXPENSE	BUDGET	
1	2100	HOUSING	150	1900	1800	FOOD	230	2500	← Added
2	4500	TAXES	75	1900	2100	HOUSING-OPER	220	1900	← Changed
3	99999	0	0	0	3200	HOUSING-RENT	200	2400	← Added
4					5000	CLOTHING	180	1300	← 4500 Deleted ← Added
5					99999	0	0	0	← Same

Figure 11-22 Contents of sequential file before and after maintenance

TRANSACTION NO.	CODE	BUDGET CODE	DESCRIPTION	EXPENSE	BUDGET	COMMENT
1	A	1800	Food	230	2500	Add to beginning of file
2	C	2000	Housing-oper	20	0	Error—change nonexistent record
3	C	2100	Housing-oper	20	0	Change descr. and expense amt.
4	C	2100	0	50	0	Change expense amt.
5	A	2100	Housing-rent	200	2400	Error—add record with same budget code as existing record
6	A	3200	Housing-rent	200	2400	Add to middle of file
7	D	4000				Error—delete nonexistent record
8	D	4500				Delete existing record
9	A	5000	Clothing	180	1300	Add to end of file
10	F					Error—invalid transaction code
11	E	99999				End of transactions

Note: Transaction codes are as follows:
  C   Change (update) record
  A   Add new record
  D   Delete record
  E   End of transactions

Figure 11-23 Transaction summary for run of program for maintaining a sequential file

A few additional points should be made regarding Figure 11-23. First look at transaction 4. The transaction code is C. The note below the table indicates that transaction code C represents a change to the record. The only column to be changed is the expense column, which contains a value of 50. The other two columns, description and budget, contain zeros. Changes will be handled this way. When there is no change to a field, a zero will be entered.

Also note how deletions are handled. Look at transactions 7 and 8, which have a transaction code of D, meaning delete. With deletions, only a transaction code and a budget code must be entered; therefore, the other fields are blank. Now look at transaction 11, which has a transaction code of E, meaning the end of transactions. In this case the only necessary entries are the transaction code and the budget code. Transactions 5, 7, and 10 are intentional errors to demonstrate error routines.

In Figure 11-24 we look ahead to what will be displayed by the file retrieval after the maintenance program has been executed. Note the line for budget code 2100 in the expense field. The amount of 220 results from adding the amounts 20 and 50 in transactions 3 and 4 to the original amount of 150. The expense field is changed by adding the transaction amount to the amount from the master record. The description and budget fields are changed by replacing the field from the master record with the field from the transaction record.

Budget code	Description	Expense	Budget	Over(-)/ under
↓	↓	↓	↓	↓
1800	FOOD	230	2500	2270
2100	HOUSING-OPER	220	1900	1680
3200	HOUSING-RENT	200	2400	2200
5000	CLOTHING	180	1300	1120

END OF FILE RETRIEVAL

Figure 11-24   Output displayed by program for retrieving a sequential file after run of maintenance program

Figure 11-25 shows the display resulting from execution of the maintenance program. Since this is a long illustration, you will probably want to examine it in detail later. Let's look at some general points. The 1 on the left in the figure corresponds to the transaction number. Each set of output for a transaction is bracketed separately. The purpose of each transaction code is indicated by labels on the right.

```
ENTER INFORMATION AS REQUESTED FOR AFFECTED RECORD
WHEN YOU SEE A QUESTION MARK.

PLEASE BEGIN ENTERING TRANSACTION.
TRANSACTION CODE ?A  ←────────────────────────────── Add
BUDGET CODE ?1800

ENTER DESCRIPTION, EXPENSE AND BUDGET
ENTER 0, IF NO ENTRY FOR AN ITEM
DESCRIPTION ?FOOD
EXPENSES ?230
BUDGET AMOUNT ?2500
```

Transaction number ⟶ 1

Figure 11-25   Output displayed by program for maintaining a sequential file

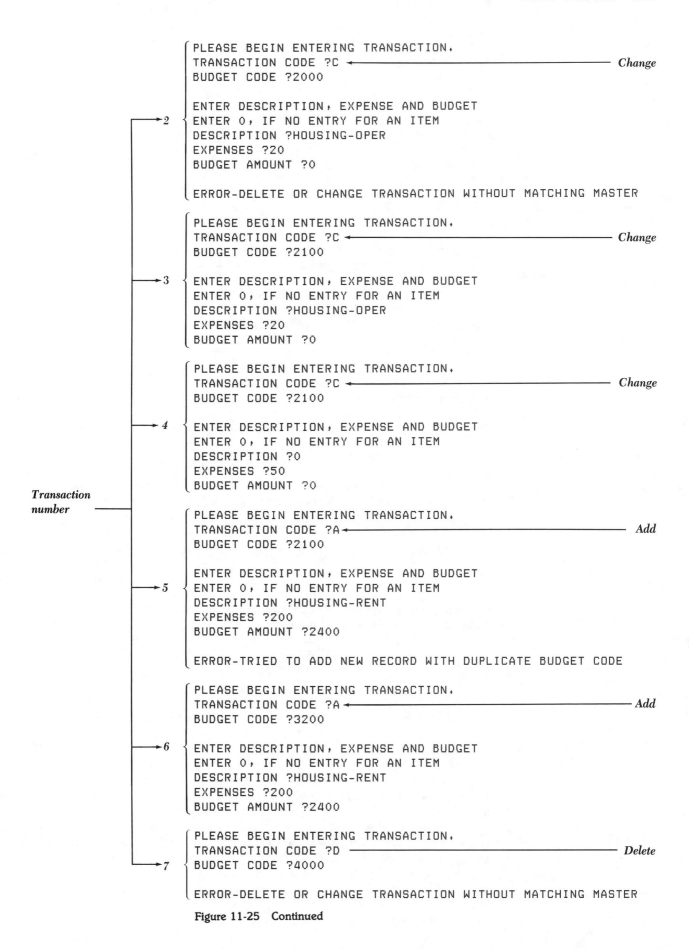

```
                 ⎧ PLEASE BEGIN ENTERING TRANSACTION,
                 │ TRANSACTION CODE ?C ◄───────────────────────────── Change
                 │ BUDGET CODE ?2000
                 │
                 │ ENTER DESCRIPTION, EXPENSE AND BUDGET
      →2         ⎨ ENTER 0, IF NO ENTRY FOR AN ITEM
                 │ DESCRIPTION ?HOUSING-OPER
                 │ EXPENSES ?20
                 │ BUDGET AMOUNT ?0
                 │
                 ⎩ ERROR-DELETE OR CHANGE TRANSACTION WITHOUT MATCHING MASTER

                 ⎧ PLEASE BEGIN ENTERING TRANSACTION,
                 │ TRANSACTION CODE ?C ◄───────────────────────────── Change
                 │ BUDGET CODE ?2100
                 │
      →3         ⎨ ENTER DESCRIPTION, EXPENSE AND BUDGET
                 │ ENTER 0, IF NO ENTRY FOR AN ITEM
                 │ DESCRIPTION ?HOUSING-OPER
                 │ EXPENSES ?20
                 ⎩ BUDGET AMOUNT ?0

                 ⎧ PLEASE BEGIN ENTERING TRANSACTION,
                 │ TRANSACTION CODE ?C ◄───────────────────────────── Change
                 │ BUDGET CODE ?2100
                 │
      →4         ⎨ ENTER DESCRIPTION, EXPENSE AND BUDGET
                 │ ENTER 0, IF NO ENTRY FOR AN ITEM
                 │ DESCRIPTION ?0
                 │ EXPENSES ?50
                 ⎩ BUDGET AMOUNT ?0

                 ⎧ PLEASE BEGIN ENTERING TRANSACTION,
                 │ TRANSACTION CODE ?A ◄───────────────────────────── Add
                 │ BUDGET CODE ?2100
                 │
                 │ ENTER DESCRIPTION, EXPENSE AND BUDGET
      →5         ⎨ ENTER 0, IF NO ENTRY FOR AN ITEM
                 │ DESCRIPTION ?HOUSING-RENT
                 │ EXPENSES ?200
                 │ BUDGET AMOUNT ?2400
                 │
                 ⎩ ERROR-TRIED TO ADD NEW RECORD WITH DUPLICATE BUDGET CODE

                 ⎧ PLEASE BEGIN ENTERING TRANSACTION,
                 │ TRANSACTION CODE ?A ◄───────────────────────────── Add
                 │ BUDGET CODE ?3200
                 │
      →6         ⎨ ENTER DESCRIPTION, EXPENSE AND BUDGET
                 │ ENTER 0, IF NO ENTRY FOR AN ITEM
                 │ DESCRIPTION ?HOUSING-RENT
                 │ EXPENSES ?200
                 ⎩ BUDGET AMOUNT ?2400

                 ⎧ PLEASE BEGIN ENTERING TRANSACTION,
                 │ TRANSACTION CODE ?D ───────────────────────────── Delete
      →7         ⎨ BUDGET CODE ?4000
                 │
                 ⎩ ERROR-DELETE OR CHANGE TRANSACTION WITHOUT MATCHING MASTER
```

Transaction number

Figure 11-25   Continued

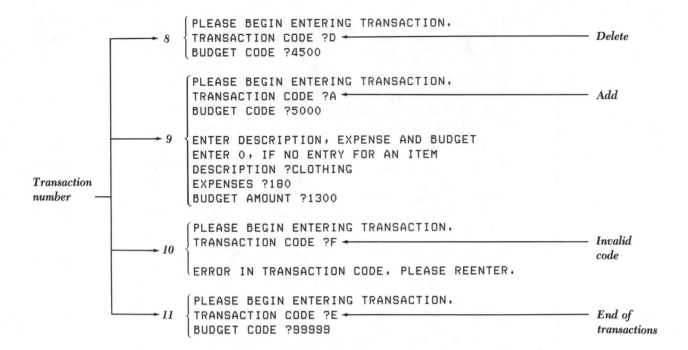

```
        ⎧ PLEASE BEGIN ENTERING TRANSACTION.
    8   ⎨ TRANSACTION CODE ?D  ◄──────────────────────── Delete
        ⎩ BUDGET CODE ?4500

        ⎧ PLEASE BEGIN ENTERING TRANSACTION.
        ⎪ TRANSACTION CODE ?A  ◄──────────────────────── Add
        ⎪ BUDGET CODE ?5000
    9   ⎨ ENTER DESCRIPTION, EXPENSE AND BUDGET
        ⎪ ENTER 0, IF NO ENTRY FOR AN ITEM
        ⎪ DESCRIPTION ?CLOTHING
        ⎪ EXPENSES ?180
        ⎩ BUDGET AMOUNT ?1300

        ⎧ PLEASE BEGIN ENTERING TRANSACTION.
   10   ⎨ TRANSACTION CODE ?F  ◄──────────────────────── Invalid
        ⎪                                                code
        ⎩ ERROR IN TRANSACTION CODE. PLEASE REENTER.

        ⎧ PLEASE BEGIN ENTERING TRANSACTION.
   11   ⎨ TRANSACTION CODE ?E  ◄──────────────────────── End of
        ⎩ BUDGET CODE ?99999                             transactions
```

Transaction number

```
END OF MAINTENANCE
```

Figure 11-25   Continued

Figure 11-26 lists the legend for variables used in the maintenance program. The names for master record fields are the same. The fields for the transaction records are named to correspond to their counterparts in the master file, by leaving off the number 1 following the letter in the variable name—for example, B instead of B1 for the budget code. In addition, T$ is the variable name for the transaction code.

MASTER RECORD	TRANSACTION RECORD	MEANING
B1	B	Budget amount
E1	E	Expense amount
N1	N	Budget code
N1$	N$	Description
	T$	Transaction code

Figure 11-26   Legend for variables used in program for maintaining a sequential file

Figure 11-27 on page 266 is the detailed logic flowchart for the file-maintenance program. As we mentioned earlier, the maintenance program is the most complicated of all file-processing programs, so it should not be surprising that this flowchart is considerably more complicated than previous flowcharts.

The opening housekeeping routine in symbol 200–242 opens the old master file named "BDGSEQ" and the temporary file named "TEMP". At symbol 302–320 a master record is read from the old budget file. Symbol 400–410 calls for the input of transaction code T$. In symbols 411 and 412 the transaction code is tested to see whether it is valid. If it is less than A or greater than E, the flow branches to symbol

414–416 to display an error message and then branches back to input another transaction code at symbol 400–410. If the transaction is valid, the flow continues to the next page at off-page connector symbol 1, which connects to symbol 420–425, which calls for the input of transaction budget code N.

At symbol 427, transaction code T$ is tested to see whether it equals E, the end-of-transaction code. At symbol 429 transaction code T$ is tested to see whether it equals D, the delete code. If it is either an E or a D, the flow branches to symbol 500, thereby skipping the input of any additional transaction data, since that is not needed for either the end of transactions or a deletion. If it is neither a D nor an E, the flow continues to symbol 430–454, which calls for the input of the remainder of the transaction data: N$, E, and B. The flow then continues to symbol 500.

At symbol 500 master budget code N1 is compared with the transaction budget code N. It is important to note at this point that *both the master file and the transaction file are arranged in ascending budget-code sequence.*

Master Budget Code N1 Is Less Than Transaction Code N

If the present master code, N1, is less than the present transaction code, N, no subsequent transaction can affect the present master record. In this case the flow branches to symbol 510–516, where the present master record is written onto the temporary master file, and at symbol 520 another permanent master record is read from the old master file. The program branches back to symbol 500 to compare once more the most recent master budget code, N1, with transaction budget code N. This cycle continues until finally, at symbol 500, an old master budget code is found to be greater than or equal to transaction budget code N; at this time the flow branches to symbol 540, to determine the exact relationship of N1 to N.

Master Budget Code N1 Is Greater Than Transaction Budget Code N

If it is determined at symbol 540 that master budget code N1 is greater than transaction budget code N, then the transaction record has a budget code that does not match the budget code of any master record. In this case the only valid transaction operation is to add a new record to the file. The flow branches to symbol 550 to determine whether this is a valid add operation, by testing transaction code T$ to see whether it equals A. If T$ *does not* equal A, an error message is displayed at symbol 580, indicating that a delete or change transaction was attempted without a matching master record. The flow branches back to the previous page at off-page connector symbol 2 to connect with symbol 400–410 to input a new transaction. On the other hand, if T$ *does* equal A, this is a valid add operation and the transaction record is written onto temporary master file as a new master record. The flow then branches back to the previous page at off-page connector symbol 2 to connect with symbol 400–410 to input a new transaction.

Master Code N1 Is Equal to Transaction Code N

If it is determined at symbol 540 that master budget code N1 is equal to transaction code N, then three valid transaction operations are possible: (1) delete a master record, (2) change a master record, or (3) end transactions. The flow branches to off-page connector symbol 3, which leads to the next page to determine which of these three actions is to be taken. On the next page, at off-page connector symbol 3, the flow continues to symbol 600 to see whether transaction code T$ is E, indicating the end of transactions and, because of the previous logic, also the end of the master file. If T$ equals E, this indicates the end of transactions. It also means that transaction budget code N is 99999 at symbol 540. Since master budget code N1 equals transaction budget code N as previously determined, the end of the master file has also been reached. In this case the flow branches to off-page connector symbol 4 to copy the temporary file onto the master file and then proceeds to the closing housekeeping routine. (This will be discussed in the "End Transaction" section, which follows in the next few pages.)

If the test at symbol 600 indicates that transaction code T$ is not equal to E, the flow continues to symbol 610, where T$ is tested to see whether it is equal to C. If T$ is equal to C, it indicates a change transaction and flow branches to symbol 670, which will be discussed in the "Change Transaction" section that follows. If T$ is not equal to C at symbol 610, the only valid transaction operation is to delete a record. The flow continues to symbol 620 to determine whether this is a valid delete operation, by testing T$ to see if it equals A. If T$ does equal A, an error message is displayed at symbol 630, indicating that an attempt was made to add a new record which is already an existing master record. Flow then branches to off-page connector symbol 2. This leads to an earlier page at off-page connector symbol 2, where the flow continues to symbol 400–410, to input a new transaction code.

Delete Transaction   If T$ does not equal A at symbol 620, then this is a valid delete transaction. Therefore, the matching master record is deleted by not writing it onto the temporary file and merely reading the next master record from the permanent master file to replace it. The flow then branches to off-page connector symbol 2 and returns to the previous page to input a new transaction code.

Change Transaction   Back at symbol 670, description N$ from the transaction record is tested to see whether it equals a string value of 0. If it is equal, the description is not changed so the flow branches to symbol 674. If N$ does not equal 0, there *is* a change in the description and the flow continues to symbol 672. At symbol 672, description N1$ in the master record is replaced by description N$ from the transaction record. At symbol 674 expense field E from the transaction record is added to expense field E1 from the master record.

If there is no change, transaction expense E will have a value of 0 and therefore will not change the master expense. The flow then continues to symbol 676 to test transaction field B to see whether it is 0. If B is 0, there is no budget change. If B does not equal 0, there is a change to master budget field B1, which is replaced by transaction field B. In either case the flow then continues to off-page connector symbol 2 and returns to an earlier page to input a new transaction code. Notice that the changed master record is not written on the temporary file, because additional transactions might change the record.

End Transactions   At symbol 600 we determined that if T$ equaled E we had reached the end of transactions. At this point since both transaction budget code N and master budget code N1 equal 99999 as previously determined at symbol 540, we have also reached the end of the master file. In this case the flow goes to off-page connector symbol 4. There the flow continues to symbol 1000–1023 to copy the temporary file onto the master file, thereby creating a newly updated master file.

At symbol 1000–1023 the last master record—the flag record with a budget code of 99999—is written onto the temporary file. At this point the old master file "BDGSEQ" is still in its original form. The temporary file "TEMP" is a new version of the master file; it contains original records, changed records, and newly added records, but it does not contain any records that were deleted. It is therefore necessary to replace the contents of the original master file "BDGSEQ" with the contents of temporary file "TEMP". At symbol 1030–1040 the pointer of each file is set at the beginning of its respective file. At symbol 1050–1056 a record is read from temporary file "TEMP", and at symbol 1060–1066 that record is written onto master file "BDGSEQ".

Symbol 1070 tests budget code N1 to see whether the last master record written was 99999; this would indicate the last (or flag) record. If N1 does not equal 99999, the flow branches back to symbol 1050–1056 to read another temporary record; at symbol 1060–1066 it is written onto the master file. This process is repeated until N1 equals 99999 at symbol 1070 and the flow branches to symbol 1700–1920 to close housekeeping routines and then to end the program. The temporary file may then be kept as a back-up file.

To help you understand the maintenance program better, we will ask you to trace various transactions through the flowchart, as part of the Application Exercises for this unit. Now that you have had an opportunity to become somewhat familiar with the file-maintenance logic, we should mention the following few assumptions applying to its design:

1. The transactions, master file, and temporary file are in ascending budget-code sequence.
2. There can be only one type of transaction per budget code. For example, if there is a delete transaction, an add or change transaction cannot occur for the same budget code. However, there can be more than one change transaction per budget code.
3. The budget code cannot be changed. Only description, expense, and budget fields can be changed.

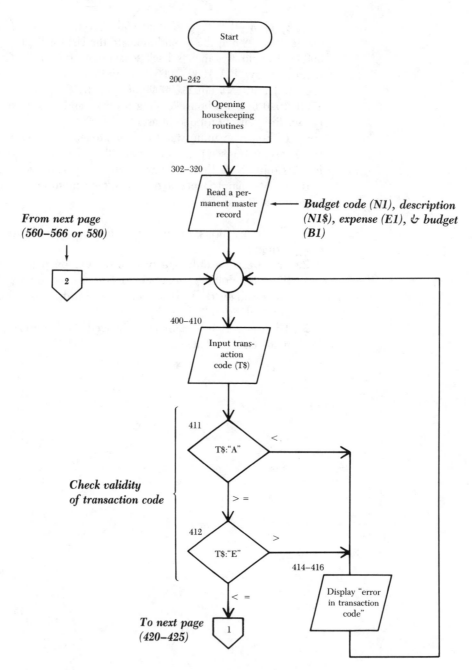

Figure 11-27   Logic flowchart for maintaining a sequential file

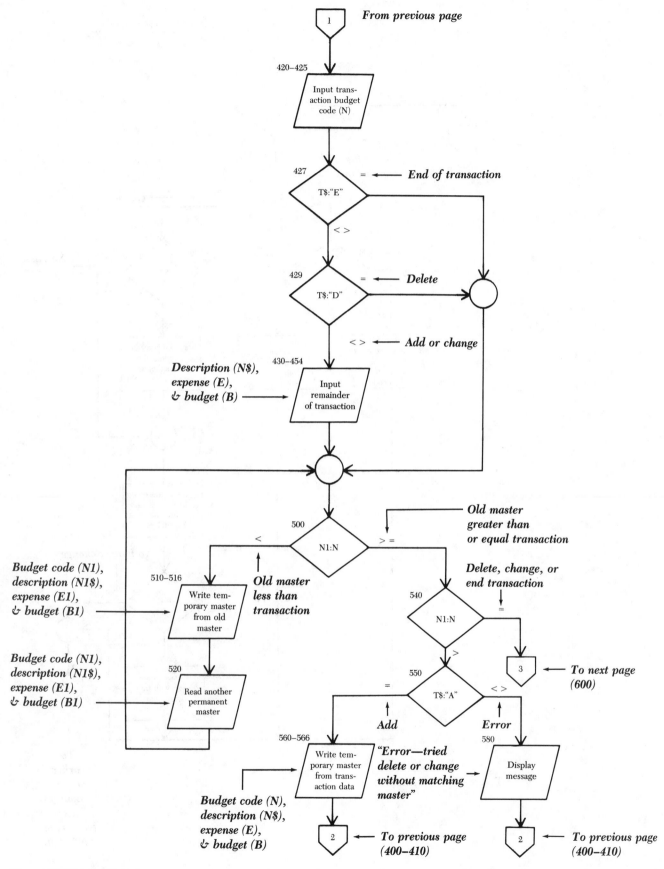

Figure 11-27   Continued

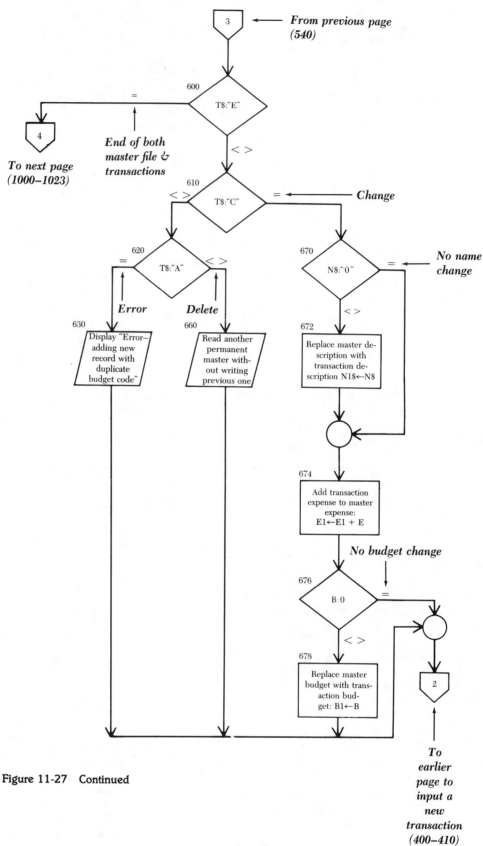

Figure 11-27 Continued

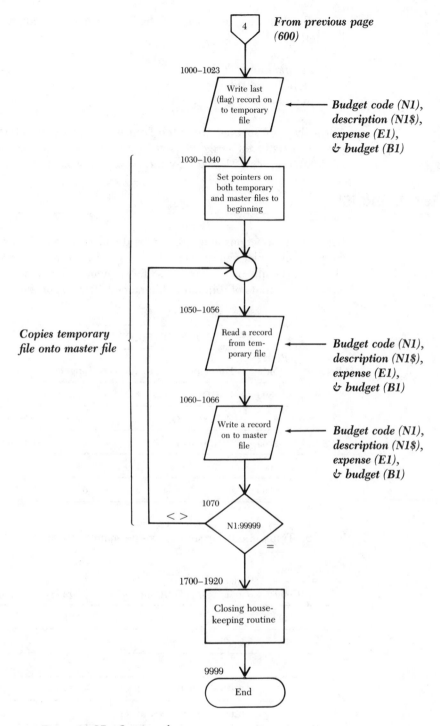

Figure 11-27   Continued

The following sections for this unit can be found in the System Specifics booklet:

Programming Techniques
Debugging Aids
Reference

Normally these sections are in the *Programming Essentials* text. However, since the procedures covered here differ significantly among various computers, these sections are located in Unit 11 of the System Specifics booklet.

APPLICATION EXERCISE

Trace the transactions in b through the detailed logic of the flowchart in Figure 11-27 for sequential-file maintenance. Enter the results in the worksheets provided in c. Base your results on the contents of a sequential file named "BDGSEQ".

    a. Contents of sequential file named "BDGSEQ" before maintenance:

		"BDGSEQ" FILE			
Record	Budget Code	Description	Expense	Budget	
1	1800	FOOD	230	2500	
2	2100	HOUSING-O	220	1900	(HOUSING-O = HOUSING-OPER)
3	3200	HOUSING-R	200	2400	(HOUSING-R = HOUSING-RENT)
4	5000	CLOTHING	180	1300	
5	99999	0	0	0	

    b. Transactions for sequential-file maintenance:

Transaction No.	Code	Budget Code	Description	Expense	Budget
	(T$)	(N)	(N$)	(E)	(B)
1	D	2000			
2	D	2100			
3	C	2200	HOUSING-RENT	220	4300
4	C	3200	HOUSING-RENT	220	4300
5	A	5000	ENTERTAINMENT	100	1200
6	A	5700	ENTERTAINMENT	100	1200
7	F				
8	E	99999			

Note: Transaction codes are as follows:
    C   Change (update) record
    A   Add new record
    D   Delete record
    E   End of transactions

c. Enter the results of your trace in the worksheet areas provided here. In the "memory contents worksheet," use a separate line to record each file record from "BDGSEQ" and each transaction record. In the section for "BDGSEQ" file records, enter ditto marks when a field does not change.

MEMORY CONTENTS WORKSHEET

FROM "BDGSEQ" FILE				Trans. No.	FROM TRANSACTIONS				
Budget Code	Description	Expense	Budget		Trans. Code	Budget Code	Description	Expense	Budget
(N1)	(N1$)	(E1)	(B1)		(T$)	(N)	(N$)	(E)	(B)
				1					
				2					
				3					
				4					
				5					
				6					
				7					
				8					

In the "error message worksheet," enter the transaction number that caused the error message.

"TEMP" FILE WORKSHEET					ERROR MESSAGE WORKSHEET	
Record	Budget Code	Description	Expense	Budget	Trans. No.	Message
1						
2						
3						
4						
5						

Answers to Application Exercise

MEMORY CONTENTS WORKSHEET

FROM "BDGSEQ" FILE

Budget Code	Description	Expense	Budget
(N1)	(N1$)	(E1)	(B1)
1800	FOOD	230	2500
2100	HOUSING-O	220	1900
3200	HOUSING-R	200	2400
3200	HOUSING-R	420	4300
5000	CLOTHING	180	1300
99999	0	0	0

FROM TRANSACTIONS

Trans. No.	Trans. Code	Budget Code	Description	Expense	Budget
	(T$)	(N)	(N$)	(E)	(B)
1	D	2000			
2	D	2100			
3	C	2200	HOUSING-O	220	4300
4	C	3200	HOUSING-R	220	4300
5	A	5000	ENTERTAIN	100	1200
6	A	5700	ENTERTAIN	100	1200
7	F				
8	E	99999			

"TEMP" FILE WORKSHEET

Record	Budget Code	Description	Expense	Budget	Trans. No.
1	1800	FOOD	230	2500	1
2	3200	HOUSING-O	420	4300	3
3	5000	CLOTHING	180	1300	5
4	5700	ENTERTAIN	100	1200	7
5	99999	0	0	0	

ERROR MESSAGE WORKSHEET

Message
Error tried to delete/ change without matching master
Error (Same as above)
Error adding new record with duplicate budget code
Error in transaction code

PROGRAMMING PROBLEMS

There are four programming problems in this unit. They are very similar to the sequential-file programs for the loading, maintenance, retrieval/display, and inquiry processes already discussed. For each problem, consult the appropriate logic flow-chart in this book and the appropriate program in the System Specifics booklet for a model to use as a guide. Also consult the System Specifics booklet for additional tips that apply to your particular computer.

11-1. Program for Loading a Sequential File

Write a program that will accept the customer credit data items listed below as input from a keyboard. For each customer, output a customer record onto a sequential file and display the record that was loaded by reading from the file as shown in the results provided in Figure 11-28.

Given data to input from keyboard:

Cust. No.	Name	Charges	Credit Limit
1200	JANICE ADAMS	500	800
2600	LEOPOLD KELLY	550	600
4000	PAT LAMENT	300	500
99999	0	0	0

Programming tips:

1. Use the logic flowchart in Figure 11-10 as a general model when preparing a flowchart for this problem.
2. Use the program for sequential-file loading in the System Specifics booklet as a general model when coding the program for this problem.
3. Carefully examine the results provided in Figure 11-28 for additional details to assist you in writing your program.
4. Note in particular the following differences between this problem and the model referenced in tips 1 and 2:
   a. The data to be loaded onto this file is input from a keyboard, rather than read from a DATA statement.
   b. After all records have been loaded onto this sequential file, they are also displayed as shown in the results in Figure 11-28. You will find additional tips regarding this file in the System Specifics booklet.

The results follow on page 274.

Results:

```
THIS PROGRAM ALLOWS YOU TO LOAD RECORDS
ONTO A NEW SEQUENTIAL FILE FROM INPUT AT TERMINAL.
PLEASE ENTER THE INFORMATION REQUESTED WHEN YOU
SEE THE QUESTION MARK (TYPE 99999 TO END INPUT)

CUST. NO. ?1200
NAME ?JANICE ADAMS
CHARGES ?500
CREDIT LIMIT ?800

CUST. NO. ?2600
NAME ?LEOPOLD KELLY
CHARGES ?550
CREDIT LIMIT ?600

CUST. NO. ?4000
NAME ?PAT LAMENT
CHARGES ?300
CREDIT LIMIT ?500

CUST. NO. ?99999

SINCE YOU ARE ENDING INPUT, PLEASE ENTER 0
FOR EACH OF THE NEXT THREE ITEMS

NAME ?0
CHARGES ?0
CREDIT LIMIT ?0

THE FOLLOWING DATA IS BEING LOADED ONTO
A SEQUENTIAL FILE FROM TERMINAL INPUT

CUST. NO.        NAME        CHARGES   CREDIT LIMIT

1200         JANICE ADAMS   500       800
2600         LEOPOLD KELLY  550       600
4000         PAT LAMENT     300       500
99999        0              0         0

END OF FILE LOADING
```

Figure 11-28   Results for "Sequential File Load Problem"

11-2. Program for Maintaining a Sequential File

Write a program to accept the following add, change, and delete transactions from a keyboard and read master records from the file loaded in the first programming problem. Your program should output onto an updated temporary file. When all transactions and all master records have been processed and the last record has been entered on the temporary file, copy the temporary file onto the master file. The input display, including error messages, should match those shown in the results provided in Figure 11-29.

Given:

1. Transaction summary for program for sequential-file maintenance:

Transaction No.	Code	Cust. No.	Name	Charges	Credit Limit	Comment
1	D	1200				Delete existing record
2	C	1600	IGOR KELLY	150	0	Error—change nonexistent record
3	C	2600	IGOR KELLY	150	0	Change name and amount of change
4	A	4000	PAM ZUBLINSKI	400	700	Error—add record with same budget code as existing record
5	A	5000	PAM ZUBLINSKI	400	700	Add to end of file
6	F					Error—invalid transaction code
7	E	99999				End of transactions

Note: Transaction codes are as follows:
C   Change (update) record
A   Add new record
D   Delete record
E   End of transactions

2. File contents before and after maintenance:

Record	BEFORE MAINTENANCE				AFTER MAINTENANCE			
	Cust. No.	Name	Charges	Credit Limit	Cust. No.	Name	Charges	Credit Limit
1	1200	JANICE ADAMS	500	800	2600	IGOR KELLY	700	600
2	2600	LEOPOLD KELLY	550	600	4000	PAT LAMENT	300	500
3	4000	PAT LAMENT	300	500	5000	PAM ZUBLINSKI	400	700
4	99999	0	0	0	99999	0	0	0

Programming tips:

1. Use the logic flowchart in Figure 11-27 as a general model when preparing a flowchart for this problem.
2. Use the program for sequential-file maintenance in the System Specifics booklet as a general model when coding the program for this problem.
3. Carefully examine the results provided in Figure 11-29 for additional details to assist you in writing your program.

Results:

```
ENTER INFORMATION AS REQUESTED FOR AFFECTED RECORD
WHEN YOU SEE A QUESTION MARK.

PLEASE BEGIN ENTERING TRANSACTION
TRANSACTION CODE ?D
CUST NO. ?1200

PLEASE BEGIN ENTERING TRANSACTION
TRANSACTION CODE ?C
CUST. NO. ?1600

ENTER NAME, CHARGES AND CREDIT LIMIT.
ENTER 0 ,IF NO ENTRY FOR AN ITEM
NAME ?IGOR KELLY
CHARGES ?150
CREDIT LIMIT ?0

ERROR-DELETE OR CHANGE TRANSACTION W/O MATCHING MASTER

PLEASE BEGIN ENTERING TRANSACTION
TRANSACTION CODE ?C
CUST. NO. ?2600

ENTER NAME,CHARGES AND CREDIT LIMIT.
ENTER 0 ,IF NO ENTRY FOR AN ITEM
NAME ?IGOR KELLY
CHARGES ?150
CREDIT LIMIT ?0

PLEASE BEGIN ENTERING TRANSACTION
TRANSACTION CODE ?A
CUST. NO. ?4000

ENTER NAME,CHARGES AND CREDIT LIMIT.
ENTER 0 ,IF NO ENTRY FOR AN ITEM
NAME ?PAM ZUBLINSKI
CHARGES ?400
CREDIT LIMIT ?700

ERROR-TRIED TO ADD NEW RECORD WITH SAME NUMBER AS EXISTING RECORD
```

Figure 11-29   Results for "Sequential File Maintenance Problem"

```
PLEASE BEGIN ENTERING TRANSACTION
TRANSACTION CODE ?A
CUST. NO. ?5000

ENTER NAME,CHARGES AND CREDIT LIMIT.
ENTER 0 ,IF NO ENTRY FOR AN ITEM
NAME ?PAM ZUBLINSKI
CHARGES ?400
CREDIT LIMIT ?700

PLEASE BEGIN ENTERING TRANSACTION
TRANSACTION CODE ?F

ERROR IN TRANSACTION CODE. PLEASE REENTER.

PLEASE BEGIN ENTERING TRANSACTION
TRANSACTION CODE ?E
CUST. NO. ?99999

END OF MAINTENANCE
```

Figure 11-29   Continued

11-3 Program for Retrieving and Printing a Sequential File

Write a program that will allow the user, through keyboard input, to specify the manner in which customer records in a credit file are to be retrieved. Once a record is retrieved, the program should calculate the amount by which the changes are either over or under the credit limit and then display the record and the calculated amount. The two methods available for retrieval are: (1) customers whose changes have exceeded their credit limit, or (2) all customers. Your output should match that shown in the results provided in Figure 11-30.

Given: A sequential customer credit file, as described in the previous two programming problems.

Programming tips:

1. Use the logic flowchart in Figure 11-15 as a general model, when preparing a flowchart for this problem.
2. Use the program for sequential-file retrieval/display in the System Specifics booklet as a general model when coding the program for this problem.
3. Carefully examine the results provided in Figure 11-30 for additional details to assist you in writing your program.
4. To get both sets of results shown, you must run the program twice.

Results:

```
THIS PROGRAM WILL DISPLAY THE FILE
IN TWO DIFFERENT MODES:
    1. ONLY CUSTOMERS WHOSE CHARGES
       HAVE EXCEEDED THEIR CREDIT LIMIT,
       IF YOU TYPE THE WORD ``OVER'',

    2. ENTIRE FILE, IF YOU TYPE THE WORD ``ALL''.

ENTER YOUR CHOICE (OVER OR ALL) ?OVER

THE FOLLOWING DATA IS BEING RETRIEVED
FROM A SEQUENTIAL FILE

    CUST    NAME            CHARGES   CREDIT   OVER(-)/UNDER
    NUMBER                            LIMIT    LIMIT


    2600    IGOR KELLY        700      600     -100

END OF FILE RETRIEVAL

THIS PROGRAM WILL DISPLAY THE FILE
IN TWO DIFFERENT MODES:
    1. ONLY CUSTOMERS WHOSE CHARGES
       HAVE EXCEEDED THEIR CREDIT LIMIT
       IF YOU TYPE THE WORD ``OVER''.

    2. ENTIRE FILE,IF YOU TYPE THE WORD ``ALL''.

ENTER YOUR CHOICE (OVER OR ALL) ?ALL

THE FOLLOWING DATA IS BEING RETRIEVED
FROM A SEQUENTIAL FILE

    CUST    NAME            CHARGES   CREDIT   OVER(-)/UNDER
    NUMBER                            LIMIT    LIMIT


    2600    IGOR KELLY        700      600     -100
    4000    PAT LAMENT        300      500      200
    5000    PAM ZUBLINSKI     400      700      300

END OF FILE RETRIEVAL
```

Figure 11-30   Results for "Sequential Retrieve and Print Problem"

11-4 Program for Inquiring with a Sequential File

Write a program that will allow the user, through keyboard input, to specify customer records to be retrieved from a credit file one at a time and displayed.

Given: A sequential customer credit file, as described in the previous two programming problems.

Programming tips:

1. Use the logic flowchart in Figure 11-15 as a general model, when preparing a flowchart for this problem.
2. Use the sequential-file inquiry program in the System Specifics booklet as a general model when coding the program for this problem.
3. Carefully examine the results provided in Figure 11-31 for additional details to assist you in writing your program.

Results:

```
ENTER CUST. NO. FOR THE RECORD YOU
WANT TO SEE. (TO STOP, TYPE 99999) ?5000

   5000         PAM ZUBLINSKI     400          700

ENTER CUST. NO. FOR THE RECORD YOU
WANT TO SEE. (TO STOP, TYPE 99999) ?4000

   4000         PAT LAMENT      300          500

ENTER CUST. NO. FOR THE RECORD YOU
WANT TO SEE. (TO STOP, TYPE 99999) ?1200

   CUST. NO. 1200         NOT FOUND IN FILE.

ENTER CUST. NO. FOR THE RECORD YOU
WANT TO SEE. (TO STOP, TYPE 99999) ?2600

   2600         IGOR KELLY     700          600

ENTER CUST. NO. FOR THE RECORD YOU
WANT TO SEE. (TO STOP, TYPE 99999) ?99999


END OF INQUIRIES
```

Figure 11-31   Results for "Sequential File Inquiry Problem"

Index

ABS function 113, 114
Absolute value function (See ABS function)
Accumulating 14, 15, 64, 71, 154, 177, 195
Adding rows and columns 190
Addition 14
Algebra rules 14
AND 61
Argument 113
Arithmetic operations 14
Array 163
Array elements 163
Arrays, one-dimensional 163
    copying 177, 203
    counting 175, 177, 196, 202
    printing 168, 174, 198, 203
    two-dimensional 185
ASCII 89, 90, 100
Assignment statement 15
Auxillary storage 5
Averaging values 147, 151, 153, 154, 177

BASIC 2
    built-in function 111 (See also entry
      under function name)
    built-in functions: general 112
    built-in functions: trigonometric 114
    command 2
    program 2
    statement 2 (See also entry under
      statement name)
Boolean expression 60
Boolean operators 61
Branch, conditional 59, 60
    unconditional 23, 24, 28

Calculating an average 63, 64
Cathode ray tube (See CRT)
Central processing unit (See CPU)
Character string (See String)
Collating hierarchy (sequence) 89, 100
Column processing 202, 204
Columns 187
Comma in a PRINT statement 36
Command (See BASIC command)
Comment (See REM statement)
Comparing values 66
Computer definition and description 4
Conditional branch 59, 60
Constants 15, 16, 26
Copying arrays 177, 203
COS function 114, 117
Counting 15
Counting with arrays 175, 177, 196, 202

CPU 1, 4
Creating a file (See File loading)
CRT 4

Data 2, 33, 34, 43
Data file 245
Data pointer (See Pointer in DATA
    statement)
DATA statement 34
Debugging aids (See contents for each
    unit)
Decision symbol 61, 73
Decrementing (FOR statement) 148
DEF statement 214
DIM statement 163, 165, 178, 188.
Dimension statement (See DIM
    statement)
Direct data file 246
Disk (See Magnetic disk)
Disk drive 5
Division 15
Dummy argument 214

E notation 16
EBCDIC 89
Empty string (See Null string)
END statement 8, 73
EQ (equal) 60
Executable statements 16
Exponent 16
Exponential notation 16, 27
Exponentiation 16, 27
Expression 16, 18, 27

Field 245
File 245
File inquiry (See File operations)
File loading (See File operations)
File maintenance (See File operations)
File operations 246
    file inquiry 254
    file loading 248
    file maintenance 257
    file retrieval and display 251
File processing (See File operations)
File retrieval and display (See File
    operations)
Flag 64
Flowchart 3
Flowcharting 16, 27
FOR variable 142
FOR-NEXT
    loop 141, 142, 143

FOR-NEXT (cont'd.)
    loop indentation 155
    loop rules 151
    statement 141, 157
Function (See BASIC built-in function)
Function (See User-defined function)

GE (greater than or equal to) 60
GO SUB statement 215, 225
GO TO statement 13, 16, 27, 28
GT (greater than) 60

Hard copy 4
Heading 16

IF-THEN statement 59, 60, 61, 62, 72
Incrementing 16, 27, 64, 71
Index variable 142
Initial value (FOR statement) 142
Initialize 17, 27, 71, 194
Input 33
Input device 4
Input prompt (question mark) 12, 39
INPUT statement 12, 34
    miscellaneous uses 39
    with string variable 88
Input/output symbol 17, 35, 73
INT function 113, 114
Integers 17, 23, 24
Internal storage (See Memory)

Keyboard 4

LE (less than or equal to) 60
LET statement 17
LET statement with string data 79
Line number 7
LIST command 10
Looping 141
LT (less than) 60

Magnetic disk 1, 4, 5, 246
Magnetic tape 1, 4, 5, 246
Main storage (See Memory)
Master file 257, 262, 276
Master record 275
Matrix 164
Memory 1, 2, 4
Multiplication 17, 18, 19

NE (not equal) 60
Nested FOR-NEXT loop 185, 186
Nested FOR-NEXT loop rules 186, 204

NEXT statement 142, 157
Null string 89
Numeric array 168
Numeric constant 17, 26
Numeric variable 14, 18, 26

One-dimensional arrays 163
Operator 18, 26
OR 61
Output 33
Output device 4, 33

Parentheses 16
Pointer in DATA statement 34, 43
Print position 37, 53, 112, 113
PRINT statement, general 7, 33
    displaying a blank line 8
    displaying calculated results 8
    displaying literal characters 7
    displaying numeric variables 36
    displaying string constants and
      numeric variables 37
    displaying string variables 82
    use of comma 38
    use of semicolon 38
    use of space for sign 39
    use of TAB function 112, 113
Print zones 36, 34, 53
Printer 4
Printing arrays 168, 174, 198, 203
Priority of operations 20
Process symbol 17
Program display (listing) 10
Program execution (running) 11
Program flowchart (See Flowchart)
Programmer 4
Programming 2
Programming—General procedure 5
Programming mechanics, displaying
  (listing) 10
    executing (running) 11
    making changes 11
    typing 9
Programming techniques (See contents for
  each unit)

Raising to a power 20
Random data file (See Direct data file)
Random number function (See RND
  function)
Random numbers 123, 125
RANDOMIZE statement 114
READ statement 34
    miscellaneous uses 43
    with string variables 87
Real numbers 21
Record 245
Reference sections (See contents for each
  unit)
Relational operators 60
REM statement 7
RESTORE statement 60, 62, 72
RETURN key 9
RETURN statement 215, 230
RND function 113, 123
Rounding function 214
Rounding numbers 118
Row processing 202, 204
Rows 187
RUN command 11
Running a program 11

Scientific notation 21, 22
Searching a file (See File inquiry)
Secondary storage 5
Sequential data file 246
Serial data file (See Sequential data file)
SIN function 114, 117
Sort subroutine 229
SQR function 113, 114
Square root function (See SQR function)
Statement number (See Line number)
Statement (See BASIC statement)
STEP 142, 143, 150
STOP statement 59, 62, 72
String 78
    array 172, 203, 207
    assignment in LET statement 79, 85
    comparison 80, 81, 90
    constant 7, 35, 37, 78, 79
    inputting 80, 88

String (cont'd.)
    output (Display) 82, 92
    reading 80, 87
    variable 22, 23, 78
Strings 22
Subroutine 213
Subroutine summary 232
Subscript 163, 164, 178, 188
Subtraction 22
Summing numbers 146
Superscript 23
System command (See BASIC command)
System flowchart 248

TAB function 113, 114
Tabulation function (See TAB function)
TAN function 114, 117
Tape drive 5
Tape (See Magnetic tape)
Terminal 4
Terminal symbol 5, 23, 24, 26, 72, 73
Test value (FOR statement) 142
Testing for end of data 71
Testing for end of input 71
Transaction file 276
Transaction record 275
Transferring values to subroutine 231
Trigonometric functions 114
Truncation 113
Truncation function (See INT function)
Two-dimensional arrays 185, 189

Unconditional branch 23, 24, 28
Updating a file (See File maintenance)
User-defined function 213, 214, 219, 231
User-defined function summary 232

Variable (See String variable)
Variable, numeric 14, 18, 26
Vector 164
Video display screen (See CRT)

Working storage (See Memory)